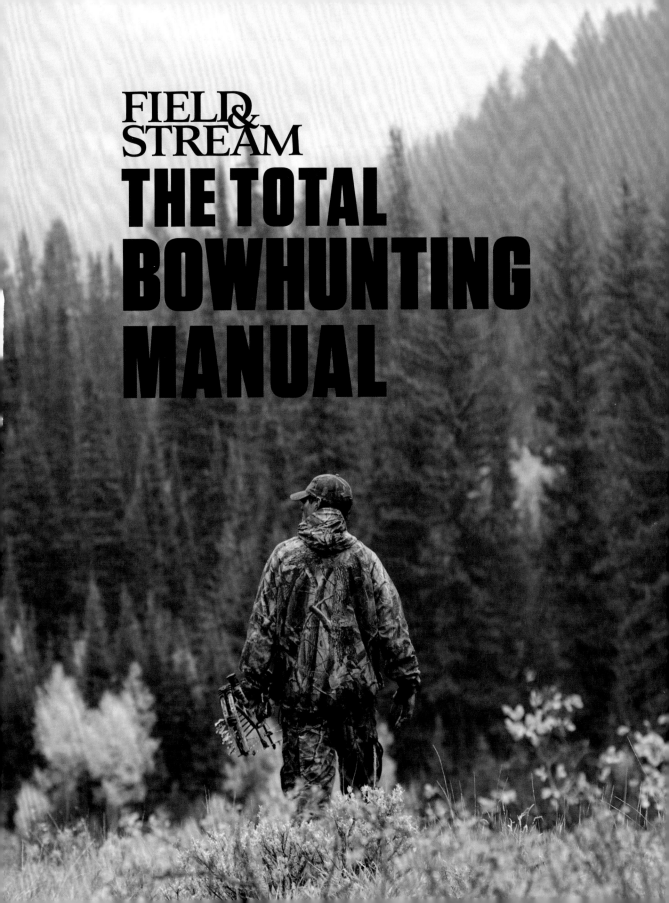

FIELD & STREAM
THE TOTAL BOWHUNTING MANUAL

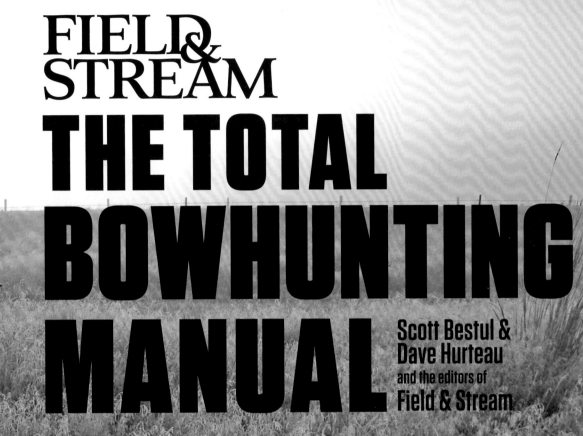

FIELD & STREAM

THE TOTAL BOWHUNTING MANUAL

Scott Bestul &
Dave Hurteau
and the editors of
Field & Stream

CONTENTS

CROSSBOWS

HUNTING

FROM THE EDITOR-IN-CHIEF

"There's more fun in hunting with the handicap of the bow than there is in hunting with the sureness of the gun."—**FRED BEAR**

Ancient as the bow and arrow are, bowhunting for sport wasn't commonplace until just a few decades ago, when iconic figures like Fred Bear introduced it to the masses. Bear was a talented archer and an excellent hunter, but just as important, he was a gifted communicator. As he traveled the world in pursuit of big game with his trusty recurve, Bear had the forethought to capture his hunts on film. Through those videos, sportsmen and women learned that not only was the bow and arrow still an effective hunting tool for even the largest game, but that bowhunting itself was an experience unlike any other.

A similar tradition of teaching through expert experience—and some great storytelling—has been the *Field & Stream* way since 1895. And since Fred Bear's day, *Field & Stream* has been on the forefront of bowhunting coverage.

Of course, much about bowhunting has changed since Bear's day—and even within the past decade. Bows have become quieter, faster, and more efficient. Arrows have become straighter, more durable, and more consistent. Today's best crossbows combine startling power with the precision to hit a nickel at 50 yards.

On one hand, the best archery equipment that was available even five years ago is hopelessly outclassed by the gear we have today. On the other, plenty of bowhunters still manage to fill their freezers each year hunting with traditional bows and wooden arrows that are no different than the ones Fred Bear used decades ago—and not much different than the equipment carried by Stone Age hunters.

At its heart, bowhunting requires the same fundamentals of today's participants that it did of ancient hunters: a deep understanding of and careful attention to your equipment—be it a new reverse-draw crossbow or an antique longbow—and the ability to get close enough to game—be it a squirrel or bull elk—to make a lethal hit with an arrow and broadhead.

The two authors of this book understand those fundamentals perfectly. *Field & Stream*'s Whitetails Editor Scott Bestul and Deputy Editor Dave Hurteau are two of the most knowledgeable and experienced bowhunting writers in America. These guys have done as much objective archery-equipment testing as anyone in this business. They are not swayed by brand loyalty or equipment sponsorships. To them, all that matters is what's proven to work.

Hurteau and Bestul are both avid, lifelong hunters, and while they still each tote a gun to the woods on occasion, I think if pressed, they would each agree with Fred Bear. There's more fun in hunting with the handicap of a bow.

ANTHONY LICATA
Editor-in-Chief, *Field & Stream*

DAVE HURTEAU

I got my first bow about 35 years ago, a hand-me-down fiberglass longbow I had to share with my brother Greg. With it, we scared the snot out of a lot of chipmunks and starlings in the little farm town where we grew up. We soon bought compounds and shot those nonstop, too. But my first big-game bowhunt, for whitetail deer, was only about a dozen years ago, and courtesy of my co-author.

Scott put me in a field-edge treestand, 20 feet up a red oak, and staked a decoy in the open, 15 yards away. Just before dusk, an 8-point buck stepped from the opposite woodline, his white rack and sleek body gleaming in long rays of sunlight reaching across the meadow. I watched him slowly close the distance, circle the fake, lower his antlers, and freight-train that plastic buck. He crashed right through it and then spun on a heel. At 17 yards, he stood there broadside, staring at two antlers, two ears, four legs, and a torso strewn in pieces over the ground. My arrow hit him just behind the shoulder. How do you not become a bowhunting fanatic after that?

Since then, as an editor with *Field & Stream* magazine, I've been lucky enough to archery hunt for a host of critters throughout much of the country, shoot and test scores of bows and crossbows, and pick the brains of the best bowhunters, the top shooters, and the engineers pushing archery's cutting edge. If you're not a bowhunting fanatic yet, we hope this book will help make you one. If you are, we want to take your skills and knowledge to the next level.

SCOTT BESTUL

I never feel like I've been shooting bows all that long until I think back to when I was 10 years old and my dad and his cousin took me to the indoor range. When Cousin Howard uncased his Allen compound bow, the joint came to a literal standstill. That bow was one of the first compounds sold in the state of Wisconsin, and the first that any of those club members had seen.

By today's standards, that Allen was a mess of cables, pulleys, and metal. But in just a few years its basic design transformed an entire sport. Not many 10 year olds, I don't guess, get to witness the start of a revolution. But I did.

Archery, I believe, is addictive because it's so intimate. I love shooting guns, but when I make a good shot, the only credit I take is in not preventing the gun from doing its job. But when an arrow flies true, I sense a piece of myself arcing through the air and landing in the target. You have to do so many things—large and small—correctly in order to shoot a bow well.

To get within bow range of an animal demands some combination of knowledge, stealth, discipline, time, and often, a whole lot of luck. Roll that all together and you get the amazing experience of bowhunting. I love it.

001 KNOW YOUR BOW HISTORY

64,000 BC
Early South African hunters fashion small stone projectile points possibly shot by bow.

20,000 BC Cave paintings in Spain are earliest proof of bow-and-arrow use.

7,000 BC Era of oldest complete bow, found in the Holmegaard Swamp in Denmark.

3,300 BC Era of "Otzi," mummified hunter found on the Italy-Austria border, carrying bow, arrows, and quiver.

1307 Swiss crossbowman William Tell shoots an apple off his son's head.

1200 Genghis Khan's archers fired 160-pound composite bows that could kill at 300 yards.

600 BC Chinese armies are using the crossbow in battle.

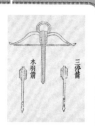

1,800 BC Assyrians introduce the recurve bow.

2,800 BC Egyptians use a composite bow, made of wood, horn, and sinew.

1363 Englishmen are required to practice archery on Sunday and holidays.

1413 English longbows beat French crossbows at the battle of Agincourt.

1545 *Toxophilus*, a book defending archery as a noble pastime, is published.

1600S Kyudo—way of the bow—is established as a martial art in Japan.

1879 The National Archery Association is established in the U.S.

1933 Fred Bear, the "Father of Modern Bowhunting" founds Bear Archery.

1946 Doug Easton sells the first commercial aluminum arrow shafts.

2015 New York and Wisconsin become the 22nd and 23rd states to allow crossbows during archery seasons.

1948 Beryl Steinbacher receives a patent for the first mechanical broadhead.

1930 Wisconsin is first state to recognize the bow as a legal weapon for hunting.

1951 Howard Hill stars in *Tembo*, a feature-length bowhunting movie during which the "World's Greatest Archer" kills a 12,000-pound elephant with a 125-pound longbow.

1990 Chuck Adams kills all 27 North American big-game species with a bow and coins the accomplishment the "Super Slam."

1923 Dr. Saxton Pope writes *Hunting with the Bow and Arrow*.

1983 Easton Archery offers the first carbon arrows.

1961 The Pope and Young Club is founded.

1981 Ohio and Arkansas grant full inclusion to crossbows during archery season.

1900 Archery becomes an official Olympic event at the Paris Games.

1969 Missourian Hollis Wilbur Allen patents the compound bow.

All bows—including modern ones, both vertical and horizontal—are very simple machines. Next to your iPhone, they are slightly more sophisticated than a rock. If they seem complicated, it may only be because the nomenclature and jargon is unfamiliar. But that's easy enough to fix. Here's a breakdown of the different types of bow you're likely to encounter in this book and out there in the real world.

TRADITIONAL BOWS

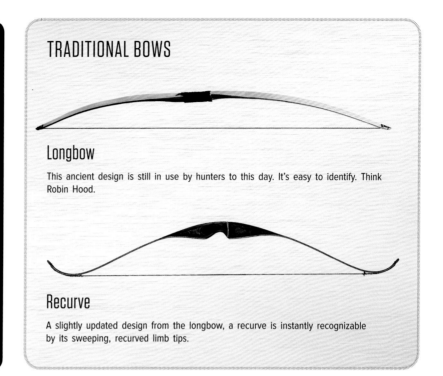

Longbow

This ancient design is still in use by hunters to this day. It's easy to identify. Think Robin Hood.

Recurve

A slightly updated design from the longbow, a recurve is instantly recognizable by its sweeping, recurved limb tips.

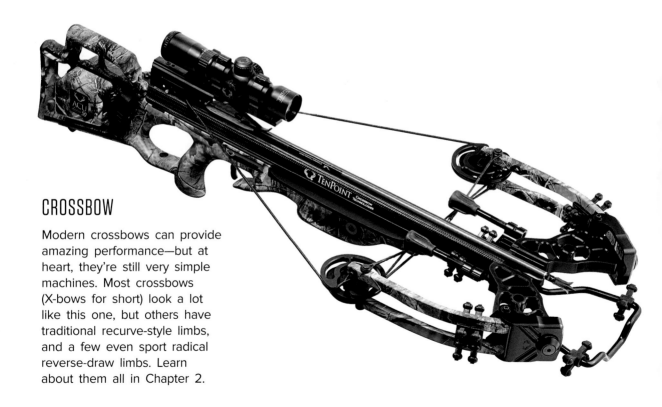

CROSSBOW

Modern crossbows can provide amazing performance—but at heart, they're still very simple machines. Most crossbows (X-bows for short) look a lot like this one, but others have traditional recurve-style limbs, and a few even sport radical reverse-draw limbs. Learn about them all in Chapter 2.

COMPOUND BOW

The compound bow could be considered "standard issue" for today's bowhunter. Though today's high-tech compounds look quite different than the original designs that debuted back in the 1960s, a compound bow is, in essence, just a standard vertical bow and with a cable and pulley system affixed to the limbs. Learn more in Chapter 1.

VERTICAL BOWS

IT'S THE BOW THAT KICK-STARTED MY PASSION

It hangs in my office—my father's first bow, a hickory self bow with a leather grip, no arrow rest, and a now-ancient Flemish string. Dad bought that bow as a kid in the 1940s and used it to hunt whitetails during some of Wisconsin's first modern archery seasons. As a boy I used to stare at that stave of wood and dream of being strong enough to launch an arrow from it.

Bows have been exerting that kind of spell on people for as long as, well, we've been people. Archeologists have found mummified hunters clutching bows. Warriors—from the ancient Chinese to North American plains Indians—made battle with the bow and arrow. And archery competitions are so steeped in lore they've spawned legends as rich as Robin Hood.

Sure, today's bows don't much look like their ancient predecessors, but the simple joys and extreme challenge of shooting a bow well remain unchanged. It doesn't matter if you're shooting a stick bow or the fastest compound on the planet; watching an arrow hit exactly where you aimed it is one addictive thrill. Here's how to make it happen.

003 GO TRADITIONAL WITH A LONGBOW

Traditional archery isn't back in vogue so much as it has never really gone away. Though traditional shooting enjoys occasional upticks in cool factor thanks to pop culture (think *The Hunger Games*), a very strong contingent of bowhunters will always prefer to keep their archery simple by sticking with the stick and string—no matter how fast compound bows get or how sexy crossbows become.

The longbow is an ancient tool, one that hunters and warriors of many cultures have used for millennia. The great exhibition archer Howard Hill rekindled interest in the weapon as an effective hunting tool, starting back in the late 1920s and wowing fans around the world over with shooting demonstrations. But Hill's true love was actually hunting with a longbow, and he used it to kill everything from bunnies to elephants.

OLD SCHOOL
Why not hunt with a tool that hasn't changed in centuries?

004 TRY A RECURVE

Like the longbow, the recurve has been around forever; reports of archers shooting bows with recurved limbs appear in the book of Psalms in the Bible. Indeed, no shortage of ancient archers from multiple cultures (including Native Americans) used composite materials and stiffening laths to bend or curve the limbs' tips away from the shooter. This design gave faster arrow speeds, greater efficiency, less hand-shock, and a shorter bow length—handy in tight quarters or while riding a horse.

The modern ambassador of the recurve bow was the legendary Fred Bear, who, like Howard Hill, achieved widespread fame through his many hunting and archery exploits. His hunt for an African elephant was featured on national radio; his hunting films played in theaters (my dad took me to see one in Madison, Wisconsin, many years ago). Bear also established Bear Archery in Michigan in 1933 and began mass-producing recurves that many used in the first modern bowhunting seasons.

As the name implies, the recurve bow's limbs curve away from the shooter; unlike a longbow, in a recurve the string touches the limbs. Recurves can also be made in multiple pieces in a "takedown" design.

Custom bowyers, who craft recurves as deadly as they are gorgeous, are largely fueling the recent boom in traditional archery. These bows can cost as much as a top-end compound. But you needn't break the bank; today's mass-produced recurve bows—including those Bear Archery still sells—are reasonably priced and deadly lethal for any big game animal.

005 MAKE IT YOURSELF

What can be more intimate—and more satisfying—than killing a deer with a bow you've built with your own hands? As the name implies, the self-bow is fashioned from nothing more than a single block (or stave) of wood, a few simple tools, and a little time. The process dates back thousands of years, to the world's first archers, and remains vital today.

Surprisingly, the selection of potential bowmaking woods is broad and diverse. In the Midwest, Native Americans adored the wood cut from the Osage orange tree. In many climes, cedar or yew was the species of choice, while hickory was the go-to tree in others. What matters most is that the tree can furnish a long blank (often as long as the archer is tall) of straight-grained wood from which an able woodworker can visualize a finished bow).

From there, the tools you need for bowmaking are relatively simple: a draw knife, a scraper or two, and a couple of wood rasps. Along with that, of course, you need a lot of long hours to transform a rough piece of raw lumber into a working weapon. Kill a deer with a self-bow and you've accomplished something that you cannot match with any bow produced in a factory.

006 COMPOUND YOUR INTEREST

Holless Wilbur Allen wanted what archers always want: more arrow speed. Knowing that a bow stores energy as you draw the string and transfers it to the arrow upon release, he looked for a way to store more energy. Allen sawed off the ends of his recurve bow, affixed an array of pulleys, and soon submitted a patent application for the world's very first compound bow—or, as he called it, an "archery bow with draw-force–multiplying attachments."

Over time, materials and designs have changed, but a compound bow is still basically just that: a bow with draw-force multipliers—also known as eccentrics or, more commonly, cams. Put simply, a cam is really nothing more than an oblong pulley with an off-center axis, but it is able to do something remarkable: It allows a bow to store maximum energy or minimum energy or anything in between, almost anywhere in the draw cycle.

Think about that for a minute.

A traditional bow starts out very easy to pull and becomes gradually harder. As such, it stores maximum energy only at the end of the draw stroke. Plus, it forces you to hold the peak weight at full draw—that's why most traditional shooters shoot substantially less draw weight than most compound shooters. But a compound bow can start out hard to pull, stay that way through much of the draw stroke—storing way more energy—and then ease up at the end so you can hold much longer at a full draw. And this is why 90 percent of today's bowhunters use a compound bow. They're easier to shoot and much more powerful than a stick bow of the same draw weight.

007 GRAPH IT OUT

Wait, don't turn the page. This isn't really as technical as it looks. It's called a draw-force curve, and it neatly illustrates exactly what a compound bow does and how various models can do it differently.

Suppose you have a 60-pound bow. That doesn't mean that you have to pull on 60 pounds the whole time you're drawing the string back; that's just the peak weight. Instead, the weight builds up to 60 as you pull, stays there for a bit, and then eases off. A draw-force curve is a graph plotting exactly how much weight you are actually pulling from the beginning of the draw stroke to the end, one inch at a time. Here's an example, with all the important parts labeled.

DRAW WEIGHT This is the *y* axis, in pounds. As you can see, it changes as you pull back, peaking at 60.

DRAW LENGTH This is the *x* axis, in inches. In this example, the bow's draw length is set at 28 inches.

FRONT SLOPE As you begin pulling back, the bow builds up to peak weight. In this example, you only have to pull the string back 13 inches to get up to 60 pounds of draw weight.

PEAK DWELL This is the distance at which the draw weight stays more or less at peak. The longer the dwell, the more energy is stored by the bow.

LET-OFF As you near the end of the draw stroke, the weight starts to ease off.

VALLEY This the distance at which the draw weight remains at full let-off. As you can see, it looks like a valley. What's commonly described as a wide or generous valley is more U-shaped. A narrow valley is more V-shaped.

BACK WALL This is where you hit the bow's draw stops and you can't pull back any farther. The weight shoots up because most shooters pull hard against the wall. The more vertical this line is, the harder the wall.

STORED ENERGY Everything under the curve is energy stored. The more shading, the more energy, the faster the bow.

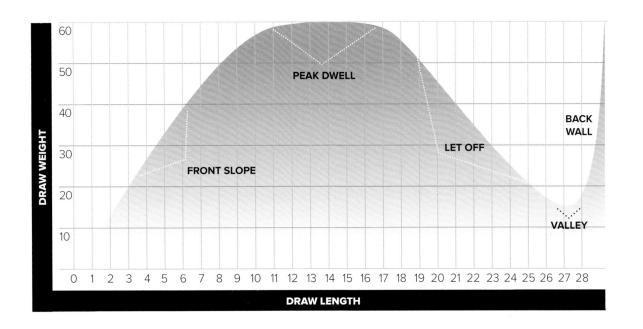

008 THROW THE CURVE

Bow engineers can design cams to get almost any draw-force curve, for smooth bows, speed bows, or anything in between. The question is, what kind of bow do you want?

NO CAM

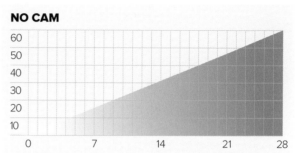

For comparison, this shows the draw-force curve of a traditional longbow. Basically, it goes straight uphill.

SMOOTH CAM

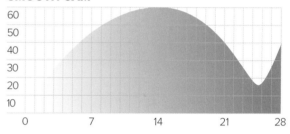

A compound bow designed for moderate speed and comfortable shooting comes up to peak weight gradually, stays there for a short distance, and drops gradually into a generous U-shaped valley. The gentle slopes and soft curves make for a smooth, easy draw stroke.

HARD CAM

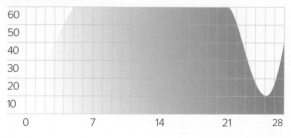

A bow with aggressive cams designed for maximum speed gets to peak weight quickly, stays there as long as possible, and drops sharply into a narrow V-shaped valley. The steep angles and hard curves make this bow much harder to handle—but notice how much more energy it stores.

THE SPEED TRAP

Dave Hurteau on

The absolute worst way you can use an ultrafast bow is to pair it with lightweight arrows—achieving the flattest possible trajectory in order to fling shafts at critters from ungodly distances. It's one thing out on the 3-D range, where extreme long-range shooting is just for fun. But your job as a hunter is to kill critters quick, not to find out from how great a distance you can hit one.

009 GO SLOW

The average bow-shot at a whitetail deer is under 20 yards; the majority are under 30. You don't need a super-flat-shooting speed bow. In theory, speed is great, but in a treestand, there's a lot to be said for a bow you can pull back easily, hold at full draw for a long time, and let down without any sudden, game-spooking motions—in other words, a slower bow.

010 BUY A NEW COMPOUND

You can hunt big game using an original Allen Speedster or a Dukes-era Martin Warthog, but ever since the first compound bow, the technology has advanced at breakneck speed. Modern longbows are much like those from the late Pleistocene, but today's compounds barely resemble those of just a couple of decades ago, and they shoot much, much better.

Over the last couple of decades, compound bow efficiencies have soared. A speed bow of yesteryear with hard cams and a demanding draw cycle might have had an IBO rating of 290 fps. Today's smooth bows routinely IBO 320—that's a huge difference. Various improvements mean that today's bows are also quieter and shoot more smoothly.

So you want to own a good compound bow? First and foremost, get a new or recent model. You don't have to drop a grand on this year's flagship bow; the latest mid-priced bows often perform better than the top models from only five or six years ago. Just go get ahold of something fairly new, and you'll be happy you did.

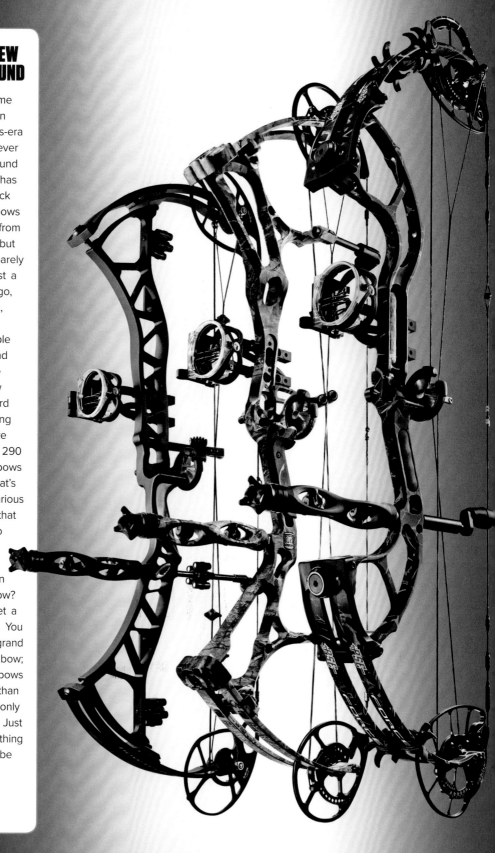

011 DON'T BE A FANBOY

Brand loyalty makes sense. If you plunk your money down for a chainsaw or a pickup truck and both it and its maker serve you well, you have every reason to buy that brand again. But in archery we have something more than mere loyal customers. We have fanboys, guys so convinced of their pet brand's superiority that all other bows are "junk" by comparison—never mind that they've never seriously shot any of the other bows.

This is stupid.

I know because I have shot the other bows. Every year, Bestul and I test all the new flagship models for *Field & Stream*'s Best of the Best Awards. We evaluate other bows for other stories. We've hunted with a wide variety of brands. And what we have both found is that: one, pretty much all of the biggest players make a heck of a good bow; two, the practical differences between the brands' top models is small; and three, which brand is at the very top of the heap changes regularly. A few years back, Mathews and Hoyt dominated. Lately, it's been all Bowtech and Elite. At the moment, Obsession is surging. And it'll change again, and again, and again.

So go on and shoot whatever you like. Doesn't matter to me. But be smart—and don't be a fanboy.

012 IGNORE THE NOISE

I was chatting recently with a bow engineer who would begin every point with, "What people don't understand about bows is . . ." He covered maybe half a dozen different topics—that brace height isn't as important as it used to be, that a short bow that's too light will give you problems, and so on. "So," I asked him, "why don't people understand these things?"

"Too much noise."

He didn't specify what he meant by noise, but it's not hard to guess. I've read one bow company's ad copy that describes a model's long 8-inch brace height as "extremely forgiving" and another's short 6½-inch brace height as "offering extreme forgiveness." Baloney. Then there's the TV hunter shilling for brand X—and hoping you don't remember that he used Brand Y last year when they offered the better sponsorship deal. And sure enough, some brands do win more shooting competitions; they just happen to be sponsoring the most shooters.

When choosing a bow, ignore the marketing hype; shoot as many makes and models as you can. Go to several dealers. Skip stores where you can't shoot. Try your buddy's bows. Decide for yourself what you like. Only then should you plunk down your money.

013 BALANCE SPEED AND "SHOOTABILITY"

When comparing bows, everyone talks speed versus shootability. *Speed* is simple: How fast does that sucker fling an arrow? *Shootability* is a ridiculous non-word that marketing people invented, and it should be chucked over a guardrail (the word, not the people). Nonetheless, it popularly refers to the ease with which you can draw and fire a bow.

As a rule, more speed will usually mean less shootablity, and vice versa. It's a trade-off, and the wild card is you. If you can shoot a blazing-fast bow and still be hell on wheels both on the range and in the deer woods, then more power to you (literally). On the other hand, a slower, easier-shooting bow can definitely help you keep your form together, especially when your knees are knocking. It's a matter of give and take. And getting the perfect bow for you means knowing how to give and take wisely.

When shopping for the perfect bow, you need to know what to look for, and how to find it. Here's a good routine to test every bow you pick up.

FIT AND FINISH Grab a bow off the shelf. Examine the materials and workmanship. Are the limb pockets plastic (okay) or aluminum (better)? Is the riser cast (okay) or extruded, forged, or machined out of a single billet (better)? Are the cutouts neat and tidy? Is the finish uniform? Is the bow durable? Do you like how it looks?

DRAW CYCLE Ask the shop owner if you can draw the bow, and then do so several times, slowly. Ideally, the motion will feel even and smooth, with a minimum of grittiness or bumps as the cam turns over. Don't expect a fast bow to draw like a slow one.

BACK WALL Draw the bow again, all the way back until it stops. How does the stop feel? Hard and solid, like a concrete wall? Or a little softer? Most shooters, especially hunters, prefer the former.

VALLEY From the back wall, ease up a little. The valley determines how much you can relax at full draw before the string suddenly lets down. Steep or narrow valleys—common on speed bows—jerk your arm forward at the slightest relaxation, while generous or wide valleys offer more leeway, which many hunters prefer.

SHOCK AND VIBRATION Ask to shoot the bow. Step close to the target so you're sure to hit it. Close your eyes, shoot, and concentrate on what you feel in your bow hand. Some bows, especially light, fast ones, will jump or vibrate a little. That's not good. A bow with no noticeable shock or vibration is "dead in the hand."

NOISE Shoot with your eyes closed again; this time, listen carefully. Some bows, even very fast ones, are noticeably quieter, and in hunting, the quieter, the better.

BALANCE AND HANDLING How does the bow feel in your hand? Does it balance naturally or list a little? Is it easy to settle on target? Grip is highly personal, but thin grips are in vogue and seem to reduce torque.

SPEED Look at the manufacturer's IBO rating, usually listed on the bow. This number is usually a little inflated, but it can still make for a serviceable apples-to-apples comparison between bows.

ACCURACY AND FORGIVENESS Critical but complicated, these qualities are hard to evaluate in the store, but we'll look at them more closely soon.

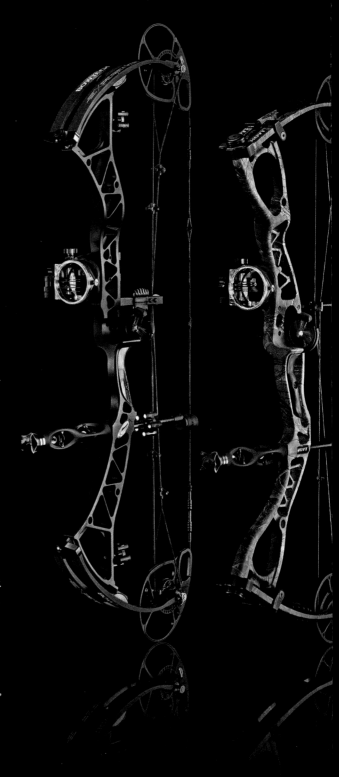

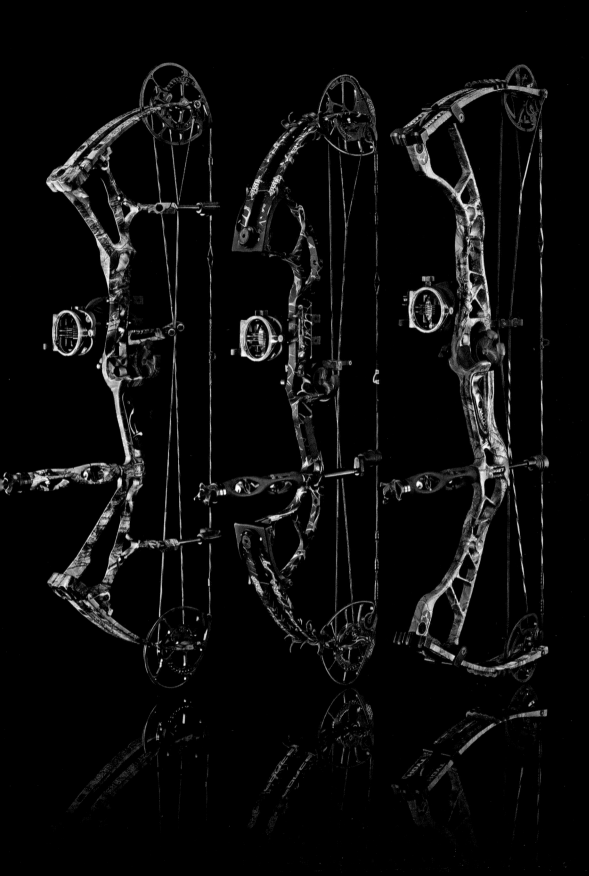

015 DON'T SWEAT BOW ACCURACY

It's natural to assume that bow accuracy is similar to rifle accuracy but, in reality, the two are very different. In riflery, you can reasonably discuss inherent accuracy because you can put a rifle on a bench rest, shoot a variety of ammo, and pretty much find out what the thing is capable of. Some rifles will shoot under a Minute of Angle; others won't put three shots into a deer-crossing sign. (Don't go shooting at deer-crossing signs.)

Although you can test bows with a Hooter Shooter (a machine that fires off arrows with perfect consistency, thus removing the human element), this exercise doesn't really tell you anything. Almost every bow can be tuned to hit virtually the same hole time and again at 20 yards, and be very close to that out to 60 or 70.

In other words, don't worry about the bow's accuracy. Worry about *your* accuracy with a given bow, which comes down to three things: forgiveness, tunability, and you. For now, let's look more closely at the first two factors.

016 READ OUR TESTS

The best way to test bow forgiveness is to get several different shooters—each with slightly different shooting form and making slightly different errors—to shoot groups at a single distance with all the latest compound bows.

The average shopper, can't do that, but we do it every year for *Field & Stream*'s Best of the Best bow testing. We invite all the major manufacturers to submit their best new bows for the test. After a variety of objective tests, such as speed and noise measurements, our four-man test panel spends a couple days on the range wringing out each new bow, tallying the results, and then averaging the final scores. And every year we find that not only do some bows shoot better than others, but they do so with obvious consistency between the shooters. In other words, they are more forgiving of a variety of shooter screw-ups. And we are not afraid to name names.

So in a sense, the easiest way to find a new, forgiving bow is to read *Field & Stream*. The only other test like it is *Outdoor Life*'s— another great reference.

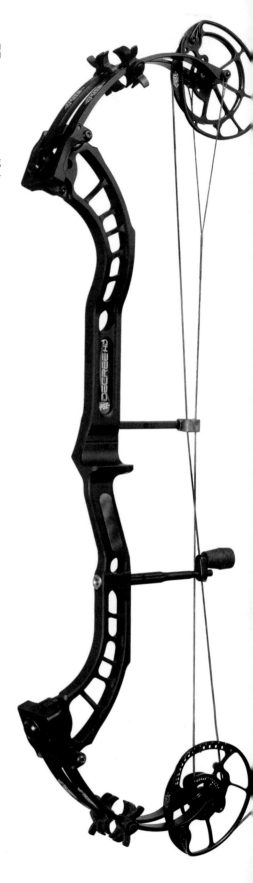

017 SEEK FORGIVENESS— BUT BEWARE

Bow forgiveness is a marketing department's dream. It has the benefit of sounding both unequivocally good (who doesn't want forgiveness?) and being impossible to quantify. And so hucksters have flogged the term senseless. Company X's latest model is not only extremely forgiving but even more extremely forgiving than all their other extremely forgiving models. It's total B.S.

A forgiving bow, by definition, forgives your mistakes. That doesn't mean you can let your shooting form go to hell and still expect to hit the bull's-eye. No bow will do that for you. But, having shot scores and scores of different bows, I can tell you that some models punish your mistakes less harshly than others. One may put you only a few inches out of the bull if you punch the trigger; another may put you in the weeds.

In the real world, a bow that's easier to shoot is more accurate. But shopping for forgiveness is tricky. There's no specific formula. As a very general rule, a heavier bow—which your twists and jerks affect less—is easier to shoot well. Beyond that, it's mostly a mystery, the answer to which you'll best find by shooting lots of bows before you buy.

018 LOOK PAST THE PEEP

You can get a decent feel for how well you shoot various bows even if they're not specifically set up for you. The best pro shops have a 20-yard or longer shooting range ,and various bows already set up with D-loops, accessories, and a good basic tune. From there, all you need is the correct draw length and peep-sight placement.

The first takes only a few minutes to set up in most cases. The latter is also easy to achieve, if the peep needs only a slight adjustment. Otherwise, just anchor up as usual, line up the top pin with the edge of the string in the same place each time, and start shooting groups.

Don't worry where the arrow hits in relation to the bull; just compare groups from bow to bow. This is not a perfect solution, but you'll still get a good idea which bows feel and shoot best for you.

019 GET DRAW LENGTH RIGHT

Many hunters shoot too long a draw length, which hurts shooting form and accuracy. A bow that's too long makes it difficult to hold against the back wall and overextends your bow arm.

Yet shortening your draw length can cost lots of speed (about 10 fps per inch), so some hunters are reluctant to do it. Also, adjusting the draw length can be a pain. You can adjust some bows with a set of hex wrenches; others require a bow press or even new cams.

So just how does too great a draw length hurt your accuracy? Our test panel, consisting of Bestul and me, as well as *Field & Stream* contributor and book editor Will Brantley, put this to the test with three different bows, each set at the correct draw length (as determined by our bow-shop pro) and then each set 1 inch too long. The results? All three of us utterly fell apart with too much draw length, and for the same reasons. It messed up our anchor points and stretched out our bow arms until they were in line with the string. Once the string whacks you in the arm a couple of times, you get jumpy, and everything falls apart.

In short, ensuring that the bow you pick is set to your exact draw length is the most important step in ensuring it hits where you aim.

020 LIGHTEN UP (BUT NOT TOO MUCH)

In bowhunting, conventional wisdom says a bow that's longer measured axle to axle is easier to shoot accurately than a shorter one because it's easier to hold it steadily on target. That must be right; why else would so many competitive archers shoot 45-inch-plus bows?

But short, lightweight bows have dominated the hunting market for years as they are handier in a treestand or ground blind. So how significant is the longer bow's accuracy edge? Is it worth carrying a heavier, more unwieldy bow in the field?

The answer is no—at least not at most field ranges. We compared short axle-to-axle bows (30 to 31 inches) to longer models (34 to 35 inches) from

three different companies, using a trio of shooters on our test panel. We shot the longer, heavier bows a bit better—but not greatly so until we stepped back to 60 yards. If you keep your shots within 30 or even 40 yards, a short, light bow is nice to have and will cost you next to nothing in accuracy.

But in my experience, there is a short-and-light threshold that, when crossed, can send everything straight to hell. In the past year, I tested four bows at or under 30 inches and 3.5 pounds. One shot well; others performed dismally, averaging almost 4 inch groups at 30 yards. Novice shooters did even worse; my brother and nephew could barely hit the target.

021 BRACE YOURSELF

As with axle-to-axle length, there is a lot of conventional wisdom about brace height (BH), the widest point between the bow's grip and string. A shorter BH—6 inches or less—makes a bow faster by as much as 10 fps per inch. A longer BH supposedly means more forgiveness, as the arrow is on the string for a shorter distance and period of time, so screwups during the shot affect it less.

But while watching slow-motion video of myself shooting a couple years back, it looked obvious that the arrow was gone before I could move a muscle. A few years ago, a bow engineer told me that BH just doesn't matter with today's fast bows for that very reason.

So we put the idea to the test. Our team compared two bows of the same make with identical specs, except BH. I shot a Bear Motive 6 (6-inch BH) and a Motive 7 (7). Bestul shot a McPherson Monster MR5 (5) and MR7 (7). Brantley shot a Hoyt Spyder Turbo (6) and Spyder 34 (6¾). None of us found more than a lick of difference in bow accuracy or forgiveness. Brantley and I actually shot the shorter-BH bow slightly better, Bestul did best with the longer, but neither shooter did appreciably better. We all found that a longer BH made for a slightly easier draw cycle, but that's a pretty minor advantage—particularly when compared against speed.

022 INVEST IN A FLAGSHIP BOW

In most pro shops, you'll see bows in a range of prices. In the flagship section, the price tag will hit you like a hammer. But if you shoot such a bow, you might consider selling your kidney to pay for it.

"How can they charge that?" your little voice of sanity asks. Well, partly because they know you'll pay it, but also because they've poured the best effort and materials into that one model for the year.

The riser is likely machined out of a single block of material, and perhaps made of carbon. It will sport the company's most advanced cam system. Usually a roller guard ensures consistent cable clearance. The overall craftsmanship will be superb.

That fanciness won't kill a deer any deader than one shot with a bow costing half as much. But for some people, buying the absolute best is important. To that end, every year four guys take the *Field & Stream* bow test, a three-day shootout that pits every major bow company's flagship model in a contest for the best. The bows are scored on a 100-point scale, and in a typical year, the difference between the winner and fifth place is about 5 points—in other words, not much. Typically, the winning bow does several things very well and almost nothing wrong. So the question is: "Is it worth a thousand-plus dollars?"

That's up to you. Flagship bows are a joy to shoot, no question, and if one model makes you a better archer than you were before, you could justify it as a wise investment. Then again, you might fall into the "fanboy fever" trap, which requires that you trade in last year's hot shooter toward next year's model. In that case, we have no advice for you except to warn that no, selling your other kidney is not an option.

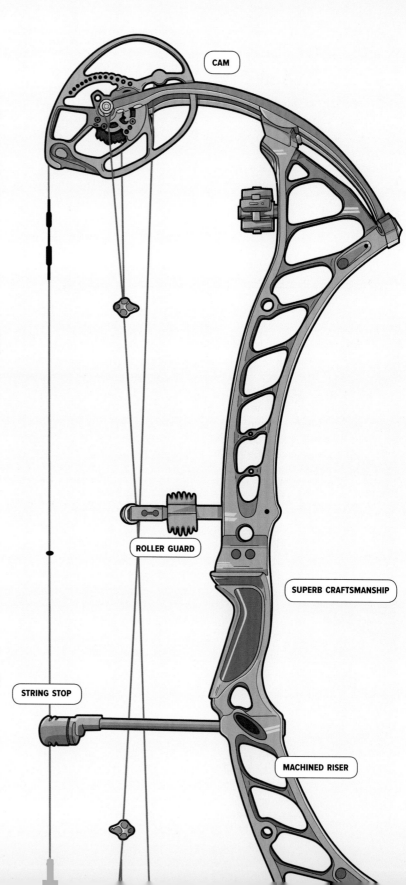

CAM

ROLLER GUARD

SUPERB CRAFTSMANSHIP

STRING STOP

MACHINED RISER

023 GET A GOOD DEAL

For the last several years, we've been testing "budget" bows. Generally, $500 is our price cap, and while these bows never quite match more costly models' performance, we are perennially blown away at how good they are for the price. This brings us to the next burning question: "What's the difference between a company's midline (budget) bows and their flagship models?"

Many budget bows have a cast riser and plastic cable guard, both cheaper to produce. Most are slower by at least 10–15 fps, often because they're equipped with older cam designs. The draw cycle may feel a bit clunky, and there may be a little extra buzz after the shot.

For some, these distinctions are huge. But the truth is, they make very little difference in most real-world hunting scenarios. If the best you can afford is a mid-line bow, there's no reason to feel handicapped. They are more than up to the job and typically represent a fantastic value. What's more, they are often sold as kits, (already rigged with accessories) and available through big-box stores.

024 BUY A USED BOW

Believe it or not, many modern bowhunters will routinely offload last year's top model for today's latest-and-greatest ones. As a result, you can find a lot of killer used bows at bargain prices. You can shop online (eBay is full of used bows), but your local pro shop is a better option because you can carefully inspect and shoot the bow before buying it. A pro shop commonly includes setup and tuning costs in the deal, too.

When shopping, give every bow a careful inspection. Make sure strings and cables are in good shape, as replacement costs can add $100 or more to a seemingly smoking deal. Worn strings look fuzzy, but be especially on the lookout for fraying, nicks,

and cuts. Examine the bottom edge of the lower cam for damage from resting against hard surfaces. Inspect limbs for cracks or splits. Run a cotton ball over each limb's surface; snagged white fuzz indicates a problem. If the limbs are compromised at all, you should walk away.

Check the draw length. Most new bows are adjustable, but a few require expensive replacement cams or modules to change this, and the wrong length will ruin your accuracy (see item 20). Also, look for quality accessories. Because dealers rarely give sellers extra money for sights, rests, and other add-ons, they don't add much to the price—but they add a lot to the value.

025 SHOOT A FIXED MULTI-PIN SIGHT

A fixed sight typically features three to five adjustable sight pins stacked vertically inside a round, stationary housing. Because most hunting arrows drop quickly after 20 or 30 yards, most hunters sight in their top pin to hit dead-on at 20 or 30, and then set subsequent pins for greater distances in 10-yard increments. A typical 3-pin arrangement, for example, is 20, 30, and 40, top to bottom.

The beauty of a fixed, multi-pin sight is that it's simple. Once you're sighted in, just tighten everything down. Then, when a buck comes in and turns broadside at 20 yards, for example, there's nothing to do but put your 20-yard pin on its vitals and shoot.

The downsides are two: First, it's easy to pick the wrong pin in the heat of the moment—say, a 20-yard pin for a buck at 30 yards—and let your arrow fly harmlessly beneath its belly. Second, having more sight pins obscure the sight picture, which complicates aiming.

026 SPLIT THE DIFFERENCE

My favorite sight type is a two-pin slider. I tend to sight the pins in for 30 and 40 yards. I'm mostly a whitetail hunter, and so the vast majority of my shots at animals are made inside 40 yards. So I use the sight just like a standard fixed-pin sight most of the time. But, the slider feature is there if I need it (especially if I have to take any follow-up shots). When I'm on the range, sliding the bottom pin down allows me to practice beyond 100 yards.

027 TRY A SINGLE-PIN SLIDER

This type of sight has only one pin inside a circular housing—but the whole housing moves up and down via a lever or knob. As you move the lever or turn the knob on a single-pin slider, an indicator tab moves up or down a tape marked with various ranges. Once you've sighted in, you simply align the tab with the appropriate yardage and shoot.

This kind of slider has three upsides. First, you never have to hold off. When you range a buck at 36 yards, you dial your sight to "36" and aim dead-on. With a fixed sight, by comparison, you'd have to either hold high with your 30-yard pin, hold low with your 40, or split the difference. Second, a slider offers more latitude of elevation adjustment, which is great for long-distance shooting on the range. With most sliders, you can take your shot from 10 yards out to 100 or more without holding off. Third, a slider provides a much cleaner sight picture, and you can't pick the wrong pin (although you can pick the wrong yardage).

On the other side of the coin, to be accurate with a slider, the configuration of the numbers on the range tape (the gaps between 20, 30, 40, and so on) must

marry with the arrow trajectory for your specific setup. These sights often come with an array of preprinted tapes, and with any luck there will be one that works for you. Online calculators also allow you to print customized tapes. But for some shooters, all of this is a hassle they really don't want to deal with. (You can mark the ranges manually, which simplifies things a little but is typically less precise.)

The more obvious downside, however, is that wild animals are not always very cooperative about waiting around while you take the time to make precise range measurements and then dial your sight in to match. To accommodate this reality, many hunters keep the pin at 30, and only make adjustments for longer shots or when there's plenty of time.

028 GO SMALL

Conventional wisdom says that a small, single pin makes for more precise aiming, which should give better accuracy. We wanted to see if this is true. Also, because smaller pins are harder to see in low light, we wanted to see if that difference in accuracy is worth the trade-off. So we conducted a test in which three shooters shot three different bows, each with a 5-pin Trophy Ridge Cypher 5 sight with 0.029-inch pins vs. an HHA Sports Optimizer single-pin slider sight with a 0.010 pin.

Here are the total average groups for large-multi-pin sight versus small-single-pin sight:

YDS	SINGLE PIN	MULTI-PIN
30	2.77	2.82
40	3.53	3.86
60	4.96	5.61

The smaller, single-pin sight really came into its own at long distance, but inside 40 yards it didn't make much difference. We could definitely see the larger pins better in low light. In other words, larger pins probably make the best sense for a whitetail woods bow—smaller ones are superior for long-range, open-country hunting or 3-D target shooting.

029 CAPTURE THE MOMENT

Bowhunters are always arguing about something. When they can't think of anything else, they squabble over rests—namely, capture rests versus fall-away rests. Naturally, one is awesome, the other is junk—but I can't tell which is which.

I exclusively shot a capture rest for years. Bestul still does, for good reason: They're foolproof. The capture rest is a non-mechanical device that provides a rest for your arrow. It also holds the shaft firmly in place so it doesn't go clanking around should you catch it on a limb or if you are shaking like a disco ball with buck fever. The most popular capture rest is the Whisker Biscuit, but several good ones are available.

Critics will tell you that because your arrow's fletchings must pass through a capture rest's bristles, this type of rest costs you both velocity and accuracy. The part about velocity is true, but not to the degree some claim (see item 31). The latter assertion regarding accuracy is a non-issue for hunters. A Whisker Biscuit doesn't cause any significant loss in accuracy, but even if it did, you could go to a capture rest with no fletching contact, such as a Hostage. The main advantage of a capture rest is that it's simple. It has no moving parts and causes no timing issues. You slap it on, and it works 99 percent of the time.

030 USE A FALL-AWAY REST

A fall-away rest is a mechanical device that, like a capture rest, provides a rest for your arrow. However, on a fall-away type, the part that holds the shaft, called the launcher, falls out of the way so fast that there is zero contact with the arrow's fletchings.

Opponents say that the moving parts and timing issues can blow a critical shot all to hell. This is theoretically true. But I've seen very few mechanical errors with fall-away rests, and the timing is not difficult to set correctly. What's more, many fall-away rests offer full containment of the arrow, just as capture rests do. They also offer a small advantage in arrow velocity, as well as more latitude in terms of arrow tuning, which can result in a slight bump in accuracy.

031 MAKE AN INFORMED CHOICE

The *Field & Stream* testers wanted to settle the capture versus fall-away rest debate once and for all, so we put them head-to-head as a part of our 10,000-arrow test to find the real speed and accuracy difference—and ultimately determine which rest style is truly better. Bestul, Brantley,

YDS	CAPTURE	FALL-AWAY
30	2.68	2.55
40	3.67	3.15
60	5.29	5.19

and I compared the Whisker Biscuit to both a Trophy Taker Smackdown and Quality Archery Design's UltraRest HD. First, using both a Velocitip Ballistic System and a chronograph, we tested the speed of one versus the other on the same bows, using the same arrow. Once that was done, we compared their accuracy in the field with our standard range test, which consists of all of us measuring 10 3-arrow groups shot at 30, 40, and 60 yards. (We actually each shoot 11 groups at each range, but we throw the worst group out to eliminate flyers.)

What did we find? Despite some claims that a fall-away offers a speed advantage of up to 15 fps, we only found a 3- to 6-fps advantage. But accuracy was the bigger surprise.

Brantley, a fall-away devotee, shot the Whisker Biscuit just as well all the way out to 60 yards. Bestul and I, both Whisker Biscuit fans, shot the fall-aways better at distance. That opened everyone's eyes a bit. Overall, the fall-away came out a bit better in accuracy, but the difference was peanuts. There's no denying the speed difference, but it too is slight. So if you're a max-performance kind of shooter, go with the fall-away. If you like to keep things simple, you can shoot a capture rest with the knowledge that you're giving up almost nothing.

032 TRY A STABILIZER

A stabilizer is simply a weight that screws into the front of the bow's riser to help balance and stabilize the bow while aiming, as well as mitigate vibration and noise. Far and away the most popular for hunting bows is a straight 5- or 6-inch model. And yet, when we tested typical hunting models for our Ultimate Bow coverage, we found that they had no significant impact on accuracy.

Given that result, we wanted to see if it would make a difference to try the longer, heavier models that are popular with long-range Western hunters. So we did. And the results were astonishing. Will Brantley and I did the shooting. Neither of us noticed a big difference out to 40 yards, but at 60, the Earth teetered a little.

Shooting a Bowtech Insanity CPXL with your basic 5-inch hunting stabilizer, I shot 10 three-shot groups that averaged 4.82 inches. Then I screwed on a $10^{3}/_{8}$-inch, 10.5-ounce Doinker EFDF and shot 10 more groups at 60. Average size was 2.97 inches. I thought it had to be a fluke, so I shot another 10 groups. They averaged 3.21 inches. Meanwhile, Brantley cut his 60-yard groups nearly in half (from 6.12 to 3.50) when he went from no stabilizer to a 12-inch, 17-ounce Fuse Carbon Bowhunter Freestyle on a Hoyt Spyder Turbo. He called the result "amazing." Although it doesn't make sense to hang such a big, heavy stabilizer on a short-range woods bow, on a long-range western or 3-D bow, carrying a little extra weight is worth all that extra accuracy.

033 SKIP THE STABILIZER

One of the main stated purposes of a stabilizer is to make a bow easier to hold steadily on target for improved accuracy. We wanted to find out if the fairly short, light 5- to 6-inch versions hunters slap on as a matter of course actually help. So we shot three different bows, each with and without a typical hunting stabilizer.

THE RESULTS With the total average group sizes for 6-inch hunting stabilizer versus no stabilizer, we found no clear accuracy advantage. Unless your only goal is to tame a bow with lots of noise and vibration, you are better off going bigger (see item 32). Or on a short-range, handy woods bow, you may want to go without any stabilizer at all.

YDS	STABILIZER	NO STABILIZER
30	2.59	2.75
40	3.66	3.61
60	5.07	5.23

034 LOSE YOUR GRIP

YDS	WITH GRIP	NO GRIP
30	3.05	2.43
40	3.88	3.62
60	6.01	4.98

More and more accuracy-obsessed archers are removing the grips on their bows or buying models with very thin or no grips. (And some new bows even come from the factory with flat panels to replace the grip, should you decide to remove it.) The idea is that a thick grip or tacky rubber model makes for better hand-to-bow contact, which ups the odds of torquing the riser during the shot. To see if this makes a real difference in accuracy, we chose three bows with substantial grips: a Bear Motive 6 with a rubber grip, a Mathews Creed with a large wood grip, and a Hoyt Charger, also with a rubber grip. Then we shot them with and without grips.

THE RESULTS Total average group sizes for grip on, grip off: All three testers shot better without the grip. For me, the difference didn't show up until I stepped back to 60. But Bestul, testing the thickest grip of all—Mathews' famous hunk of walnut—shot a full inch better at 30, 40, and 60 after removing it. There's no doubt: Going without a grip is better.

BOW SLINGS

Dave Hurteau on

Every serious bowhunter installs a sling on his bow (which attaches at the base of the riser and wraps around your wrist when you're gripping the bow). Because proper form requires shooting with an open hand, you need one to catch the bow after the shot, right? Baloney. In real life, almost every hunter catches the bow before the sling does. I'm not convinced a sling does much of anything for anyone. If you want one, if it makes you feel you're less likely to drop your bow from the treestand, God bless. But I can't, in good faith, tell you that it will really help you.

035 GO SHORT

If, like most hunters, you keep your field shots inside 30 or 35 yards, this is your perfect bow. You're probably after whitetails, turkeys, and perhaps pigs in the woods or elk in the timber. You don't routinely practice or shoot 3-D at long ranges.

> SIGHTS AND PINS

FIXED, MULTI-, MIDSIZE PINS: You don't need an extra-fine pin or a sliding sight at close ranges. Keep it simple: Go with a fixed three-pin sight, or use a five-pin for long-range practice and drop the two or three bottom pins right out of the sight picture for hunting.

> REST

NON-MECHANICAL, FULL- CAPTURE: There's no real advantage to a fallaway here. Unless you must have that extra 3 to 6 fps, go with a foolproof, no-fail Whisker Biscuit rest.

> GRIP

NONE: The grip test was one of the few that showed a clear difference in accuracy at all ranges. Take it off.

> STABILIZER

SMALL OR NONE: It makes no sense to put a long, heavy stabilizer on a short, handy bow. Go short or go without.

> BRACE HEIGHT

6 INCHES: You get an extra 10 fps or so compared with 7 inches, and no lost accuracy. The bump in speed offsets shooting with a fail-safe rest or turning your bow down a bit for an easier, stealthier draw on close-range critters.

> AXLE TO AXLE

30–32 INCHES: Going longer won't help accuracy these ranges. Why not have a short, handy bow? It won't hurt you in the treestand and will help greatly when you're still-hunting, stalking, or hunting from a blind.

> ARROW

HEAVY, SMALL-DIAMETER, BLAZER VANES: QuickSpin vanes offer very little accuracy advantage inside 40 yards and they will quickly mangle the bristles of a Whisker Biscuit rest. Go with standard Blazer vanes.

036 GO LONG

If you are one of the few who can, in good conscience, shoot at an animal beyond 40 yards, this is your bow. It's well suited for both hunting and long-distance 3-D shooting. Odds are you hunt the West, where open country tends to make for longer shots.

> SIGHT AND PINS

SINGLE, MICRO-PIN SLIDER: We clearly shot better at long range with this type of sight. The small single pin type allows for fine aiming and gives an uncluttered sight picture.

> REST

FALL-AWAY REST: A fall-away rest adds long-range accuracy, and the extra speed helps mitigate range-estimation errors.

> GRIP

NONE: We shot a full inch better with no grip at 60 yards.

> STABILIZER

LONG AND HEAVY: A small stabilizer's effect on accuracy was varied in our tests. But a long, heavy model did tighten our groups at long range.

> BRACE HEIGHT

6 INCHES: Again, why not? It's faster, with no accuracy trade-off.

> AXLE TO AXLE

33–35 INCHES: Lean toward the shorter (and likely lighter) side of this range if you'll do a lot of hiking and climbing, the longer if not or if you are just crazy-obsessed with long-range accuracy.

> ARROW

ARROW MIDWEIGHT, SMALL-DIAMETER, QUICKSPIN VANES: The narrow shaft lets you shoot a somewhat lighter, flatter-shooting arrow and still get great penetration.

037 SET UP YOUR OWN BOW

If you find the information on the next four pages intimidating, there's a simple solution: skip ahead and have a shop pro set up your bow. Those guys can use your support, and you'll have some added confidence in knowing an expert did the job. On the other hand, setting up your own bow is not terribly difficult. The basic procedure involves installing a rest, finding the nocking point, tying a D-loop, attaching a sight, finding the center shot, installing a peep sight, and serving it in. How much of this you take on yourself depends mostly on what tools you want to invest in. You can do all but install the peep with nothing more than a $15 bow square. For another $100 or so, a bow vise, string level, and arrow level will let you do the same with considerably better precision. Add a basic bow press—anywhere from $50 to $500—and you can do it all, plus more.

If you decide to do your own setup, take this preliminary step right now, before you do anything else: Grab your bow and look at the middle of the riser to locate the two threaded holes positioned side by side just above the arrow shelf. These are called the Berger holes. On the outside of the riser (opposite the shelf), they accept your arrow rest's mounting screw. If that were all they did, they wouldn't merit this discussion. But they also help you set up your bow correctly because on the inside of the riser, they provide a visual guide for how high your arrow should rest above the shelf. Viewed from the side, a nocked, level arrow should ideally cover up both holes evenly. If it doesn't, use the rest's elevation adjustment to get it as close as possible. It doesn't have to be perfect, but it's a good starting point.

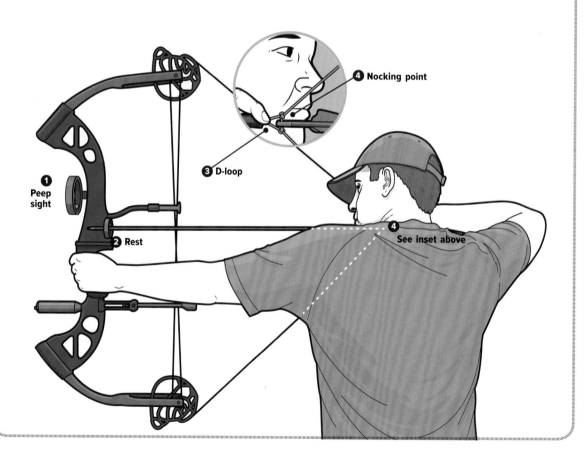

4 Nocking point

3 D-loop

1 Peep sight

2 Rest

4 See inset above

038 CHECK CAM LEAN AND TIMING

A problem with either cam lean or timing can complicate basic bow setup, so rule out issues with both before you even take your new bow home. Ask your shop pro to help you check the following.

LEAN ON THE CAM Take a straight arrow and lay it flat against the cam(s). If the shaft runs parallel to the bowstring, your cam is straight. If not, it's leaning. A little cant can be fine, as some models shoot best that way; discuss this with your pro. Lots of lean is usually a problem, though, and one that the shop should fix for you before the sale is final.

DON'T BE A TWO-TIMER If you're buying a two-cam bow, ask the pro to draw it back manually or on a draw board. The cams should roll off peak weight and into the valley exactly at the same time. Most cams have a pair of timing dots or lines. The string should run between them, both top and bottom. If it doesn't, ask the pro to fix the timing.

039 INSTALL A FALL-AWAY REST

This is a two-part process. First, simply bolt the rest onto the riser; make sure it's square, level, and aligned with the Berger holes; and then tighten it down.

The second part requires that you install the D-loop (see item 42). With that done, you need to attach and time the activation cord to ensure that the launcher falls out of the way quickly enough to avoid fletching contact. In most cases, you'll attach the cord to the down cable, and the easiest way to do this is with a clamp typically included with the rest. Another option is to serve it into the cable.

The key is to initially leave the cord loose enough so that it will slide through the clamp (or cable) as you draw the bow. With most fall-away rests, the cord will automatically slide to the proper position when you reach full draw. Then just let down and tighten the clamp, or cut and melt the cord so it can no longer slide through the cable.

040 ATTACH A CAPTURE REST

This is a piece of cake. Simply attach the rest by threading the provided bolt into the first Berger hole. Many capture rests, including most Hostage and Whisker Biscuit models, automatically square up to the riser and align with the Berger holes, right out of the box. In this case, just tighten the screw(s). (Some models include a second set screw.) Otherwise, adjust the rest to get it square and level, and then nock an arrow and adjust the rest's height if necessary to align with the Berger holes. Tighten everything down.

041 FIND THE CENTER SHOT

Finding the center shot simply means moving the rest left or right until the arrow appears to align perfectly with the string and the center of the riser. Nock an arrow and hold your bow at arm's length, or square it up in a bow vise and step straight back. Close your weak eye and visually align the string with the vertical center of the riser. Have a look at the arrow. Odds are the tip is pointing off to the left or right.

Another way is to nock an arrow and set the bow's bottom cam on the ground between your feet, close one eye, look over the bow, and align the arrow shaft with the center of the riser shelf (a long stabilizer helps as a reference in this method).

You can also nock an arrow and take equal measurements from the front and back of the riser to the arrow. Or you can use a laser level, which is how many pro shops do it. In each case, the idea is to get the arrow running as straight out of the bow as possible before hitting the range.

042 TIE A BETTER D-LOOP

Tying your own D-loop is fairly easy, but the standard method can give you a loop that's too long, unnecessarily adding to your draw length and potentially causing a host of problems (see item 50). Try this approach.

STEP 1 Start with a 12- to 18-inch length of loop material, tamp one end to flare the fibers, and melt them with a lighter to form a ball.

STEP 2 Loop the cord under and around your string and feed the end back through the loop as shown (A). Be sure to snug it tight (B).

STEP 3 Instead of preforming the D at this point, let the rope lie flat between the knots as you loop and snug the second one (C).

STEP 4 Cut off the tag end about $^1/8$ inch away from the knot, flare out the fibers, and melt them into a ball, being careful to keep the flame away from the bow string and loop (D).

STEP 5 Finally, open the loop with pliers (E), and you've got a nice, tight D-loop.

Caution: No D-loop you or anyone else ties is 100 percent fail-safe.

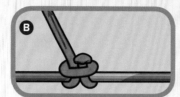

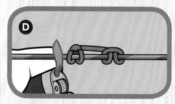

043 ADD A BOW SIGHT

Ninety percent of the time, this is a walk in the park, too. Just bolt the sight's attachment arm firmly to the backside of the riser. Then nock an arrow and visually align string, riser, and shaft. If the sight pins are not lined up along that same plane, adjust the sight's windage until they are.

That usually does it. However, not every bow sight runs perfectly level and square off every riser. And because a cockeyed sight can wreak havoc with accuracy, it's a good idea to double-check, which is process all its own (see item 46).

044 INSTALL A PEEP SIGHT

First, pick your peep. They come in a variety of colors, weights, and aperture sizes. The lightest model will result in a tiny bit more arrow speed. Ideally, the peep's aperture should exactly match the outside of your sight housing as seen from full draw. For most hunters, this is a $^1/4$- or $^3/8$-inch model. You need a bow press; an inexpensive portable model will do, but if you lack that, just have your shop pro put in your peep, which shouldn't run you much more than about $20.

Next, press the bow and use a string separator to evenly split the fibers about $5^1/2$ inches up from the D-loop. Put the peep in, with half of the string fibers (one color) running along one side, and the other half (and color) running along the other side. When the peep is squarely seated, take the bow out of the press.

Nock an arrow and draw back, closing your eyes as you settle into your anchor point. Now open and aim. Odds are the peep is too low or high. Don't move your head or change your anchor point to compensate. Instead, let down, slide the peep to where you think it needs to be, and repeat the process until you open your eyes and find that you're looking right through the center of the peep to your sight.

045 SERVE IN A PEEP SIGHT

Do not serve the peep in right away. First, you need to take your bow to the range and shoot a minimum of 20 shots. In the process, the peep will likely rotate but it will eventually settle into the spot where it will stay. When it does, you may find that you will need to turn it around or put a half twist in the string in order for the peep sight to come back and meet with your eye correctly.

Press the bow, make adjustments, and then take a few more shots to make sure the peep stays put. Finally, you can press the bow one more time and then serve in the peep sight.

046 WATCH YOUR AXES

An installed bow sight can be cockeyed in relation to the first axis, the second axis, the third axis, or any combination thereof. Look at the round sight housing as if to aim. If the top or bottom of it is tilted toward or away from you, the first axis is off. This has the least effect on accuracy. Still, you can check it by measuring off the string to the top and bottom of the housing.

Now think of the housing itself as a trap door, with the hinges on the right (if you're right-handed). If the left edge is tilted up or down, the second axis is off, which can wreck accuracy. To check it, put a speed level against the riser, and compare its bubble to the one on the sight.

Finally, picture the sight housing as an entry door, with the hinges on the right side. If the door is ajar—toward or away from you—the third axis is off. For most hunters, this is a non-issue, but if you're apt to be taking long-range shots at steep angles, see item 76 for the fix, which is more akin to advanced tuning than it is to basic setup.

047 WAX IT

The string is your bow's lifeline. Of course it flings arrows, but it's also the conduit that keeps the whole package—limbs, cams, and riser—tied together and functioning as a single unit. It endures incredible stress, and, like any working implement, your string needs some TLC.

That TLC comes in a simple tube of wax. The multiple strands of a bowstring can become frayed through simple use, and also by weather (such as ice, snow, or rain) or debris. Waxing these strands helps them stay lubricated and resist rot, fraying, and breakage. It's simple to do: Just rub some bowstring wax (available in any pro shop) along all non-served areas of the string, and then work it thoroughly into the strands with your fingertips.

If it's possible to over-wax a string, I've not heard of it. But in general, if you shoot three times or more per week, wax your string every couple of weeks. When your string becomes genuinely frayed, it's time to buy a new one. This isn't just a cosmetic thing; frayed strands can break, which at the least will cause the string to stretch and your bow's timing to go awry. At worst, the string could break, and then you've got real problems that wax can't fix.

048 CHANGE YOUR DRAW WEIGHT

At some point, you may want to raise or lower your bow's draw weight. Most have an adjustment range of 10 pounds, and this is one of the easiest tweaks to make. Most manufacturers even include the proper Allen wrench to do this, as well as instructions in the manual. If you're not a manual reader, here's the quick-and-dirty version.

Put a pencil mark right on the limb bolt that extends across the bushing surrounding it. You adjust draw weight by tightening or loosening the limb bolts, and the pencil marks will serve as a marker that ensures you loosen or tighten the top and bottom bolts exactly the same number of turns.

To increase draw weight, tighten the top bolt the appropriate number of turns—typically 2–3 pounds per complete turn, but you'll need to read the owner's manual for exact specs on your bow—using the pencil marks to count a complete revolution each time the marks meet. Repeat the process on the bottom limb, and you should be good to go. To decrease draw weight, just crank the bolts in the opposite direction.

050 CHANGE YOUR DRAW LENGTH

Shooting a bow with the incorrect draw length is an accuracy-robbing disaster (see item 19). To recap what we've said elsewhere, a bow that's too long is downright impossible for you to anchor consistently, and it will slap your forearm and wrist to boot. A bow that's too short will send your form all to hell too, not to mention robbing you of extra speed.

Measuring your draw length isn't difficult, but you must be precise. The fastest way to reach a starting number is by measuring your arm span from one fingertip, across the shoulders and chest, to the other fingertip, and then dividing that number by 2.5.

When you're close, use a premeasured and marked arrow (most pro shops have one) to try out a few different bows of slightly varying draw lengths to finally settle on the one that fits you perfectly. A half-inch can make a world of difference, and you may find that two bows set to "identical" draw lengths actually fit you a little differently.

Given all that, you may also find that the bow you've already purchased needs adjusting. For many modern bows, this is a simple matter of repositioning the draw-length module on the cam (usually held in place with two hex screws) for several full inches of possible adjustment, no bow press required.

You can adjust some other bows with draw-length modules, but they are going to require a different module for each increment of draw-length adjustment, and you will have to use a press on many of them to change those modules out. A few bows still require changing out the cams altogether.

ARM SPAN ÷ 2.5

049 BREAK IN YOUR BOW

Getting a new bow set up and smacking arrows into the 10-ring of a target is undeniably thrilling. But after a few dozen shots, you may start noticing some hiccups.

Maybe your arrows aren't grouping well. Or maybe your peep sight (assuming you have one) has gotten slightly twisted. Or your arrows are hitting the target a little askew.

If you think you're suddenly doing something wrong, you're probably not. Your string is simply stretching a bit as it wears in, and that slight length increase can mess with your peep alignment and tuning. With today's quality string materials, this isn't the problem that it once was, but it's still not uncommon. Fixing it takes all of 10 minutes at the pro shop.

All you need to do is press your bow, add a couple twists to your string or cables to compensate for the stretch, and put it all back under tension. Draw your bow and check your peep. When it's perfectly realigned, you should be good to go.

051 RELEASE EASY

Modern compound bows are designed for shooting with release aids. Curling three fleshy digits around the bowstring means three more ways to screw up a shot. Today's relatively short axle-to-axle compounds also create string angles so severe that holding the bow at full draw with your fingers is impractical or even painful. Almost everyone who shoots a compound bow these days uses a release aid, making for far less contact with the string and far better repeatability—and both of these can lead to improved accuracy.

Most hunters use a wrist-strap–style release (commonly referred to as a caliper release, though some types do not incorporate a caliper). Here, you cinch the strap onto your

wrist, clip the jaws or a hook onto the string or string loop, and then pull the trigger to release the arrow.

There are many nuanced options within this category, including caliper-style jaws versus string-loop hooks and spring-loaded calipers versus non–spring-loaded. Having shot the lot, I can't say that one style is any better or more accurate than another. The key is to try a variety to find out what feels right to you and allows you to shoot your best. That said, here are a few general rules:

MAKE A CLEAN BREAK The trigger on your release should have the same qualities as a good rifle trigger: no creep, no mush, no grittiness—nothing but a crisp, clean break.

GET OPTIONS Make sure that you can adjust the length of the barrel (or strap), as well as the weight of the trigger.

BUCKLE UP Most models offer the option of a buckle or hook-and-loop enclosure. Both work, but I prefer a buckle because it's quieter and it closes in the same exact place every, offering better consistency.

DON'T SKIMP I have watched cheap releases wreak havoc on people's shooting. If you have to spend less on a bow to afford a good release, do it. It's worth it.

052 HAND-HOLD IT

Some hunters and many competition shooters prefer a handheld release. The most obvious difference is that these typically lack a wrist strap and are designed to be held in the hand. There are two types: thumb-button and back-tension or hinge style. The former has a thumb-activated trigger. While taking aim, you rest your thumb against said trigger and slowly apply pressure (via back-tension or not) until the shot fires. Many fans of handheld releases prefer this type for hunting because the trigger adds a degree of control. The back-tension or hinge style looks similar except there's no trigger. Instead, you fire it by rotating the release. It is called a back-tension type because

you can use back-tension to affect that rotation, creating a smooth, surprise shot. But you don't have to; many pros simply relax their fingers or shift finger pressure to achieve the same. You'll want plenty of practice with a hinge release before hunting with one. If your not careful it can fire at mid-draw, causing you to punch yourself in the teeth. That may be just what you need on the range—but probably not what you want in the woods.

053 BEWARE OF CHANGE

While you should try a variety of releases, once you've settled on one and used it to sight in and practice, any change you make afterward will likely alter your point of impact. Putting a glove or an extra sleeve under your wrist strap, for example, can make you miss. So can using a backup release (which you should always have with you) because you forgot your primary. This doesn't mean you can't wear a glove or use a backup. It does means you need to use these items on the practice range first to see how they affect your shot so you can make any necessary adjustments.

054 GET A GOOD FIT

Adjust the length of your caliper-style release so that the top of the head lands somewhere between the first and second knuckle of your forefinger. Any longer and you'll be reaching for the trigger with the tip of your finger, which encourages slapping instead of squeezing in. Also, it's worth noting that a shortened release combined with a forward trigger style, which is increasingly popular, allows you to shoot a slightly longer draw length (for a little more speed) with the same anchor point.

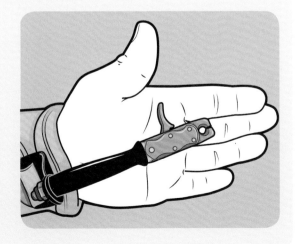

055 DON'T BE A MACHO MAN

There's something inherently macho about draw weight. The more we pull, we figure, the manlier we are, and the better we can kill stuff. We figure wrong. Successful bowhunting is all about accuracy, and you'll never shoot a bow well if you can't draw it smoothly and hold it at anchor comfortably. Besides that, today's bows are so efficient that heavy draw weight just isn't needed for most hunting scenarios. I know women and kids who routinely kill whitetails with bows drawing 30 to 40 pounds.

So how do you know what's too heavy? Perhaps the easiest test is to sit in a chair, hold the bow straight in front of you, and draw straight back. If you can't do that without twisting and flailing about, lower your draw weight a bit. You can always increase it as you build your muscles.

056 KNOW YOUR CAMS

Here's a look at the four basic cam systems in use on today's compounds.

SINGLE This type features a cam on the bottom limb and a plain wheel, called an idler, on the top. A single cam is typically pleasant to draw and easy to tune, but it's rarely the fastest option.

TWIN This system features an identical, independent cam on each limb. For the bow to work most efficiently, you must perfectly synchronize (or time) these cams to each other, so they tend to be the most difficult systems of them all to tune.

HYBRID This system sports two elliptical cams that work together, but the top is a control cam, while the other is a power (or speed) cam. It's typically easier to tune than a dual cam, and as a rule, it's faster than a single cam.

BINARY This is the newest system, which joins or slaves two cams together with a cable that replaces the cam's connection to the limbs. This supposedly eliminates the need for tuning and other problems—such as cam lean—inherent to other designs.

057 GO FASTER—IF YOU CAN

Some bowhunters are fond of saying, "Speed doesn't kill." And they're right; with the perfect shot, you could kill a deer with a sharpened oil dipstick, shot from a washtub bass. But bowhunters don't always make perfect shots.

Of course you need to understand the trade-offs (see item 13), but a faster bow has major advantages, as long as you can shoot it accurately. All things being equal, it shoots a flatter arrow, which makes exact range estimation less critical and typically allows you to shoot one pin out to 30 yards. But the biggest upside to a blazing bow is that, in my opinion, it lets you shoot a heavier arrow without giving up too much in trajectory. This adds up to more momentum and better penetration, neither of which matters if you make a perfect shot.

But if you screw up, a fast bow can turn an iffy shot into a good one. Who doesn't want that?

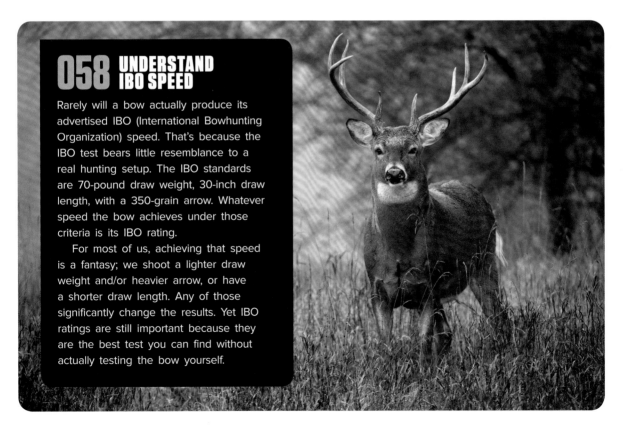

058 UNDERSTAND IBO SPEED

Rarely will a bow actually produce its advertised IBO (International Bowhunting Organization) speed. That's because the IBO test bears little resemblance to a real hunting setup. The IBO standards are 70-pound draw weight, 30-inch draw length, with a 350-grain arrow. Whatever speed the bow achieves under those criteria is its IBO rating.

For most of us, achieving that speed is a fantasy; we shoot a lighter draw weight and/or heavier arrow, or have a shorter draw length. Any of those significantly change the results. Yet IBO ratings are still important because they are the best test you can find without actually testing the bow yourself.

059 GET THE RIGHT SHAFT

Cavemen, Robin Hood, Ishi, and Howard Hill all had one basic arrow-shaft material to choose from. You have the modern luxury of at least four times more choices. Here's a breakdown.

GO OLD SCHOOL Wood ruled as a shaft material for about 10,000 years, from the end of the Upper Paleolithic era until the second half of the last century. Many traditional archers still use wooden arrows—typically made of laminated birch, pine, fir, spruce, or cedar—not just because they are beautiful but because they remain accurate and hard-hitting enough to stop big game. They also have the advantage of being very quiet in flight. However, these shafts warp or bend easily and therefore require frequent maintenance. They are also unsafe to shoot from most compound bows.

BE A METALHEAD Introduced in the 1940s, aluminum arrows dominated the archery scene by the '70s, and remained the top choice of hunters until only a handful of years ago. Extremely straight and quiet, with precise weight and spine consistency, they offer outstanding performance for the price, thus remaining a top choice for archers on a budget. Aluminum is comparatively heavy, which makes for a slower arrow, but its weight is a plus for penetration, which is why many hunters consider it the shaft material of choice for very large game. The biggest downside to aluminum is that it bends easily with use—and in most cases a bent arrow is a ruined arrow.

GET BACK IN BLACK Most modern archers have switched to carbon arrows, for two key reasons: speed and durability. In comparison to wood and aluminum, carbon is lightweight, allowing modern archers to get the full flat-shooting advantage from ever-faster bows. And today's carbon shafts, unlike the ones introduced in the early '80s, are exceptionally strong and durable, and possess increasingly precise tolerances. They maintain their straightness with use; as the saying goes, "They're either straight or they're broken."

If they have a downside, it's price. The best carbon arrows can approach $200 per dozen. Still, archers on a budget can find affordable basic models; traditional archers can choose carbon finished to look like wood; and those who want ultimate penetration can opt for weighted or micro-diameter models. In short, there's a carbon shaft for everyone.

TRY OTHER OPTIONS Some manufacturers are combining aluminum and carbon to marry the exceptionally consistent spine, weight, and straightness tolerances of the former with the standout durability of the latter, as with Easton's Full Metal Jacket series. Another option is fiberglass, which is inexpensive and extremely durable. It's the top choice for kids and for bowfishing, because it can handle whatever abuses an 8-year-old boy or an 80-pound carp can dish out.

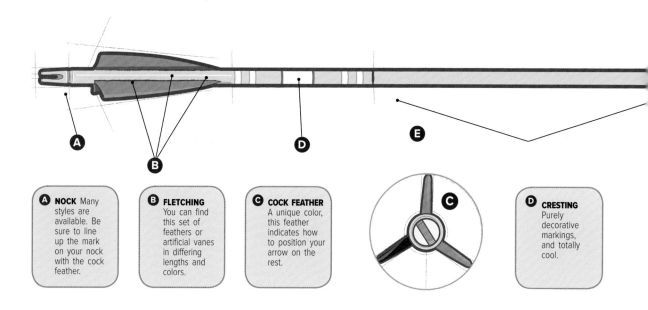

A NOCK Many styles are available. Be sure to line up the mark on your nock with the cock feather.

B FLETCHING You can find this set of feathers or artificial vanes in differing lengths and colors.

C COCK FEATHER A unique color, this feather indicates how to position your arrow on the rest.

D CRESTING Purely decorative markings, and totally cool.

060 WATCH YOUR WEIGHT

Just as dry firing can damage your bow, so can shooting an arrow that's too light. That's why the International Bowhunting Organization recommends a minimum arrow weight of 5 grains for every pound of your bow's draw weight. So if you shoot a 60-pound bow, your finished arrow (including the point) should weigh no less than 300 grains. Above that minimum, the weight of your arrow should depend on what you'll fling it at (see item 71), and from how far.

A lighter arrow is a faster arrow, which means it has a flatter trajectory, making accurate shooting a little easier, especially at longer ranges. For this reason, target archers usually stay near the 5-grain minimum. But, all else being equal, a heavier arrow is going to have more momentum, which makes it more likely to slice through a critter's vitals and create an exit hole for easier blood trailing. That's why most hunters go heavier, typically between 7 and 10 grains per inch.

E WRAP OR DIP This is mostly decorative, but does add weight and aids in-flight visibility.

F SHAFT inspect the shaft often for nicks, cracks or bends. Any damage can foil accuracy.

G INSERT Largely standardized for most screw-in points; new narrow-diameter and/or heavier options are available.

H POINT The business end of the arrow can be tipped with a field point or a broadhead.

061 DON'T COME UP SHORT

Arrow length is slightly less complicated than arrow weight. At an absolute minimum, your cut arrow should extend 1 inch forward of the rest with the bow at full draw. Anything shorter risks a misdirected shaft not clearing the shelf when fired, which could cause serious injury. An even safer standard is to make sure your arrow is long enough so that the blades of a broadhead will stop just forward of your grip hand at full draw. Of course, you should never allow a finger to get above the arrow shelf, but following this guideline prevents bloodshed if you do.

To measure, nock an uncut arrow, draw it back, and have a friend (safely keeping himself and his hand to the side) use a permanent marker to mark the arrow either 1 inch forward of the rest or just forward of your grip hand. Now remove the arrow and measure from the throat of the nock to your mark. This is the correct arrow length for your setup, so write it down.

Alternately, you can measure draw length as the distance from the nocking point at full draw to the throat of the grip, plus 1¾ inches. So, measuring from the throat of the grip away from the string 1¾ inches shows you the terminus of an arrow cut to match your draw length. Assuming you know the latter, you can adjust and figure from there. (For a stick bow, start about an inch long, as trimming the arrow back is part of the tuning process.) If you have the slightest doubt, go to your bow shop for help.

062 GO MICRO

Micro-diameter arrows are all the rage right now, and our own tests show that they do indeed penetrate better than standard-diameter shafts. They also reduce wind drift. A smaller-diameter arrow is harder to perfectly center on the bowstring, making it potentially less forgiving to tune and shoot, but not enough to affect most bowhunters. The only real downside to these arrows is their heart-stopping price, and the fact that some do not accept standard ⁸⁄₃₂-thread broadheads and field points.

063 DON'T SWEAT FOC (TOO MUCH)

An arrow flies better if it's a little front-heavy. Front of center (FOC) measures how front-heavy that arrow is. Calculating FOC is a simple matter of finding the difference between the center of a finished arrow and its balance point, which should be closer to the tip, or—you guessed it—front of center. (If it isn't, you have problems.) Finally, you divide the total arrow length by the difference. For example, a 30-inch arrow that balances 3 inches forward of the center has an FOC of 10 percent. You can change FOC by adding or subtracting weight at one end of the arrow (with different-sized heads, inserts, and weights) or the other (with vanes and nocks).

Some target archers tinker obsessively with FOC, trying to eke out the smallest advantage. All that a bowhunter really needs to know is that your arrow's FOC should be somewhere between 7 and 14 percent, which virtually every hunting arrow is. Within that range, a little more FOC hits slightly harder downrange and can help steer a large fixed-blade broadhead. However, this percentage also causes the arrow to nosedive a bit more. As usual, it's a trade-off.

064 GET IT STRAIGHT

Not all new arrows are equally straight; there is a range of straightness tolerances, typically from +/- .006 inch to +/- .001. The tighter the tolerance, the straighter the arrow, the better the accuracy (in theory), and the more you pay for them.

Now, if you've just got to have the best, go crazy. But here's a plain fact: +/- .006 inch, the least straight of the choices, is not only pretty damn straight, but as straight as most guys at typical bowhunting ranges will ever need.

To see any difference between +/- .006 and +/- .003, you need to be a good long-range shooter. And to gain anything by going to +/- .001, you need to be Levi Morgan—or, at least, see him at some of your shoots.

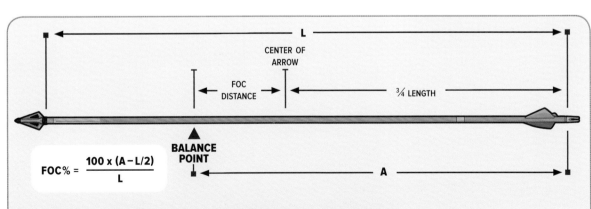

$$FOC\% = \frac{100 \times (A - L/2)}{L}$$

L = Distance from bottom of nock groove to end of shaft (also known as correct arrow length).

A = Distance from bottom of nock groove to finished arrow balance position (includes weight of point [+insert], nock system and fletching.)

Chart courtesy of Easton

065 SPINE IT

The concept of arrow spine tends to make folks' heads spin. So here's the least you need to know about static and dynamic spine:

Static spine refers to an arrow's stiffness at rest. Manufacturers sell arrows in a range of static-spine values. Because arrows with the same static spine will bend differently when shot through different bows (this is the arrows' dynamic spine), you need to buy shafts whose static-spine value best matches your individual rig. Otherwise you'll likely have tuning and/or accuracy problems.

That's it. You can stop right there if you want, because bow-shop pros and customer-support techs will gladly help you choose appropriately spined shafts. Make sure to ask. Don't just guess and grab from the big-box store's arrow bin. Don't wing it with an online spine chart. Speak up or call, and say, "Hey, can you help walk me through this?"

The reply will almost definitely be, "Of course." If it isn't, go somewhere else.

COCKAMAMIE SPINE VALUES

Dave Hurteau on

Do you need a 400 or a 340 spine? As if only to confuse us further, manufacturers do not strictly follow any standard expression of spine stiffness—even though there is a perfectly good industry standard for measuring it, called *spine deflection* (SD).

It's simple: Hang a 1.94-pound weight on an arrow supported in two places 28 inches apart, and if the center sags half an inch, the spine deflection is .500. If it sags .4 inch, it's .400. Lately, more makers are listing SD on their charts or in their specs, or a version thereof, such as Easton's familiar carbon-shaft values; the lower the number, the stiffer the arrow. Still, everyone should just use straight SD.

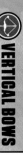

ARROW SHAFT SELECTOR (spine deflection values)

COMPOUND BOW		ARROW SHAFT SELECTION							
Medium Cam 100g tips	Single or Hard Cam 100g tips	ARROW LENGTH							
Draw Weight	Draw Weight	25"	26"	27"	28"	29"	30"	31"	32"
37–41 lbs	32–36 lbs	500	500	500	500	500	500	500	400
42–46 lbs	37–41 lbs	500	500	500	500	500	500	400	400
47–51 lbs	42–46 lbs	500	500	500	500	500	400	400	400
52–56 lbs	47–51 lbs	500	500	500	500	400	400	400	340
57–61 lbs	52–56 lbs	500	500	500	400	400	400	340	340
62–66 lbs	57–61 lbs	500	500	400	400	400	340	340	300
67–72 lbs	62–66 lbs	500	400	400	400	340	340	300	300
73–78 lbs	67–72 lbs	400	400	400	340	340	300	300	300
79–84 lbs	73–78 lbs	400	400	340	340	300	300	300	–
85–90 lbs	79–84 lbs	400	340	340	300	300	300	–	–
91–96 lbs	85–90 lbs	340	340	300	300	300	–	–	–

Chart courtesy of Easton

066 CHART OUT SPINE

Manufacturers offer an array of dynamic-spine charts and calculators to help guide you to the correct spine value for your equipment. The simplest of these take into consideration only your bow's draw weight (as set by you) and arrow length. This may work out fine, but remember that such a basic chart assumes that the other factors affecting dynamic spine—including IBO speed, let-off, and head weight—are roughly average on your rig. If they aren't, adjust them accordingly. An especially fast bow, for example, will require a stiffer spine. The more factors a given chart or calculator takes into account, the better, and there are some very precise aftermarket calculators out there. When in doubt, err on the stiff side.

067 GO FLETCH

Vanes—or fletching, as they're referred to collectively—help stabilize your arrow while it's in flight. How they work is simple: when the tail of the speeding shaft veers out of line with the tip, the vanes catch extra air and steer the tail back in line. They come in a huge variety of styles, most of which fall into one of the following categories.

GO TRADITIONAL The fletching material for millennia, real feathers are exceptionally lightweight. Their textured surface catches air particularly well, and they fold down flat when contacting a non-center-shot riser, making them ideal for use with stick bows. They are expensive, though, and not as durable or weather-resistant as synthetic models.

KEEP A LOW PROFILE Typically available in 3-, 4-, and 5-inch versions, the synthetic, low-profile style vanes popularized by Duravane are generally inexpensive and have the advantage of being quiet in flight, impervious to weather, and very durable.

GO HIGH Shorter high-profile vanes, popularized by Bohning's 2-inch Blazer, are all the rage now. Made of a particularly stiff material, they tend to distort less when shot through a Whisker Biscuit rest. The popularity of Blazers reflects that of mechanical broadheads, which don't need as much stabilization as a large, fixed-blade vane. But part of the appeal is nothing more than fashion.

068 OPTIMIZE ARROWS

If you like to keep things simple and just want to take your bow out in the field and get down to hunting, and you've read everything we've said about arrows so far, you've got what you really need to know.

If, on the other hand, you're interested in optimizing your setup, things will, as usual, get a little more complicated.

For optimization, you'll need to consider a number of factors and trade-offs, the most important of which are the following.

VANE WEIGHT The vane's weight affects dynamic spine, trajectory, and FOC. The greater the FOC, the less vane stabilization is required, and vice versa.

AERODYNAMICS Similarly, the less aerodynamic the tip is (as would be the case with a big fixed-blade broadhead), the more vane stabilization it requires, and vice versa.

TURN More turn in the vane configuration—whether offset or helical—means better stabilization and accuracy, but it also creates more air resistance, slowing the arrow.

SPIN Finally, spin can create vane-clearance problems with some rests.

069 BUILD THE ULTIMATE ARROW

What does the ultimate hunting arrow look like? We conducted several tests to find out which variables matter most.

The first finding is that smaller-diameter arrows penetrate better. We compared Easton's micro-diameter Carbon Injexions to Easton Flatline 340s. Both were 29 inches, but the Injexions were heavier (8.9 grains per inch versus 8.2), so we evened it out by adding a 125-grain tip to the Flatline, which made it very slightly heavier. Still, the Injexion shafts penetrated a full 4 to 5 inches deeper on average into every layered foam and 3-D target we shot them into. Targets are not flesh and bone, but that is a significant difference.

Next, long-range hunting requires stabilization. New Archery Products' QuickSpin vanes use a kicker and grooves to accomplish the same thing archers have for years with helical fletching: more spin on the arrow for better accuracy. So we fletched up some of our test arrows with QuickSpins and shot them alongside arrows from the same batch fletched with standard Blazer vanes. At 30 and 40 yards, there was no noticeable difference. At 60 yards, the QuickSpin-fletched arrows produced a group average of 4.81 inches, while the standard Blazers averaged 6.75 inches. For accuracy-obsessed long-range shooters, that's a huge difference.

Lastly, we swapped our correctly spined 340s with both 300s and 400s. For each arrow weight, we tipped one set of three arrows with field points and two other sets with fixed-blade broadheads, since incorrect spine is supposedly most noticeable with the latter. After adjusting the sight to match the point of aim for a given shaft, we fired multiple three-shot groups with each arrow type. The only measurable difference was that the broadheads consistently hit an inch higher than the field points with the 300s. There was no point of impact difference with the 340 or 400. In other words, although tuning your broadhead may be a little more difficult if you're slightly underspined, that should not affect the size of your groups.

070 CHOOSE YOUR BROADHEAD

A broadhead has two requirements: It must hit where you aim it, and it must be sharp and sturdy enough to kill quickly and humanely. Any broadhead that meets those simple criteria is a winner. Still, bowhunters love to debate the merits of their favorite broadheads, and some styles are much better suited for some bowhunting tasks than others. Before we get into all that, though, you need to know the three basic broadhead types.

CUT AWAY Typically crafted from a single piece of steel, the cut-on-contact style is the simplest of broadheads. Since the edge of each blade extends to the broadhead's tip, this type begins cutting as soon as it makes contact, and so it typically penetrates better than other broadhead styles. It's a favorite style for large game, as well as for traditional bowhunters and anyone shooting a lightweight setup.

USE REPLACEMENTS On a replaceable fixed-blade broadhead, a slotted ferrule accepts two to four replaceable blades. If a blade breaks or gets nicked or damaged, simply remove it and slip in a new one, and you're back in business. Most replaceable-blade heads have a chisel-like tip that's pretty good at breaking

bone (if you're shooting enough bow) that also assists in locking the blades in place.

BE A MECHANIC The ferrule retains the blades of mechanical broadheads within flight, only opening them upon impact. The deployment method of the blades varies widely: Some swing open from the top, while others have slotted blades that pivot around a pin within the ferrule and deploy from the rear of the broadhead. Mechanical broadheads typically provide large cutting diameters and accurate flight—although their advantages in the latter category aren't as stark as you might think (see item 75).

HITS AND HEADS

Dave Hurteau on

As a rule, fixed-blade heads penetrate better, and mechanicals make a bigger hole. So ask yourself: When you don't make the perfect shot, where do you tend to miss? If you usually hit the shoulder, you could benefit from the added penetration of a fixed head. If you tend to hit a little back, penetration isn't an issue, and a bigger hole will help. If you miss all over the place, maybe broadhead choice isn't the main issue.

071 USE ENOUGH BOW

Some states still have minimum draw-weight rules left over from when recurves were in vogue. But with today's compounds producing impressive power from even short-draw, light-poundage setups, several states are now dropping those minimums.

Most bowhunters hunt whitetails with a setup that launches a 400-grain hunting arrow in the neighborhood of 250 to 280 fps, producing between 55 and 70 foot-pounds of kinetic energy and .44 to .50 slug-foot per second of momentum. That's more than enough for whitetails, but is it enough to drive an arrow through an elk or moose? What if you want to use a 2-inch-wide mechanical broadhead? What if you try a heavier arrow or increase your draw weight?

If you know the weight (or mass) and the speed of your finished arrows, you can determine your setup's kinetic energy and momentum with a couple of high-school–physics formulas. But we thought we'd spare you the math. Instead, just take a look at this chart to get an idea of the type of broadhead to use from your bow on the game you're hunting. Each letter represents the combination of kinetic energy and momentum required to cleanly kill the animal pictured.

THE POWER MATRIX

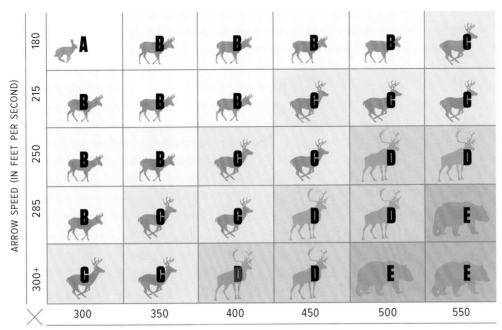

ARROW SPEED (IN FEET PER SECOND)

	300	350	400	450	500	550
180	A	B	B	B	B	C
215	B	B	B	C	C	C
250	B	B	C	C	D	D
285	B	C	C	D	D	E
300+	C	C	D	D	E	E

ARROW WEIGHT (IN GRAINS)

A 25 foot-pounds of kinetic energy and <.28 slug-foot per second of momentum: small game.

B 25–55 and .28–.40: whitetail-size game at close range with a cut-on-contact or replaceable fixed-blade broadhead.

C 40–75 and .40–.52: whitetail-size game with any broadhead.

D 60–90 and .52–.64: big game such as elk with any broadhead.

E 90+ and .64+: whatever the hell you want to shoot. We recommend a cut-on-contact or replaceable fixed-blade broadhead.

072 BADASS YOUR BROADHEADS

Keeping your cool at the shot doesn't offer a guarantee against a shattering result. Your broadhead also makes a huge difference. A good one kills in seconds. A bad one can turn a perfect shot into a lost deer. Here's how to avoid the latter situation.

SAMPLE SEVERAL Broadheads are expensive, but they're reusable. Go in on a variety of heads with a couple of buddies to find the ones that you shoot best.

WEIGH THEM I've found as much as a 13-grain weight difference between the heaviest and lightest broadhead from the same package of six. Make sure that your hunting heads all weigh the same.

SHOOT AT 50 Tune your broadheads at 20 or 30 yards, and then back up to 50. If that head consistently hits its mark at the longer range, it's just about perfect. Put it in your quiver.

SHARPEN Nicking your finger with a broadhead should ruin a t-shirt and make you queasy, but that's no way to test one. Instead, use a rubber band—each blade should slice a stretched-out band at the slightest touch. If it doesn't, keep on sharpening (see item 73).

CHECK THEM out In addition to new blades, many broadheads—especially mechanicals—have replaceable washers, rubber O-rings, and tiny set screws. Make sure these are all in place and serviceable.

073 KEEP 'EM SHARP

Most new broadheads look wickedly sharp at first glance, and some of them actually are. But a good many aren't, and no matter what, they all will need a touch-up after you practice with them or shoot them through an animal (or into the dirt).

With both replaceable fixed-blade and mechanical heads, you can just swap the old blades out for new ones. But you can resharpen cut-on-contact fixed blades, as well as replaceable blades that don't have obvious nicks and burrs.

The basics of sharpening a broadhead are no different than the steps in sharpening a knife: You're simply removing material on each side of a bevel to create a clean, acute, sharp edge. You can use a specialized broadhead sharpener, a stone, or a sharpening stick, the same as you'd use for your knife.

I keep an 8-inch mill file (available at any hardware store) in my archery toolkit, and I've used that file to touch up broadheads of all styles. I like a sharp but somewhat rough edge, and the file is perfect for getting that done.

Regardless of the sharpener you use, the idea is to make smooth, even strokes on both sides of the blade, and decrease the pressure as you work. One neat trick to ensure that is to color in each beveled edge with a permanent marker. This helps you to remove the same amount of material on each bevel; simply work the bevels against the sharpener until the marker is gone, and recolor as necessary until the edge is sharp. Once you attain that final edge, you can preserve it against oxidization—the slight rusting that can occur in even a well-protected quiver—by coating the blade with a light application of petroleum jelly or bow wax.

074 TAKE YOUR ARROWS FOR A SPIN

Spin-testing your broadheads proves that the head and the end of the arrow shaft and insert are in perfect alignment. If they aren't, erratic flight can result.

Spin testers are available for purchase; most pro shops also have one on hand. These devices typically hold the arrow shaft parallel to a table or other flat surface. The nock end fits into a small housing next to a motor, and a V-shaped rest supports the shaft. Switch on the motor and the arrow spins on the rest. If the head doesn't spin true, you have a problem.

You can also check broadhead alignment without buying a spin tester. Simply lay the arrow shaft diagonally across the corner of a table or countertop and spin it by drawing a finger across the shaft. Other hunters put a dot on a piece of paper or cardboard, set it on a table, place the head point-down on the dot, and spin the arrow by twisting the nock between two fingers, just as you would spin a top. If the broadhead wobbles off-center as the arrow spins, there's an alignment problem.

Realignment can be as simple as unscrewing the problem head and trying a different one; the new head might match the arrow insert better and eliminate the problem. If that doesn't work, try an arrow-squaring

device, which removes a little material from the face of the insert so that it's perfectly even and marries to the broadhead base. Color the face of the insert with a marker before you start. This ensures you're removing the same amount of material around the entire surface. When you're done squaring the end of the arrow, screw in a broadhead and spin-test it again to check your work.

Traditional archers (and some compound shooters) often use fixed broadheads glued to the end of a tapered shaft. If such an arrow fails a spin test, that usually means the glue isn't evenly distributed on the tapered end. To fix this, leave the broadhead on the shaft and heat it gently on both sides with a lighter. With a gloved hand, slowly rotate the broadhead once to spread the heated glue more evenly. Allow the head to cool and spin-test it again.

075 MAKE A HEAD-TO-HEAD COMPARISON

When we're not arguing over rests, sights, and other gear, bowhunters love to argue over broadheads. There are two familiar sides: One says that fixed-blade broadheads are the more reliable killers; they deliver consistent penetration and are impervious to mechanical failures that lead to lost game. The other holds that mechanicals fly just like field points, require no special tuning, and are more accurate, especially at longer ranges. But recent, real-world data blows gaping holes in both assumptions.

STUDY THE REAL THING For years, outdoor writers have struggled to come up with the definitive test. Problem is, there's only one perfect test medium: living deer. Then,

in spring of 2014, Maryland's Naval Support Facility Indian Head, a 3,000-acre military installation, published findings of the kind that no one could simulate with ballistics gel and frozen rib cages: the first ever multiyear study comparing recovery rates of real whitetail deer shot with each type of broadhead.

DOCUMENT THE DIFFERENCE In 1989, Indian Head employee Andy Pedersen started a bowhunting program at the facility, and he documented everything from hunter effort and equipment to shots taken and animals recovered. "When we first allowed mechanical broadheads for the 2007 season, I was eager to document their failure. I'd been bowhunting since 1974,

and I knew what worked and what didn't," he says.

But when he crunched the numbers at the end of the 2013 season, Pedersen was in for a surprise. Hunters using conventional broadheads from the program's inception recovered 821 of 1,001 deer shot, for a recovery rate of 82 percent. Hunters using mechanical heads starting in 2007 shot 161 deer and recovered 143 of them, for an 89 percent recovery rate. "I was shocked," Pedersen says. He had assumed that the deployment and penetration problems commonly associated with mechanicals would result in more lost deer. But the numbers say otherwise.

Still, they don't quite reveal the full story. Pedersen's hunters must pass a special course and proficiency test (though he notes that many are newbies who take their first bow kill at Indian Head). Also, because deer are abundant, most shots are close, and a tracking team (complete with dogs) is available for the recovery. The study does not, therefore, mirror the typical field

scenario. Nonetheless, it is the best head-to-head test to date, and its results turn conventional wisdom on its ear.

MAKE AN ACCURATE CHOICE So what about the other supposition—that mechanicals are more accurate? To find out, I assembled a test team consisting of Trent Kleeberger (a Minnesota indoor-archery state champion), Bob Borowiak (a veteran bowhunter and competitive 3-D shooter), *Field & Stream* deputy editor Dave Hurteau, and myself (both of us are members of the bow-test team and seasoned bowhunters). We shot over 2,000 arrows, pitting four of the top-selling mechanicals against four popular fixed-blade heads. First we tested out-of-the-box point of impact compared with field points at 20 yards. Then each tester shot 10 three-shot groups with each head at 40 and 60 yards (see our findings below).

FIX YOUR MIND It's hard to say which is the more surprising result of all this experimentation—that the mechanicals bested fixed blades in a recovery-rate study, or that fixed blades ranked right alongside mechanicals in an accuracy test. But I personally find the latter result more compelling and actionable. The Indian Head study does not account for the longer shots for which many archers favor mechanicals. Like most of you, I will keep my shots at game inside 40 yards, where I now know that my fail-safe fixed blades will shoot just as accurately as mechanicals, and maybe even a tiny bit better.

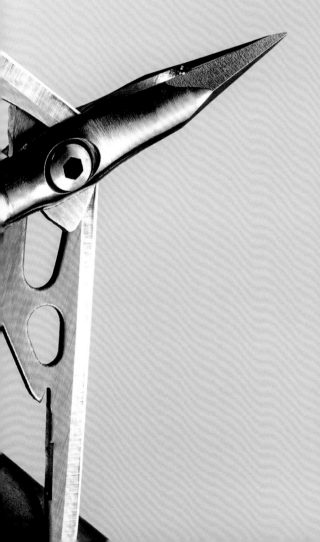

THE BOTTOM LINE

> Fixed heads grouped slightly better at 40 yards (2.99 inches fixed blade versus 3.27 inches mechanical). This was a surprise, and no anomaly of averaging. Every one of the testers shot the fixed blades better here, although the difference was very small.

> Mechanicals grouped slightly better at 60 yards (4.83 inches mechanical versus 5.03 inches fixed blade). If you're the kind of guy who needs to eke out every smidge of accuracy at long range, you might find a tiny advantage with mechanicals. More likely, the difference is statistically insignificant.

076 GET TUNED UP

You want your arrows to go where you aim them. But to do so from various distances, they must leave the bow on a straight and level plane. If the tip of a nocked arrow angles to one side, it will not only hit to that side, but will do so progressively more as the distance to the target increases. You can adjust your sight to account for this at one distance, but you'll still be off at all others. This is no good. An up or down angle is a little easier to deal with, but you don't really want those either.

Once you've correctly set up a bow, basic tuning is a simple matter of making fine adjustments until that arrow flies straight and true. An archery-shop pro can help you get your bow shooting straight. (The service is often part of the purchase of a new bow, so be sure to ask.) It's important to do the shooting yourself; don't just leave or drop off the bow. Some shops even offer a service called "supertuning," which promises to fine-tune your entire setup—bow, arrows, heads—until every shot from a Hooter Shooter hits in virtually the same hole.

But very few of us need that level of precision. For hunting, the methods on the next two pages are not just adequate but can produce excellent field accuracy even at long ranges. There's nothing mystical about them—they're just straightforward skills that most of you can tackle on your own.

077 TUNE IT EASY

Tuning means making adjustments until the arrows shot from a bow fly consistently straight and true. It's fairly easy to get perfect arrow flight with some bows, but not with others.

Out in the real world, most archers won't spend hours fine-tuning their equipment, nor will they pay someone else to do it. So you want a bow that's easy to tune from the get-go.

It's difficult to shop for tunability. If you're buying your bow at a pro shop and paying to set it up, ask to have it tuned for you, too. The answer you want to hear goes something like this: "I'll have it shooting perfectly before you leave. If you have any problems, bring it back for a tweak." That's a good sign that the bow is easy to tune.

If you're buying a bare bow and setting it up yourself, make sure you can bring it back—and exchange it at the least—if you have tuning problems. Get the salesperson's name.

078 DO A DOUBLE-CHECK

Before you try any specific tuning method, double-check that your bow is ready for tuning. Preexisting conditions can sabotage the whole process otherwise. Here's a quick checklist.

- ☐ Make sure it doesn't have any excessive cam lean.
- ☐ Confirm that the bow's timing is correct.
- ☐ Ensure that you have the correct draw length.
- ☐ Get the bow all set up, including the center shot.
- ☐ Ensure that the arrow spine matches your bow.

079 READ THE PAPER

Once your bow is all set up and you've run through the checklist (see item 78), the typical next step is *paper tuning*, which involves shooting through a sheet of paper stretched vertically in a frame at roughly eye level. (A simple wood frame tacked together with nails will do.) Place a target behind the paper as a backstop, making sure it's far enough away so that it doesn't interfere with the shaft's clean passage through. Then step 6–8 feet back from the frame, and concentrate on using good form (see item 87) as you take a level shot into the paper. Your goal is to produce a neat, round bullet hole. Adjust your rest or nocking based on what you see. That said, don't go moving your rest or loop based on one arrow, as even a slight error on your part can cause a bad tear. Take several shots and make adjustments based on consistent results.

Tears in any direction indicate that the arrow is coming out of the bow at an angle, which you can correct as follows:

TEAR TO RIGHT: Move rest to right.

TEAR TO LEFT: Move rest to left.

TEAR UPWARD: Adjust nocking point down. (To move a string loop up or down, rotate the whole thing completely around the string serving. A counterclockwise rotation usually moves it up, but not always, so watch it closely.)

TEAR DOWNWARD: Adjust nocking point up.

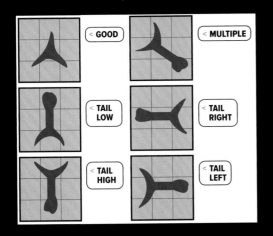

< GOOD

< MULTIPLE

< TAIL LOW

< TAIL RIGHT

< TAIL HIGH

< TAIL LEFT

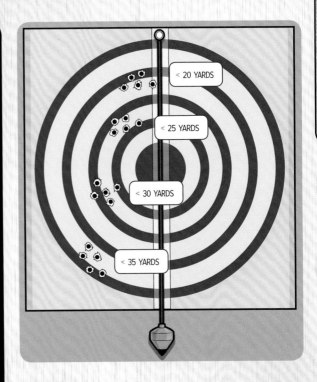

< 20 YARDS

< 25 YARDS

< 30 YARDS

< 35 YARDS

080 TAKE A WALK

Many serious archers these days either skip paper tuning and go straight to what is known as *walk-back tuning*, or they paper tune to verify their up and down and ball-park their side-to-side tuning, and then they walk-back tune to more precisely dial in the latter. Point is, they all walk-back tune, because it's easy to do and it adds a degree of exactitude. Here's how.

Use a level or plumb bob to affix a perfectly vertical strip of masking tape on the center of your target, and then add a small dot at the top for aiming. Shoot that dot at 20 yards. Back up to 25, aim at the same dot with the same pin, and shooter another arrow. Back up to 30 yards and repeat. Do the same thing clear out to 40 or 50 yards. Ideally your arrows, while hitting progressively lower, should be in line vertically. If you notice a trend of all the arrows gradually "walking" to one side or the other of the tape, a fractional rest adjustment is in order. And when I say fractional, I mean about $1/64$ inch, so be very careful here. (It's a good argument for buying a rest with good, positive micro-adjustments.)

It is pretty easy for you to screw up the process here, so shoot when you're fresh (as opposed to after a long practice session), and disregard any flyers you know were your fault.

081 TUNE THE VERTICAL

Walk-back tuning helps perfect arrow flight on the horizontal plane. For the vertical plane, try this method I learned from Kris Christensen of Spot Hogg, the staff of which comprises tuning fanatics.

First stretch a line of tape horizontally across a target. Then step back to 30, 40, or 50 yards. The farther back you go, the better, as long as you can normally shoot a decent group from that distance. Now go ahead and fire five arrows at the line, all from the same distance. Then walk up to the target and inspect your group.

Hitting the line of tape is not as important as hitting on the same side of the tape (above or below), and about the same distance from it. In other words, you will want all of your arrows to hit at more or less the same elevation along the vertical plane.

If your rest or nocking point is slightly off up or down, your groups will open vertically—even at a single distance. If your flyers tend to hit above the average point of impact, just move the rest slightly down or the nocking point slightly up, and vice versa if they trend below.

Repeat until your groups are as tight vertically as you feel you can get them.

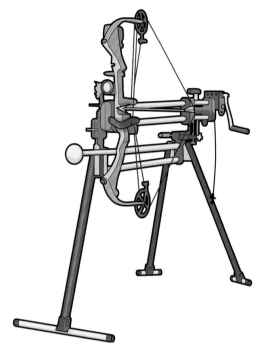

082 NOCK-TUNE YOUR ARROWS

To shoot your best, it's not enough to tune your bow. You have to tune your arrows, too. Even a dozen brand-new, high-end, correctly spined arrows won't all hit the same spot out of the box. "Typically, you'll have seven or eight that hit close to the same spot and four or five that are way off," says Spot Hogg's Christensen. The way to fix that is by nock tuning. The most precise method is to use a Hooter Shooter, which some pro shops have and which Christensen employs routinely. Here's how he does it (typically taking all shots at 20 yards).

STEP 1 Shoot all of your arrows through the machine to see which group together best. Then take any one of those and shoot it several times to make sure it hits in the exact same hole each time. Assuming that it does, mark it as No. 1.

STEP 2 Now take any other arrow, mark it No. 2, and shoot it through the machine. If it doesn't hit in the same hole as No. 1, turn the nock slightly and shoot again. Repeat this until it hits the No. 1 hole, or as close as possible. If you have a fall-away rest with good clearance, you can turn the nock to any position. Otherwise, you need to work within the limitations of your rest. There aren't any set rules for which way or how much to turn a nock to make certain corrections. "It varies," says Christensen, "but with each setup you can often find a pattern that helps speed up the process."

STEP 3 Do this for all your arrows. You may not get all 12 to hit in precisely the same hole, but you can usually get very close. If one or two arrows really give you trouble, replace their nocks and try again.

If you don't have access to a Hooter Shooter, you can—and should—do exactly the same thing by hand. You won't have the same degree of precision, but you will have better groups when you're done.

083 TUNE WITH BROADHEADS

Because the terms paper tuning, walk-back tuning, and nock tuning each refer to a specific process, many people assume *broadhead tuning* does, too. In fact, it means doing any of those tuning methods, but with broadheads on your arrows. Most shooters initially tune and practice with field points. Then, as the hunting season draws near, they'll switch to broadheads. But here's the rub: That switch—even with the broadheads you've already weighed and spun—often throws a little wrench into your previously perfect arrow flight. The remedy is to redo some of your tuning. Often a quick walk-back session solves the problem.

084 YOKE AROUND

For simplicity's sake, we've assumed until now that you'll make tuning adjustments by moving either the rest or the nocking point. That's exactly what you'll do on most bows (and part of what you can do on all bows). But with many models, you can also alter arrow flight by yoke tuning. Many bows have a Y-shaped split on one or both ends of the cables, and that split is called a yoke. By twisting either side of that split cable, you can change its length to precisely control cam lean.

Single-yoke systems are limited in this respect in that you can only adjust the lean of one cam, but sometimes that's all you need to do to bring to bring both cams into balance (so they have the same lean or lack thereof), which can solve major shooting or tuning problems.

However, you can tune some double-yoke systems, such as Bowtech's Binary Overdrive, almost entirely via the yokes. The process is a little complicated, but here's the idea in a nutshell. Most shooters introduce torque into the riser, which alters the angle of the arrow in respect to the rest, string, grip, sights, and so on. Purposely introducing a small amount of lean to both cams via yoke tuning can true the arrow in relation to the entire system in a way that simply moving the rest cannot, making for less horizontal nock travel and better arrow flight.

The process isn't difficult, but it does require a bow press and a little time to master. You need to understand that going in, or just have your shop pro do your tuning.

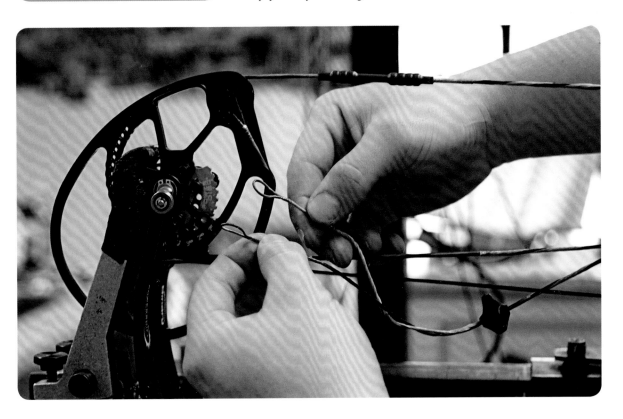

085 SHOOT THE SHAFT

For traditional archers—and finger shooters in general—the most common method of evaluating and correcting arrow fight is called *bare-shaft tuning*. (The name is a little misleading because while the technique involves shooting an unfletched shaft for aluminum and carbon arrows, wood shafts tend to explode when shot when unfletched, so most shooters leave the feathers on.) Competitive stickbow archer Johnathan Karch of 3 Rivers Archery explains how he does it.

GO LONG Assuming you know how long you want your finished arrow and approximately what weight tip you want to shoot, use a chart or calculator to get arrows that are appropriately spined for your setup. "For wood arrows, or if you have an aluminum or carbon arrow saw, get them about an inch long so there's room to trim if necessary," says Karch.

RUN A CHECK "Before I shoot, I double-check my bow's brace height, the rest, the nocking point, and that the arrow nocks themselves do not seat too tightly." Any problems here can throw off your results.

SHOOT AT FOAM Next, using just one arrow equipped with a head and nock but no fletching (unless it's wood), step 10–15 yards back from a chest-high foam target, nock the shaft, and take a level shot. Karch takes several shots with the same arrow to ensure consistent results.

CHECK THE HIGH AND LOW Inspect the angle of the arrow in the target. Unless the nock is in line with the point, you need to make some tweaks. "If the nock is high, for example, you need to move your string's nocking point down, and vice versa."

DON'T BE WEAK If the nock is left or right of the point of impact, you have a few options. On some traditional bows, you can adjust the rest; otherwise, you need to change the arrow spine. If the shot is nock-left, the spine is too weak; you can trim the arrow length a little, go with a lighter head, or add a little weight at the nock. It's okay if a bare shaft is slightly weak—adding fletching will stiffen it a bit. If it's nock-right, it's too stiff. The typical fix is to add weight up front.

FLETCH AND CHECK "Once I have the bare shaft plunging straight into the target, I fletch it up and then paper tune it—or, for wood, go straight to paper tuning. If that's good, and it usually is, I outfit the rest of my arrows exactly the same way and then fine-tune on the range if necessary."

086 GET INTO HEAVY METAL

Broadhead adapters used to be made of aluminum, and generally weighed about 35 grains. Now they also come in steel, in 100 and 125 grains, allowing you to double the weight of your arrow tip and significantly increase its front of center. A very front-heavy arrow doesn't usually make sense for compound shooters because it dramatically affects trajectory. But for traditional shooters taking shots inside 20 yards, the extra weight up front results in better penetration and, ultimately, cleaner kills.

Bob Morrison, founder of Morrison Bows, tests tip-heavy arrows by shooting them into 3/4-inch plywood boards with a 50-pound recurve. For comparison, he brings one graphite arrow up to 560 grains by sliding plastic tubing inside the shaft. Then, using an identical arrow without tubing, he achieves the same overall weight by attaching a steel adapter, loading the blunt tip up to 315 grains.

"The arrow without the heavy tip rarely sticks in the board," Morrison says. "The tip-heavy arrow not only sticks—it cracks the board on every shot and occasionally punches through it."

Over the years, Morrison has taken numerous deer and hogs with tip-heavy arrows that weighed 520 grains. Every shot was a pass-through, with the exception of one whitetail he hit in the hindquarters. In that instance, the arrow continued through to penetrate the vitals. Morrison claims that the tip-heavy arrows fly well, but they may require additional tuning and possibly a stiffer arrow shaft.

Compound shooters also can reap benefits from heavy tips, especially on thick-skinned game shot at close range. I know of a Texas pig hunter who was able to significantly increase his recovery rate on big hogs just by increasing his arrow tip weight, which resulted in better arrow penetration and more obvious blood trails. That's a result that deer (and especially bear) hunters should mark well.

087 SHOOT A STICK BOW

Shooting a recurve or longbow is a fluid, instinctive process, like throwing a baseball. You can show someone the basics, but to truly learn the art—accuracy, consistency, range estimation—requires lots and lots of practice. To practice correctly, your form needs to be correct, as described below.

STAND Point your left foot slightly toward the target (if you're a right-handed shooter), bend your knees slightly, and lean your torso in a bit.

GRIP The bow's grip should hit the base of your palm, meeting bone. Relax your fingers.

SET Some shooters put three fingers under the arrow, others put an index finger above, middle and ring fingers below. Use whichever position feels better to you.

ANCHOR Some anchor up by their eye, others high on the cheekbone. I stick my middle finger in the corner of my mouth and drop my nose down on the string. Go with what's most comfortable; the key is consistency.

DRAW Cant the upper limb to the right (right-handed shooters) so you get a clearer vision of the target and the arrow stays on the shelf. As you draw, your eyes should burn a hole in the spot you want to hit.

RELEASE Simply relax your fingers. Don't overthink the release. Focus on the target and just let go.

088 MIND THE GAP

Instinctive shooting is, as the name implies, a sort of dead-reckoning aiming method. Just as when you throw a ball, you focus on the target, letting your brain do the necessary calculations as your arms, hands, and body posture make the physical stuff happen. Naturally, this takes lots of practice. Let's be honest: Some people are naturally better at it than others, just as some people can throw a fastball well enough to play for the major leagues.

But following your instincts isn't the only way to shoot. Gap shooting is on the other end of the spectrum. With this method, the shooter focuses on the target, keeping the tip of the arrow in his vision. Using the arrow's tip as a reference, the shooter estimates a predetermined gap, or approximate distance, to hold the arrow above his target. For example, at 15 yards or less, the shooter might hold the tip dead on the target. At 15–20 yards, he holds the tip slightly above the spot; at 20–25 yards, he holds the tip one arrow width high, and so on. Naturally, you can only perfect this method with intense practice, and it requires the shooter to know the distance to the target (or estimate it closely).

A gap shooter needs to be able to see the end of the arrow and the target in the sight picture, which usually requires making an adjustment in form. Gap shooters typically shoot with three fingers under the arrow, and frequently have an anchor point higher than instinctive shooters—often on the cheekbone or near the eye itself. I've talked with gap shooters who shoot a longer arrow than necessary and/or slightly elevate their nocking point, so they can see the arrow tip more readily. Some traditional shooters are pretty snooty about gap shooting, since the method isn't truly instinctive, and therefore, they feel, is less pure. I say any technique that allows you to shoot good groups with a stick bow and no sights is A-OK. After all, Howard Hill perfected a style of gap shooting that made him one of the greatest bow shots of all time. Who am I to argue with him?

HUNTING WITH A STICK BOW

Scott Bestul on

I know I can shoot farther and more accurately (and with less practice) with a compound than I can with a recurve. But I still love the challenge of a stick bow—the commitment to extra practice, the added hurdle of getting a little closer to game, the intimacy of sending an arrow right where I'm looking with no sights or gadgetry for help.

And then there are situations where a stick bow can outshine a compound. One of the biggest bucks I've killed nailed my wind before he walked into my shooting lane. As he walk-trotted behind my tree to escape, I rotated against the tree trunk and drew in one motion, and just as his shoulder entered a small gap in the cedars, I released. The arrow zipped through his lungs as if I'd willed it. I'd never have been able to make that shot with a compound. Hours of practice had crystallized into a few amazing seconds that are forever burned into my memory. I'd like to think Fred Bear would have approved.

089 SHOOT LIKE LEVI MORGAN

Morgan is the world's top-ranked professional 3-D archer and host of Name the Game on the Sportsman Channel. He has 10 world titles and 42 national titles, and is an 11-time Archery Shooting Association Shooter of the Year. He has also tagged more than 50 Pope & Young animals. So he's a pretty good guy to emulate. Here's exactly how he shoots a bow.

STAND STEADY Morgan sets his feet perpendicular to the target about shoulder-width apart, and then he turns his toes out slightly for better stability. "Stand on a piece of cardboard, get your feet just right, and have someone trace them," he says. "Whenever you practice, put that cardboard down and stand in the outlined footprints. After a month you can ditch the cardboard, and you'll take the exact same stance every time you address a target."

ANCHOR UP Consistent anchor points are critical at full draw. Morgan uses three: First, he puts his release hand against his face in exactly the same spot on every shot. Second, he rests the tip of his nose on the string. Third, he holds the release in the very same way, shot after shot. "Not everyone thinks of this last one, but if you change how you grip the release, it will affect your shooting."

RELAX YOUR GRIP Don't grab the bow's handle like a hammer; that just introduces torque to the shot. Instead, rest the bow's grip against the bony part of your palm's heel, between the two fleshy pads. "I favor the thumb side some," says Morgan. "Otherwise the pads on either side can influence your grip inconsistently." Lower your fingers safely under the shelf, but leave your hand relaxed as you shoot.

KEEP IT STRAIGHT Form as straight a line as possible from your grip hand back to your lead shoulder, and keep that shoulder low and extended. "Don't entirely lock out your bow arm, but don't bend it much either," Morgan says. You also want a straight line from the tip of the arrow all the way to the point of your string-arm elbow. "It's easy to put a kink in that line where your release meets your face, so try to keep that straight."

DON'T PUSH AND PULL Conventional wisdom would have you push toward the target with your bow arm and pull away with your string arm at full draw. "That's becoming old-school," says Morgan. He shoots static, meaning he pulls just hard enough to stay against the back wall. "Otherwise it's too easy to push or pull a little harder from shot to shot, making the method difficult to repeat."

FLOAT THE PIN No one can hold a bow steady enough while aiming to keep the sight pin perfectly centered on a distant target. So don't try. "I let the pin float over the target while I concentrate on the center," says Morgan. "It's amazing how much pin movement you can get away with and still make a good shot by just thinking about the middle on the bull."

FORGET BACK TENSION For more than a decade now, experts have said that the only correct way to shoot a bow was via back tension (see item 91). But learning this method isn't easy; using it in a hunting situation is something many competitive shooters describe as "unthinkable." If you've struggled trying to shoot this way, forget it. Today's best pros prove that there are other valid methods.

BE SURPRISED Morgan typically uses either a thumb or a hinge release, but the principle is the same with a caliper style. "Slowly squeeze the trigger, or press the thumb button, or rotate your hand until the release goes off. It should be a surprise every time."

END NATURALLY Don't exaggerate the follow-through. Don't consciously throw your string arm back at the release. "If you have correct form and a surprise release, proper follow-through is just going to happen—along with better accuracy."

090 PUNCH IT

Most hunters punch the trigger when the sight picture looks good—and most of them have been told it's the wrong way to shoot. "Don't let anyone tell you that punching is a negative," says Gold Tip's Tim Gillingham, who won the last two IBO 3-D World Championships doing just that. "It can work really, really well." If the word *punching* is already poisoned for you, do like Gillingham and call it 'command-style' shooting. Here's how he does it.

VISUALIZE Before you even draw the bow, you should visualize the shot. "Your body will do what your mind tells it to," Gillingham says. "If you worry about missing, you'll miss. If you see the perfect shot in your mind, your body will repeat it." Gillingham imagines the motion of the pin slowly getting smaller and smaller over the target until the sight picture is perfect—then thunk, 10-ring.

AIM AND PULL It's impossible to hold the pin perfectly still, so concentrate on slowing it down. "You want to focus on the middle of the target and make the shot the moment the pin passes over the center. That's a lot easier if the pin is moving slowly," he says. "For me, the key is pulling hard—straight back—with my string hand." When you get nervous over a big shot or a big buck, pulling hard really helps slow the pin down.

SEE AND SHOOT "Let the sight picture fire the shot," says Gillingham. "If you make a conscious decision to shoot, you'll anticipate the shot, which any pro will tell you is the kiss of death." You're also going to need to have to have a light trigger, because if you feel resistance as you pull, you'll anticipate the shot. "Trust that your body will perform what you've visualized, and the trigger will just go off when the sight picture is right."

091 PUT YOUR BACK INTO IT

Plenty of top archers still trigger a mechanical release with back tension, and a few use a pure back-tension release. Shooting with back tension is more complicated than simply punching the trigger, but it works. If you suffer from target panic, it may be just the thing for you.

Back tension is essentially squeezing your shoulders together instead of punching the trigger with your index finger. Many hunters never try it, assuming that it's too difficult to master. In fact, anyone can learn the technique. The regimen below will have you using back tension and shooting better in weeks.

GET COMFORTABLE During the first week, stand just a few feet in front of a target. Come to full draw and settle into your anchor point. Hook your index finger firmly against the trigger. Now, instead of pulling it toward you to fire the release, close your eyes and begin squeezing your back muscles together, drawing your release elbow rearward. When the bow fires, it should come as a surprise. Repeat this 15 to 20 times a day to get comfortable with the basic motion.

MAKE MUSCLE MEMORY The next week, start each session with the same 15–20 shots as before—point-blank, eyes closed. Then back up 10–15 yards and shoot 30–40 arrows with both your eyes open, using exactly the same procedure. End each day's practice with another 15–20 shots up close with eyes closed, concentrating on how it feels to release the trigger by using your back muscles instead of by moving your index finger.

PUT IT ALL TOGETHER Return to your normal practice distance in the third week. Take a deep breath and then focus on burning the pin into your target. Let your back muscles take over and just shoot. If you get off track, take some point-blank, eyes-closed shots as a refresher. By the week's end, your flyers will be fewer, your groups will be tighter, and you'll have the confidence to take your new and improved shooting technique into the field.

092 DON'T PANIC

It came out of the blue: One minute I could nail the bull's-eye without thinking; the next it was all I could do to place my sight pin on the target. I shot prematurely. I jerked the release trigger. I flinched as if I was shooting an elephant rifle. Eventually, I laid down my bow, wondering: "What's happened to me?"

In sports, this is known as "the yips." Archers call it "target panic," and it afflicts thousands of shooters, from Olympic competitors to casual hunters. Some believe target panic is psychological—anxiety caused by fear of missing. Others suggest it's a disorder caused by overworked neurons. Regardless, learning to live with target panic is important, but it's not easy; once you've fallen victim to the syndrome, it can flare up at any time. These simple steps have helped me keep it under control and enjoy shooting a bow—and hunting effectively—again.

ACCEPT IT Being hard on yourself just makes it worse. Acknowledge the problem and resolve to fix it.

RETURN TO BASICS Stand in front of a target. Draw your bow and settle your pin on the target—but don't shoot. Just visualize a perfect shot, and then let down. This process alone has all but cured some top shooters.

SHOOT BLIND Follow the blank bale practice regimen (see item 94), which removes the target face and therefore eliminates the fear of missing.

GET UP CLOSE After shooting blank bale, take a single arrow and stand 10 feet from a target. Focusing on the perfect form, drill bull's-eye. Take several shots and end on a good one—it's very important to finish on a positive note.

TAKE BABY STEPS When 10 yards becomes easy, step back, but only 5 feet at a time and over the course of a few days. Don't shoot more than a couple dozen arrows per day. Even a little shooting fatigue can wreak havoc.

FLOAT THE PIN Many panic-stricken archers seize up because they're trying to lock the pin on the bull. Forget this. Remember to float the pin on—or trace little circles around—the bull as you execute a smooth release.

PULL SMOOTHLY If you're still having trouble, try a no-punch release such as the Golden Key Futura Answer. This model will simply not fire unless you are squeezing the trigger smoothly. It'll be maddening at first, but it's an excellent teaching tool.

094 SHOOT BLANKS

Students of well-known archery coach Terry Wunderle have spent endless hours shooting "blank-bale"—at a target butt with no target face—from 10 to 15 feet. And his world champions are the ones who spend the most time doing it. Here's his suggested routine 30-day routine.

DAYS 1–10 With the target at chest level, shoot blank-bale for 30 minutes, focusing on form: Draw and let the pin float and settle; then pull the bow apart (unless you shoot static, in which case focus on a smooth release). Do not aim. Your goal is consistency. You want each shot to feel like the one before and the one to come. If you can safely shoot with your eyes closed, try it. It helps some guys feel the shot better.

DAYS 11–20 Shoot blank bale for the first 10 minutes. For the next 20 minutes, alternate every other shot between shooting at the blank bale and shooting at a dot or other small target. Even with the latter target, do not aim. If you're in good form, the pin will find the target. Judge success by how good your form is.

DAYS 21–30 Continue to shoot blank bale for the first 10 minutes. Spend the remaining 20 shooting at the target. You should be settling into a rhythm where once you begin the shot process, the arrow goes off within a second or two each time. If you have any hiccups, go back to the blank bale.

093 TEST YOURSELF

The only meaningful test of a bowhunter is how he shoots under pressure. Before you begin a practice session, team up with a buddy and try to intimidate each other as you each shoot five arrows at a 3-inch bull's-eye at 20 yards. The only rule is that you may not physically touch the shooter or interfere with his line of sight to the target. Monetary wagers, standing close, yelling, making choking noises, and singing "neener, neener, neener" are all permitted. If you each get all five in the bull, increase the distance in 5-yard increments until one of you misses.

THE HARDEST THING

Dave Hurteau on

The hardest thing to master in archery is learning to mentally separate aiming from pulling the trigger. Too bad this is also the key to good shooting. It helps to practice aiming without shooting, and shooting without aiming. It's smart to do the latter so much that a smooth release becomes automatic—something you don't have to think about—thus freeing your mind to focus entirely on aiming. As countless top archers prove every day, achieving this focus is possible—but it's a constant struggle. If you come up with an easy way, let the rest of us know.

095 ADD 10 YARDS

Expert archer Anthony Dixon says that most bowhunters can extend their range by 10 yards with a little work. Here's his formula.

MATCH PEEP AND PIN GUARD Most modern sights have a round pin guard. Make sure it lines up perfectly with your peep sight at full draw. "If there is space between the outside of the guard and the edges of the peep, downsize the peep."

GET A SINGLE-PIN SLIDER SIGHT "A movable pin that can be precisely adjusted in 1-yard or even ½-yard increments gives you a big advantage over guessing where to hold with multiple pins, especially at longer ranges where the arrow is dropping faster."

CALIBRATE TO ONE RANGE FINDER "Because different range finders can give slightly different readings, it's critical to calibrate your sight to a specific range finder and then use the same model in the field."

PRACTICE LONG RANGE Dixon practices at 100 and 120 yards. "If your goal is to double-lung deer every time at 35 or 40 yards, practice at 60-plus," he says. "It'll make those shorter shots seem easy."

096 MAKE THE FIRST SHOT

"In hunting, it does you no good to shoot the last 299 of 300 arrows really well," says Steve Toriseva, of Border Country Outfitters in Ontario, Canada. "You need to make that first shot really well, in any conditions." Don't just take more shots. Take more first shots. Here's how.

SHOOT COLD "There are no warm-ups in the field, so you shouldn't have any in your practice," says Toriseva. Just take a shot at any range. Then change the distance, angle, or shooting position, and shoot again. Do this one more time, and then take a 20-minute break. After that, come back for another set of three "first" shots. "Shoot only four sets per day; more than a dozen shots risks fatigue, which leads to poor technique."

KEEP YOURSELF GUESSING Deer don't just stop broadside at exactly 20 yards, so why arrange your targets that way? "Stalk a foam deer target, stopping in a random spot to shoot," Toriseva advises. Or pick a spot, sneak to it, kneel down, and shoot. "You'll hone your abilities to judge range and choose the proper impact point."

GET REAL High winds, low light, rain, heat, and cold all affect your shots in the field, so practice under these conditions. Shoot from the blind or stand you'll use in the field. "As opening day nears, treat each session like a dress rehearsal. Put your target in the woods. Shoot broadheads. Wear your camo." When the season opens and a giant walks into range, you'll get the shot right the first time.

097 HAVE A FIELD PLAN

Here's what to do in the field when a shooter buck walks in.

VISUALIZE Ignore the rack (I know, it's hard!) as your buck steps broadside into range. Focus on a small spot, such as a tuft of hair behind the foreleg, and visualize your sight pin on it.

DRAW YOUR BOW Do so when the buck is looking away or his view is obstructed. Pull back slowly. Mentally check your anchor point.

GAIN A SIGHT PICTURE Hold your focus for a slow count of three to keep from rushing the shot.

TAKE THE SHOT Squeeze the trigger if you're using a mechanical release aid. Otherwise, smoothly relax your fingers. Keep looking at that tuft of hair; hold your shooting form until your broadhead's struck.

WATCH THE BUCK Take note of his reaction after the shot and the exact location you last see him.

LISTEN Wait several more minutes. You may hear him fall, change direction, jump a fence, or cross a stream. Study that area carefully with your binocular, trying to get another look at the buck.

MARK YOUR POSITION Use a hat, glove, or flagging tape if you're hunting from the ground. If you're in a treestand, shoot a practice arrow into the spot where the deer was when you shot him.

TRACK THE BUCK Go to where the buck was standing and look carefully for sign. Then sift through all the evidence to evaluate the hit and decide whether to wait until morning to take up the trail, wait a few hours, or simply go now and collect your trophy.

098 MAKE A 100-YARD SHOT

Hitting a target at 100 yards with a bow is not as difficult as you think. Try it. Not only does long-range practice make shots at hunting ranges seem like gimmes; it also magnifies subtle mistakes in shooting form. If you mess up your form at 30, you may still be in the kill zone. If you mess up at 100, you'll miss the whole damn target and lose a $12 arrow. This forces you to bear down and shoot well.

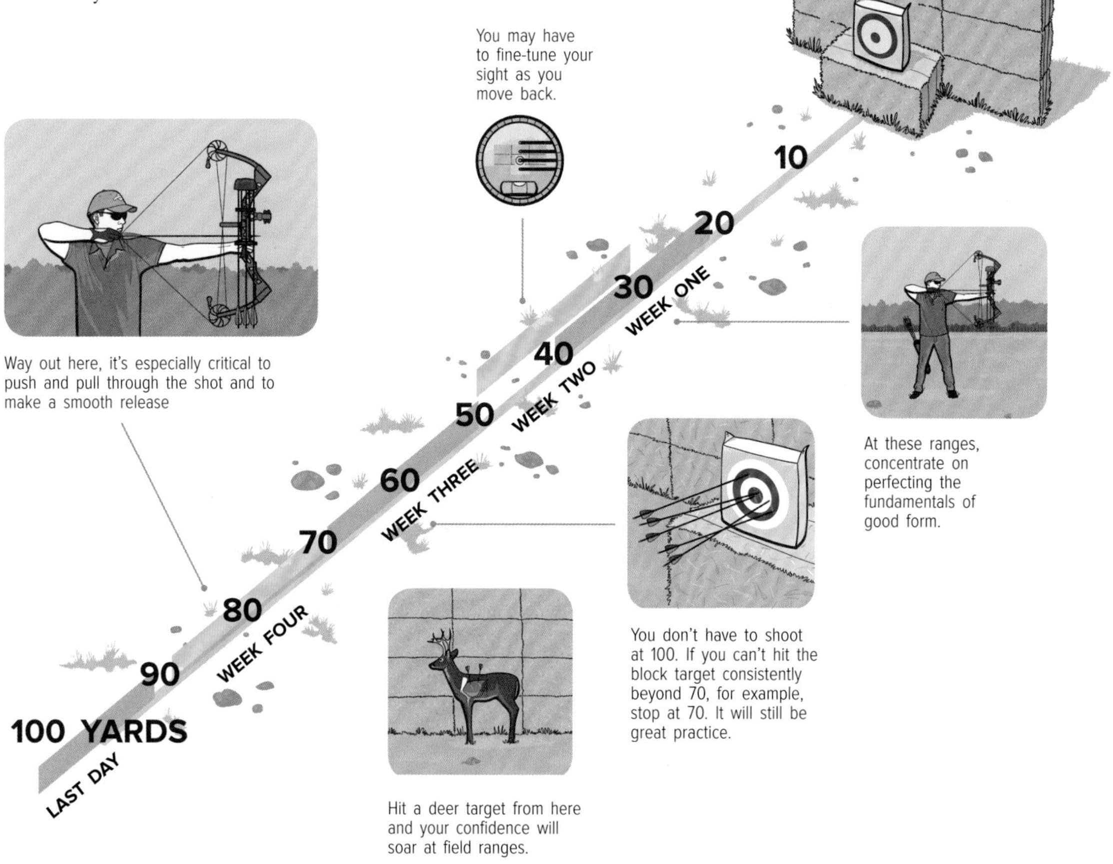

You may have to fine-tune your sight as you move back.

10

20

30 WEEK ONE

40 WEEK TWO

50

60 WEEK THREE

70

80 WEEK FOUR

90

100 YARDS

LAST DAY

Way out here, it's especially critical to push and pull through the shot and to make a smooth release

At these ranges, concentrate on perfecting the fundamentals of good form.

You don't have to shoot at 100. If you can't hit the block target consistently beyond 70, for example, stop at 70. It will still be great practice.

Hit a deer target from here and your confidence will soar at field ranges.

099 TAKE THE LONG-SHOT REGIMEN

Want to be sure of your accuracy in the field once you get out for the hunt? Here's how to hit at 100 before the opener.

In the first week of practice, work on your form at a 30-yard range. At the second week, move out to 40 yards; fine-tune your sight if needed. After that, back up to 60 yards and keep working on your accuracy in the third week. Make sure you can consistently hit the target before extending your range. In the fourth week, you'll hopefully be able to execute a smooth shot with good form at 80-plus yards. By the time the last day before the opener rolls around, you should be trying to hit the target from 100 yards. If you can put your arrow into the target at this distance, it'll be no trouble at closer ranges in the field.

100 SHOOT 3-D

For guys like Levi Morgan, 3-D shoots are serious business; perhaps they are for you, too. But you don't have to compete on the pro circuits to enjoy 3-D archery. A shoot hosted by your local club with nothing more at stake than bragging rights and a 10-dollar entry fee is good practice and lots of fun.

Most 3-D shoots are set up similarly to a golf course, with 20–40 targets ranging from ground hogs to bull elk placed at varying distances along a walking trail. And most shoots follow similar rules. Shooters can get a score of 5 for a hit anywhere on the target, 8 in the large vital ring, 10 in the small vital ring, or 12 for a hit in the tiny 12-ring, which is typically offset just a bit within the 10-ring. You can shoot in various classes, depending on your skill level and equipment. Shooters in traditional archery classes, for example, are allowed to get much closer to the targets.

Some events are "known distance" shoots, with targets set at known distances and range finders allowed. In others, the shooter must judge the distance to the target himself, no range finder. Sanctioned shoots typically set targets at a maximum of 50 yards, but plenty of club shoots stretch that out.

The competition is fun, and it teaches you to shoot well under pressure. In the heat of the summer, it's about the best practice you can get.

101 HIRE A COACH

If you're double-lunging every deer you shoot at and drilling quarters from 50 paces in the back yard, there's little reason to spend money on an archery coach. But, sooner or later, every bowhunter endures a slump. A few bad shots in the woods or a severe case of target panic on the range can get in your head, big time. Soon you're second-guessing every detail of the shot, and your confidence ebbs. For that, a coach is sometimes the only cure.

"Most shooting problems, including target panic, are caused by self-doubt," says Laval "Dee" Falks, the National Federation Director for the ASA and a USA Archery level 5 coach. "It's an archer's worst enemy. A good coach can watch you shoot, figure out pretty quickly how you can improve, personalize your instruction, get into your head a bit, and ultimately help you get your confidence back."

Falks, of Mount Juliet, Tennessee, typically charges around $50 per hour of instruction, or $300 for the day. He says that's a pretty standard rate for most certified coaches. "When you're looking to hire a coach, always get references," he says. "Hiring a coach is like buying a car. Do your research first, and you'll be happier with your investment."

102 LADIES, GET A BOW THAT FITS

Only a few years ago, a female hunter leafing through a bowhunting catalog had to first thumb through eight to 10 pages of premium compound bows for men before finally reaching the half-page selection of "youth and ladies" models. These bows did offer the shorter draw lengths and lighter draw weights suited to most female bowhunters—but they looked like they were built by bow-company interns and were inevitably equipped with outdated cam designs (or two wheels, circa 1984). Frequently, they were sold as "kits," complete with sights and rests that could best be described as, well, junk.

Not that you can completely blame the bow companies. There just wasn't much call for high-quality women's bows then. But it's different today. Female hunters have been the fastest-growing segment of the hunting population for a few years now. Bear, Bowtech, Elite, Hoyt, Mathews, and other heavy hitters in the archery industry are all now building flagship-quality women's bows to meet the new demand.

These models are designed with efficient cams and feature many of the same top-end components, construction, and price as a men's bow. The only real difference is that they're purpose-built with shorter draw lengths, lighter limbs, and perhaps a few pink accents for a feminine touch (which quite a few serious female bowhunters seem to despise).

Bottom line: If you're a female bowhunter who's in the market for a serious hunting outfit, you've got lots of great options now. The advice found throughout this book will serve you just as well as it serves the guys.

103 GO TO SPRING TRAINING

Want your young hunter to join you in the woods next fall? Get a bow in his or her hands this spring. "You want everything to be able to grow with your child," says Margaret Knupp, marketing manager for Bowtech, "from the bow to the training program." Here are five ways to make sure your kid is ready for fall.

BUY A BOW THAT GROWS Find a bow with an adjustable draw length that can move up to 28 inches (the average adult draw). There are numerous "infinite adjustment" bows available on the market today.

GET THE RIGHT ACCESSORIES An arm guard and capture-style arrow rests are essential for beginners. "Capture rests reduce the risk of an arrow slipping, and until your child develops proper form, an arm guard will keep him from getting injured," says Knupp.

START LIGHT Keep the draw weight very light—no more than 20 pounds. "You don't want your child to associate shooting with work," Knupp advises. "You can graduate up to a 40-pound draw weight, which is a good standard minimum for hunting."

104 CONSIDER A BOW THAT GROWS

If you could buy shoes that grow along with your kid, you would, right? That's why bows featuring extreme adjustability are so popular right now. How popular? The Diamond Infinite Edge—a perfect example of the type, made by Bowtech—is the company's best-selling bow ever. You can set its draw weight anywhere from 5 to 70 pounds and its draw length anywhere from 13 to 30 inches, with no need for extra modules or a bow press. In other words, with the turn of a few screws, you can set it up for anyone in the family, and it can grow along with any young or new shooter. Like most such bows, it's also inexpensive, at around $400. It sounds great—and it is—but don't rush out and get one just yet.

High-adjustability bows fill an important niche to a tee; they're just about perfect for youngsters coming up, for multiple young shooters in a family, and for some adult newcomers. In general, they offer more than enough power and accuracy for hunting at modest ranges. But they do have some drawbacks. Priced for beginners, their lower-end materials, as well as all that adjustability (to a lesser degree), puts limits on performance. Sized for beginners, they tend to be particularly short and light—not ideal for accuracy. The ones I've shot (which is most, if not all of the available models) have not been especially forgiving.

So be smart. If you don't need a bow that grows, spend your money on higher-end performance and forgiveness. On the other hand, if you can put all that remarkable adjustability to good use, it can be worth every penny.

KID STUFF With the right bow, kids can learn to shoot accurately.

FORGET THE RELEASE Having your child learn to shoot by using his or her fingers (with a glove or tab) is more natural and allows them to shoot instinctively.

KEEP THE TARGET LARGE The first archery target should be big and forgiving. A target on a 4x4-foot backstop is just that. While your kid probably won't be drilling many bull's-eyes at first, just making contact with the target is positive reinforcement. "You can think about precision as you get closer to the season," Knupp says. "In the early months, you just want to make sure that your kid is having fun."

105 MAKE IT STOP

Ultimately, the idea is to shoot your arrows into dinner. But in the meantime, you need something else to aim at. That is, you need a target or two.

You can make your own. A box full of old clothes will stop most arrows, as will a stack of compressed sheets, cardboard, foam, or carpeting. But most folks break down and buy their targets. Here are your options.

TARGET TYPE	PROS	CONS	BOTTOM LINE
BAG	Inexpensive. Very easy arrow removal.	They don't weather well. Fairly heavy. You can't shoot broadheads into them.	Easy arrow removal makes these the primary target for practice mainly with field points. If you remember to take the bag out of the weather between sessions, it'll do well.
FOAM BLOCK	Stops field points and broadheads. Comparatively light and portable. Weathers better than a bag target.	Removing arrows requires more effort. Can be a little pricey.	This is the do-anything, take-anywhere target. If ease of arrow removal isn't a big deal to you, this is probably your target.
3-D PRACTICE	Best target for real hunting scenarios. Fun to shoot. Can also double as lawn art.	Expensive. Heavy. Weathers poorly. Arrow removal is a real pain.	If you can, buy one. Game animals don't have bull's-eyes, so as hunting season nears and you switch to broadheads, there's no better practice. Be sure that yours has a replaceable core.

106 ADD SOME FOAM

Want to get more life out of your foam archery target block? After a few seasons, when your arrows start to enter the target up to the fletching, apply spray foam insulation to the most heavily punctured areas. Place the spray nozzle about halfway into each hole, deploy the foam, and make sure not to overfill. Wait 24 hours for it to cure, and you'll be ready to take aim again.

107 BUILD A TARGET STAND

Tired of your bag targets rotting from the ground up and becoming an eyesore in the yard? Then build a more attractive covered stand that will hold the target off the ground, shield it from rain and snow, and allow it to more easily absorb the repeated pounding of your practice arrows. Here's how.

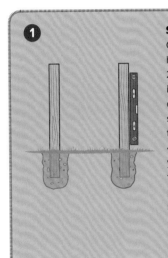

STEP 1
Cut a 10-foot 4x4 in half. Dig a pair of 1- to 2-foot-deep holes 38 inches apart, centered on where you want the stand. Add concrete to the holes, then set each 4x4 up vertically. As you backfill, lay a string flat on the face of both posts to ensure they are square to each other, and use a carpenter's level to make sure they are perfectly vertical.

STEP 3
Use two 40-inch-long 2x4s to connect the two trusses at the base, front and back. Make the roof by sheathing the framework with two sheets of plywood, cut to fit. Then lay and nail down the shingles (home-repair stores usually have already-opened packs of shingles they'll sell for a few bucks).

STEP 2
Once the concrete dries, center a 28-inch-long 2x4 to the very top outside edge of each 4x4. Nail or screw in place. Make 45-degree miter cuts at both ends of two 16-inch 2x4s. Fasten them together at the top and to one of the 28-inch bases to create a small truss. Repeat on the other side.

STEP 4
Screw two eyebolts high enough on the 4x4s to allow your bag target (attached with rope via its grommet holes) to swing freely off the ground. Stain all of the wood to guard against the elements, and you're done. Grab your bow and a quiver full of arrows, and shoot to your heart's content.

108 DON'T RUIN YOUR BOW

Beyond blatant abuse of your bow, here are six things you don't want to do.

LEAVE IT IN THE SUN Excessive heat can destroy the limbs and string, and leaving a bow in the sun is a recipe for disaster. After I left my case in the bed of my truck one October morning, I opened it to find a warped, ruined bow. Now, when I'm done hunting, my bow case goes inside, every time.

MOVE A PEEP WITHOUT A PRESS If your peep isn't aligned just right, don't try to separate the string with a butter knife or screwdriver. You'll end up with a broken string or a peep that gets stuck sideways.

OIL THE CAMS After you've hunted on a rainy day, resist the temptation to spray down the cams or other parts with gun oil or WD-40. This is bound to eat up the string. It's best to leave your bow out of the case, wipe it off, and just let it dry.

DRY-FIRE IT If your friend wants to try your new bow, nock an arrow and let him shoot it. Drawing a bow in the house without an arrow is a recipe for a dry fire.

OVERADJUST DRAW WEIGHT Be very careful when adjusting your bow's draw weight. Too many rotations out can result in the bow's coming to pieces the next time you draw it. Some bows have stops on the limb bolts to prevent this; many don't, and the number of turns required to adjust the draw weight by a certain amount varies widely between manufacturers. Also, a difference as small as an eighth of a turn between the two limb bolts can throw your bow out of time.

SHOOT YOUR BUDDY'S ARROWS Shooting a shaft that's too limber or too light for your bow can cause the same damage as a dry fire, flat-out ruining it. New arrows are cheaper than a new bow.

109 KEEP AN ARCHER'S REPAIR KIT

Bows can be prone to breakdowns at the worst times. When it happens in the woods or at camp—say, a peep sight falls out—you have two choices: go home or, if you have this kit, go hunting.

1. BOW OIL
2. SUPERGLUE
3. STRING WAX AND CHAMOIS
4. STRING SPLITTER
5. DENTAL FLOSS
6. MATCHES OR LIGHTER
7. BROADHEAD SHARPENER
8. SPARE STRING NOCKS
9. SPARE PIN
10. REPLACEMENT SILENCERS
11. FLEECE OR MOLESKIN
12. NOCK PLIERS
13. SERVING JIG AND MATERIAL
14. PORTABLE BOW PRESS
15. REPLACEMENT PEEP AND TUBING
16. STRING LOOP MATERIAL
17. REPLACEMENT INSERTS
18. REPLACEMENT ARROW NOCKS
19. REPLACEMENT BROADHEADS
20. HEX WRENCH SET

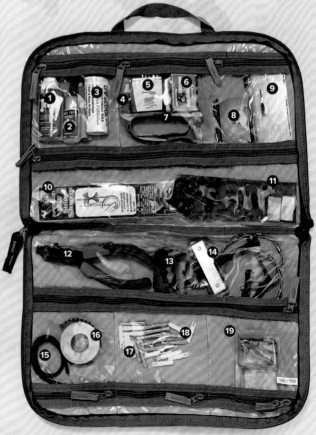

110 PREPARE FOR THE SEASON

Is your bow ready for the season? Even if your bow is only a year old, normal wear and tear can cause less than perfect broadhead flight, which could cost you your next trophy. Take your bow out of its case before season and go through this list of potential problems—and their solutions—before you hit the field.

 GET A GOOD REST Worn-out bristles in a capture rest or a drop-away rest that's out of time will affect arrow flight. Repair, readjust, or replace as needed.

 SERVE IT RIGHT A worn center serving can alter your nocking point, causing arrows to fly inconsistently. Luckily, tying a new serving is easy (for you or a shop pro).

 AVOID NOCK PINCH When you draw, the release jaws push against the nock, causing the nock to pop off the string. The solution is to install a D-loop.

 LOSE THE HOSE A few bowhunters still use old-style peep sights with a rubber hose. These inevitably break. Have a shop pro swap yours for one without a hose.

 CHECK FOR CRACKS A cracked or splintered limb can cause erratic arrow flight and is potentially dangerous. Have them replaced by a shop pro.

 LISTEN FOR CREAKS Older bows may creak as you start to draw, which of course scares game away. Have your pro grease the limb pockets.

 REPLACE CAM SERVINGS Worn end or cam servings can abrade the string and potentially cause it to snap. A new season means time for new strings and cables.

 CLIP ON A sudden jolt could cause the axle to slip out of place if the C-clip is missing. That would be disastrous. Order a few new clips and keep the extras handy.

111 GET SOME PROTECTION

Odds are you've got somewhere between $500 and $1,500 wrapped up in your outfitted bow, maybe more. It makes sense to protect it from bumps, bang-ups, and baggage handlers. Here are the major categories of cases to check out.

BE A SOFTIE Typically padded, lined on the interior, and wrapped in a durable outer fabric, these are lightweight and handy—perfect for everyday transport, as well as road trips. Toss it in the truck with your other stuff and you're off. Thirty bucks or so will get you a basic model; more buys a tougher exterior (usually high-denier nylon) and additional pockets for arrows and accessories.

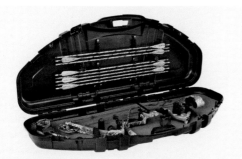

HARDEN UP The ubiquitous plastic case with the lightweight foam pad inside is all most people really need. It's a little heavier than a soft case but provides better protection and can handle airline travel. The $50 Plano Protector case I've used for more than a decade (including several flights per year) wound up battered, but never broken. Another $50 to $100 can get you a sturdier plastic shell and better latches.

GO TRAVELING Just in case you have to throw your bow out of an airplane and parachute to your next hunting destination, there are cases such as the SKB iSeries, made of military-grade high-density polyethylene, which resist impact, water, dust, UV, solvents, corrosion, and fungus. Priced in the ballpark of $250 and weighing about 25 pounds, these bombproof wheeled cases are the ultimate in airline protection, impervious to the gooniest of baggage goons.

HYBRIDIZE IT Hybrid cases combine a hard or semi-hard shell with plenty of padding and a soft fabric exterior. There are a few mid-range examples, but most of them are very high end and snazzy, approaching $350. Designed to handle airline travel, they combine solid protection with reasonably light weight, plus lots of smartly designed features. Some have room for two target bows.

112 MAKE AN ARROW CASE

Whether I'm going off on a long-distance hunt or just a regular jaunt to my local deer woods, I always like to have plenty of practice and backup arrows at hand. To keep all of my arrows organized and safe from damage, I used a PVC pipe and some fittings to build this inexpensive carrier that will handle the roughest ride in the back of my truck, as well as the worst that any airline baggage handler can throw at it.

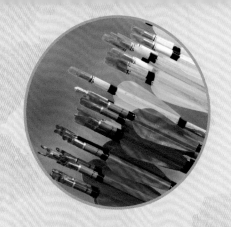

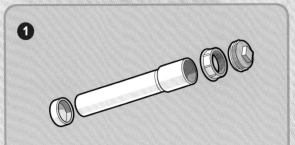

STEP 1

Buy a 3-foot length of 3-inch-diameter schedule 40 PVC pipe with a flared end from the plumbing section of your local hardware store. Get one basic end cap for the bottom of your arrow tube and one threaded cap (with cleanout adapter) to fit on the flared top end, which will provide the opening for loading and unloading your arrows.

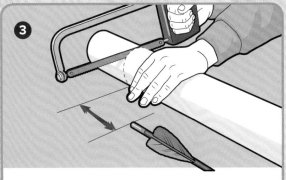

STEP 3

Measure your arrows and cut the PVC tube to accept them, with 3 inches to spare. The easiest way is to align the point of the arrow with the flared end of the pipe, add 3 inches, and then make the cut. The best way to ensure a square cut is to use an electric miter saw, but a hacksaw will do the job.

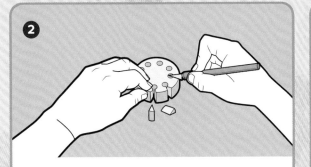

STEP 2

Visit your archery shop and ask for a pair of the foam placeholder disks that arrow companies use to ship arrows. Your shafts will fit perfectly into the disk's round slots (see above), and the disks fit perfectly inside the PVC tube. If your shop pro doesn't have any, the local hobby or crafts store should have foam disks you can cut slots into with an X-Acto knife.

STEP 4

Sand the rough-cut edge with 120-grit paper until smooth, and clean off any debris. Glue on the end cap with PVC cement, and then slide your shafts (held by two foam disks) into your new arrow tube. Finally, screw on the threaded end cap—which renders your holder waterproof—and you're ready for anything.

113 GEAR UP FOR BOWFISHING

All you really need in order to enjoy bowfishing is a fish arrow tied to a line that's tied to a bow. But you'll find that you enjoy it a lot more if your bow shoots where you point it and if your arrow doesn't snap back into your spleen because of a line tangle. As bowfishing has soared in popularity, good gear has become plentiful. Build a rig using the hints that follow and you can kill rough fish for years to come.

114 USE A TOUGH BOW

Bowfishing shots are close, fast, and instinctive, so you don't need the heavy draw weights, blazing speed, or high let-off of today's top big-game rigs. What you need is a bow that's either tough as nails or disposable because it's apt to get shot several hundred times in a day, baked in the sun, and walloped upon by a giant, hemorrhaging goldfish. It's the perfect game for recurve shooters, but compounds provide more power with less draw weight, so that's what most bowfishers use.

A retired hunting bow can work just fine, but specialized bowfishing bows are better and readily available. You'll snap-shoot most of them with your fingers; they have relatively long axle-to-axle lengths and peak draw weights of 50 pounds or less. A few have moderate let-off—the AMS Swamp Thing, for example, has 20 percent—while others have none at all. Get a bow built with stainless steel components because it will get wet and rust otherwise, and definitely add a set of rubber finger savers to the string because a leather shooting tab becomes crusty and unrecognizable after a good day of impaling carp.

115 PICK YOUR ARROW

Although some bowfishing arrows are made from carbon or other materials, most are solid, full-length fiberglass shafts that weigh in the neighborhood of 1,500 grains. Such a heavy arrow carries a lot of momentum and will produce startling penetration on a carp in 4 feet of water, even when plodding along at 100 fps. They're inexpensive and rugged; you'll probably lose them long before you break them.

Tip your arrow with the barbed bowfishing point of your choice (they all work), and then add a safety slide for securing the line to the arrow. This slide moves freely up and down the arrow shaft, and in the event of a line tangle, it keeps the arrow from snapping back at you, which will certainly happen if your line is tied directly to the arrow.

116 TAKE A REST

Bowfishing rigs don't require precision tuning, but to hit a fish under water, you do need an arrow that flies straight. Shooting right off the shelf works, but it can be tricky to set the correct nocking point for straight arrow flight. An arrow rest speeds that process along and is a little more convenient on the water.

A few styles of simple bowfishing rests are available; a containment model makes the most sense. A standard Whisker Biscuit won't support the weight of a 1,500-grain fish arrow; many bowfishermen get around that by supergluing the bristles of the rest together, which works just fine. Trophy Ridge also sells a bowfishing version of the Whisker Biscuit called the Fishing Biscuit that has more rigid bristles and is adjustable for both windage and elevation.

CROSSBOW

THE CROSSBOW ISN'T A NEWCOMER BY ANY MEANS

It's easy to think of crossbows as the newest thing on the bowhunting scene, but that's not really accurate. The idea of mounting the limbs of a bow to a stock that makes holding and aiming simpler has been around forever; medieval armies made use of them, and even Leonardo Da Vinci drew up plans for a huge crossbow to use in war.

Crossbows are often considered deadlier than their vertical cousins these days, but that hasn't always been true. As a matter of fact, medieval longbows were equally accurate and soldiers could reload them more quickly than the crossbows of the day.

In fact, the only real reason that armies in the middle ages switched to the crossbow is that it took years of training to make a competent longbowman, and only weeks to achieve the same goal with a crossbow.

Today's average crossbow is indeed more powerful than the average vertical bow. Once you pair it with a good scope, that crossbow is, on average, more accurate, too. That user-friendliness is the very bias working against the crossbow's inclusion in modern bowhunting seasons—but it's a short-sighted bias.

The number of hunters is shrinking daily, and if the less challenging learning curve afforded by a more effective tool attracts new hunters and allows veterans to remain afield, bowhunters need to embrace crossbows as the long-lost cousins they are.

And as when you hunt with a compound, a crossbow still requires you to get within arrow range. Crossbows have their own unique set of challenges, both on the practice range and in the woods. Here's what you need to know.

117 TAKE AN ANATOMY LESSON

Regardless of the style of crossbow you choose—recurve, compound, or reverse-draw compound—you need to have some knowledge of the basic nomenclature. A crossbow's working parts are, in essence, a blend of bow and rifle, so there's a lot of crossover from both in the jargon. But some features and accessories are unique to crossbows.

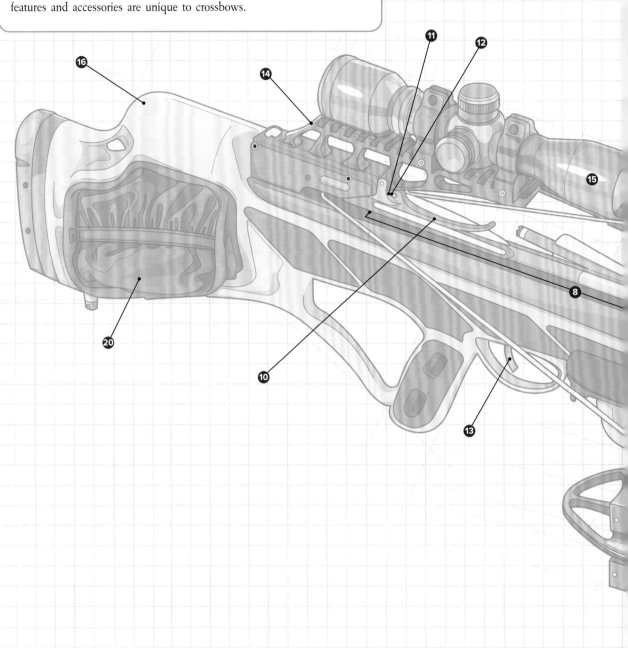

HERE'S A RUNDOWN OF THE MINIMUM YOU NEED TO LEARN.

1. LIMBS
2. CAMS (COMPOUND CROSSBOWS)
3. STRING
4. CABLES (COMPOUND CROSSBOWS)
5. RISER
6. COCKING STIRRUP
7. BARREL
8. POWER STROKE
9. BOLT TRACK
10. BOLT RETENTION SPRING
11. ANTI DRY-FIRE DEVICE (NOT ALL CROSSBOWS ARE EQUIPPED WITH ONE)
12. STRING LATCH
13. TRIGGER
14. OPTIC RAIL
15. OPTIC
16. STOCK
17. FOREGRIP
18. QUIVER
19. BOLTS
20. COCKING ROPE

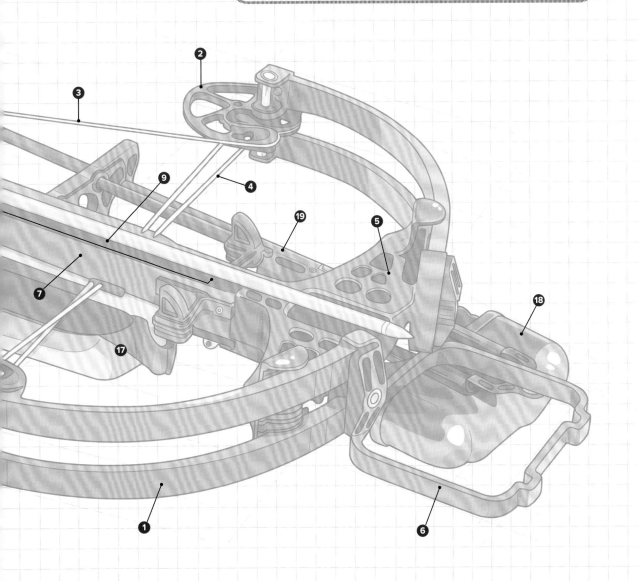

The question of whether crossbows will be a part of modern American deer hunting is no longer an issue; they're here to stay, and not just for elderly or physically challenged hunters. In many states and provinces, crossbows enjoy full inclusion into the general archery seasons. The new questions: How many new "bowhunters" will be created because of crossbows? How will the new blood affect the archery harvest, management goals, and the hunting experience?

The future looks very bright for crossbows and those who shoot and hunt with them. In my mind, the crossbow stands where the compound bow did back in the 1970s, when I first started bowhunting. Stick-bow hunters feared that the strange-looking contraption adorned with wheels and cables would jeopardize the sport they loved, but instead the compound launched thousands of new people into bowhunting and legitimized the bow as a serious hunting tool. The crossbow will do the same, and if it attracts more new hunters to our sport, and allows older sportsmen and sportswomen to remain in the woods, we should embrace this ancient weapon and celebrate its new popularity.

GET NEW HUNTERS The relative ease of use and shorter learning curve for the crossbow certainly attracts new hunters, and encourages higher participation and increased license sales, which is a good thing. During the 2003 season in Georgia, the first year crossbow hunters enjoyed full inclusion in the general archery hunt, the state sold 9,300 more bow tags than in the previous season. Over one-third of those licensees had never hunted with archery equipment previously, and 46.4 percent of those crossbow hunters were over 50 years old (declining license sales to hunters over the age of 50 is a problem noted in many states).

INCREASE THE HARVEST Gaining numbers is a great thing when we struggle to attract and hold people to the sport, but it's legitimate to question how this boost will affect overall deer harvest. In 2011 when crossbows were legal in Indiana but only under restrictions, the crossbow harvest was 1,091 whitetails. The next year, under full inclusion, nearly 10,000 additional bowhunters signed up. Crossbow hunters registered 8,452 deer, and by the 2013 season that number jumped to 10,171.

UP THE SUCCESS RATE Wisconsin is one of the nation's top states for bowhunting whitetails; in 2014 it granted full inclusion to crossbows during the archery season. That fall, 47,449 hunters purchased a crossbow permit. The percentage of first-time participants in the archery season is not yet known, but bowhunters set a single-season buck harvest record of 46,201 animals. While crossbow hunters only killed an estimated 15,768 of those bucks, their success rate (29 percent) was higher than that of vertical bow users (23 percent).

HUNT LIKE A WOLVERINE Statistics like that may be important if the number of crossbow hunters continues to climb as it did in neighboring Michigan. In 2009 (the first year of full inclusion), only 19 percent of bowhunters toted a crossbow. By 2013, that percentage had risen to 49 percent, and the success rate for crossbow hunters was the highest (32 percent) for any weapon type, including firearms.

FEAR NOT If deer harvests increase, does that mean that bag limits will be lowered or seasons shortened? Will more hunters in the field (with any weapon) increase competition for prime hunting ground, possibly reducing opportunity to take game? These concerns are legitimate, but they've proven largely unwarranted in Ohio, where the archery hunt has included crossbows since 1976. While bowhunters may kill only one buck, antlerless opportunities continue to abound, and archers enjoy a nearly four-month season.

GO TO TOWN There are places where the crossbow is a veritable godsend, especially if bowhunters are the primary agents of herd control. In Connecticut, firearms restrictions and outright bans are common, so bowhunting is the best tool to keep suburban deer numbers in check. In the 2014 season, for the first time in modern history, the archery harvest (estimated at 6,046 deer) topped the firearms kill (4,340); much of that bow harvest was attributed to the rise in crossbow hunters.

119 COMPARE YOUR OPTIONS

Is a modern crossbow really a deadlier hunting tool than a modern compound? To try to settle this question, I decided to put a couple of modern crossbows head-to-head against my hunting compound—a Hoyt Spyder Turbo rigged with a single-pin HHA slider sight and a drop-away rest—in a test of hunting effectiveness. Here's what I found.

	COMPOUND BOW	CROSSBOW	THE TAKEAWAY
LEARNING CURVE	Mastering even the basics can take quite some time.	Mastering a crossbow requires only basic rifle shooting skills and an understanding of the cocking procedure, which requires some physical strength but is basically idiot-proof.	The crossbow learning curve is significantly less challenging.
GROUPING	Shooting with the bow at 40 yards resulted in 3.75-inch groups.	Shooting even an okay crossbow from a rest at 40 yards—which is standard procedure when hunting—produced 2.63-inch groups.	The crossbow is easier to shoot accurately, especially with a rest.
EFFICIENCY	My 60-pound compound is a speed bow that shoots a 370-grain arrow to 300 fps for 74 foot-pounds of kinetic energy.	Even a slow crossbow such as the Mission MXB-320 fires a 437-grain bolt at 307 fps for 91 foot pounds of energy.	Crossbows typically fire heavier projectiles faster than compound bows, and so they're more powerful.
FIRST SHOT SPEED	Time taken to remove the loaded bow from a bow hanger and center a 20-yard target: 10.3 seconds.	Time taken to remove a cocked crossbow from a bow hanger and center a 20-yard target: 8.3 seconds.	The crossbow provides a faster first shot.
FOLLOW-UP SHOT	Repeating the same drill, two more times (the first shot sitting, the next two standing), to fire three killing arrows: 35.3 seconds.	Repeating the same drill, two more times (the first shot sitting, the next two standing), to fire three killing bolts: 58 seconds.	The vertical bow has the edge in speed of follow-up shots.
OVERALL CONCLUSIONS	The compound bow is lighter, smaller, and quieter, but requires more effort to master.	The crossbow is larger, bulkier, and makes more noise, but is easier to learn to use and more powerful.	The crossbow is unequivocally the deadlier hunting tool.

THE DEADLIEST
On most points of comparison, the crossbow takes the edge.

TRADITIONAL KILLER
The compound bow still shows a few advantages.

Last spring, I camped on the western Nebraska prairie with fellow writers to chase the area's mix of Merriam's, Eastern, and hybrid turkeys. Armed with a Cabela's Instinct Lancer crossbow, Will Brantley and I belly-crawled to the edge of a cornfield where a big Eastern gobbler and eight jakes milled at 60 yards. Brantley raised a tail fan he'd brought from Kentucky and spun it slowly left and right. Seeing this, the gobbler started to close the distance. He got a little edgy—and then, Brantley dropped him at 48 yards. Never in a million years could he have pulled that off with a vertical bow.

The next morning, Brantley and I were belly-crawling again, this time across a long stretch of rolling short grass, toward a big Merriam's tom courting a couple of hens in the wide open. Creeping over the last knoll, we finally spotted him at 70 yards. Brantley raised the fan again, but this tom wasn't edgy. He barged in, looking to kick some turkey butt, and I bolted him at 30. He dropped like he'd been poleaxed, with not so much as a flop or a flap. When we walked up to the bird, he looked like he'd been hit with a .308.

Whereas most guys would consider 30 yards a fairly long shot on a turkey with a compound, it was a chip shot with the crossbow. In short, crossbows are just plain deadlier.

Even more to the point for hunters, when it comes to making quick, clean kills on live animals in the field—when your brain is swimming in adrenaline and your nervous system is in revolt—you are going to do better with the weapon you can steady on a pack or sticks: the one with the 7x range-compensating scope.

121 WAIT FOR IT

As good as today's crossbows are, they are getting better at a faster rate than ever before. Their recent explosion in popularity—and sales—means more money for research and development and heightened competition among manufacturers. The predictable result is that in just this past year alone, we've seen major strides in ergonomics and trigger quality, which hint at improvements to come.

The typical modern crossbow is flatter-shooting and harder-hitting than the average vertical bow, but it's still a pain to carry and wield. I'd call it a club, though in some cases a club would be an improvement. Crossbows are also louder, with more recoil and vibration. One of the top models in 2014 actually slapped you in the face at the shot. That sounds like an exaggeration, right? It's not. And while triggers

are getting better, they've got a long way to go before they'll match even any good rifle trigger.

These are the areas where we are going to be seeing the biggest improvements. Companies already have the ability to make crossbows that shoot a 425-grain arrow well over 400 fps—even 450 or more, but with the current designs and technologies, today's arrows simply can't keep up with that and still fly straight. For the time being, at least, speed is not the issue. Right now, manufacturers are concentrating on making crossbows that are handy, quiet, and smooth-shooting, with rifle-quality triggers, and still plenty fast. That's what's coming—and soon.

COMING SOON Crossbows are getting better every year, so just look out!

It's easy to find an opinion on which crossbow is the best. Trouble is, those opinions are usually either from fanboys who need to justify their purchase or from salesman masquerading as hunting pros. The only way to truly make an objective comparison of crossbows is to gather up a bunch of them and spend significant time shooting and testing them all with the exact same procedure. That's out of the realm of possibility for most potential crossbow buyers.

Fortunately for you, we follow our annual compound-bow review with a crossbow review. And where testing compound bows has a few subjective aspects, crossbow testing is mostly a cut-and-dried, objective procedure, akin to testing a rifle. Here's how we do it.

FACTORY SETUP Most crossbows are sold as a kit that includes a scope and some bolts at minimum. Sure, you can buy a new scope and new bolts after the fact and fine-tune your setup—but we want to test what you get when you open the box. So we set up the bows with the supplied accessories, weigh them after setup, and then test them. We also evaluate the quality and value of the accessory package. Scopes on Excalibur crossbows, for example, are typically outstanding. One year, Barnett sent us a bow with a skinning knife in the stock. Ridiculous? Of course. Cool as hell? Absolutely.

ACCURACY This is the reading that matters most. We do accuracy testing from a bench with a paper target pinned to a crossbow target. We use the same bolt to fire three 3-shot groups at 20 yards, and then we average the size of those groups. It's a slow process. The top-tier crossbows will put every shot through the exact same hole. Most of them will print a nice, cloverleaf cluster. A few might stay within a baseball-size circle. Those bows also make good boat anchors.

SPEED AND ENERGY We weigh the factory bolts and take the average speed of three shots through a chronograph. With those numbers, we calculate kinetic energy and momentum. A crossbow's advertised speed ratings are usually pretty dang close—so long as they're using the factory-weight bolts, which is another reason why we test them with the provided accessories. Unlike vertical bows, which have IBO arrow standards, crossbow bolts have no standard at all. A bow that claims 380 fps may well be able to do that—but it could be with an 18-inch, 350-grain bolt, while the 365 fps bow is shooting a bolt that's 75 grains heavier.

SAFETY Does the crossbow we're testing have an anti–dry-fire device? We dock it serious points if not. What about the cocking stirrup? Is it comfortable and easy to use, or is a heavy boot likely to slip on it on a snowy day? Is the stock designed so that it keeps your fingers away from the rail, or could a careless hold lose the shooter a thumb?

TRIGGER PULL We measure pull weight with a trigger scale, and take subjective notes on the overall feel. Is there a bunch of take-up at the beginning? Does the trigger break crisply, or is there some creep?

COCKING EFFORT A bow generates extra speed in one of two primary ways—a longer power stroke or increased draw weight. As each of these increase, so does the cocking effort. Cocking effort is definitely important to many buyers, but a slower bow usually has an advantage in this category.

NOISE AND VIBRATION Crossbows are, on average, much louder than vertical bows, and you'll experience far more recoil and vibration as well. Right now, many crossbow manufacturers are working to make bows that are quieter and softer shooting, above all. But these bows aren't there yet. Determining which crossbow kicks and vibrates the most is pretty easy. Figuring out which is louder on an indoor range is a little more difficult. We use a tripod-mounted decibel meter for assistance.

123 KNOW WHAT YOU WANT

There are three basic styles of crossbows. All are deadly hunting weapons, but each has unique advantages—and some disadvantages. In deciding of the crossbow of your dreams, there are a number of factors to take into account, detailed below. Compare and contrast the features in the articles that follow to decide what works best for you.

124 REACH FOR A RECURVE

The oldest crossbow design has been around for centuries, and is so named for its curved limbs. Recurve crossbows function like a vertical recurve with a trigger; they rely solely on the power of the limbs to propel the bolt.

ADVANTAGES

WEIGHT Typically lighter than a compound, recurves are often easier to hold and shoot accurately offhand.
RELIABILITY Because they have fewer moving parts, recurves are pretty much bulletproof.
MAINTENANCE You can usually perform simple fixes, such as changing the string, without a bow press.

DISADVANTAGES

PROFILE The broader profile can be a problem in the confines of a ground blind or treestand.
COCKING EFFORT With no wheels or cams for assistance, recurve crossbows must have a heavier draw weight to achieve speeds comparable to those of compounds. Cocking them can be difficult.
STRING WEAR Because a recurve's trigger mechanism is holding the entire peak weight when the bow is cocked, servings and strings wear fast.
NOISE Recurves are typically louder than compounds.

125 TRY A COMPOUND CROSSBOW

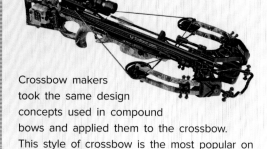

Crossbow makers took the same design concepts used in compound bows and applied them to the crossbow. This style of crossbow is the most popular on the market right now.

ADVANTAGES

EFFICIENCY Thanks to their wheels or cams, compound crossbows store and transfer energy more efficiently than recurves do.

COCKING EFFORT Able to produce more speed with less draw weight, compounds are usually easier to cock than recurves.

PROFILE Compounds have shorter limbs, making them easier to maneuver in close confines.

VARIETY Manufacturers make compound crossbows in a wide range of styles, draw weights, and prices. You can shop until you find the perfect bow to fit your budget.

DISADVANTAGES

MAINTENANCE Virtually every service needed on a compound crossbow (including changing the string) will require the use of a bow press. For the majority of hunters, that means a trip to the pro shop.

WEAR AND TEAR A compound has more moving parts, which means more can go wrong.

HANDLING Because there's more weight toward the limbs of a compound, some shooters find them front-heavy and less comfortable to hold and shoot. And when manufacturers want to increase the speed on a compound, they typically lengthen the barrel to increase the power stroke, which places even more weight away from the body of the shooter and makes the bow more cumbersome.

126 PUT IT IN REVERSE

Rather than mount the riser of the bow on the end of the barrel, reverse-draw compound crossbows swap it around so that the riser points toward the stock. As the shooter draws the string toward the riser, rather than away from it, the limbs flex inward against the crossbow's barrel. This allows for a longer power stroke on a bow that's more compact overall. A reverse-draw compound has all the advantages and disadvantages of a standard compound, but with a few caveats.

ADVANTAGES

SPEED All else being equal, a reverse-draw design has a greatly increased power stroke, and so it is inherently the fastest design. The longer power stroke also allows the use of a cam instead of a wheel, and—as vertical bow makers learned long ago—cams generate more speed than wheels.

BALANCE AND PROFILE The heavy part of a reverse-draw bow sits 12 to 14 inches farther back toward the shooter's body, which does wonders to improve the bow's balance. Overall weight of a compound and a reverse-draw bow may be identical, but the reverse draw will be more comfortable to handle. Also, since the

limbs sit closer to the barrel and flex inward when the bow is cocked, this style is usually more compact.

REDUCED NOISE AND VIBRATION Reverse-draw crossbows sport a nearly parallel limb design. As vertical compound shooters have learned, this eliminates much noise and vibration, since the limbs effectively cancel each other out as they travel during the shot.

DISADVANTAGES

PRICE Again, a reverse-draw is typically more expensive than a compound or recurve. For one, it's more difficult to build. And as of this writing, the patent for the reverse-draw design has not expired, requiring other manufacturers to pay a royalty to the patent holder, a fee that they of course pass on to consumers.

AVAILABILITY Due to patent issues and the higher manufacturing costs, there aren't many reverse-draw options on the market.

X-FACTOR Let's face it, the reverse-draw design has had less time to prove itself than the compound or recurve design. That said, it has been around long enough so that major issues inherent to the design probably would've shown up by now. They haven't.

Most crossbows come with accessories, and prices on these kits range from fairly reasonable to nearly ridiculous. So what does your money buy? Extra bucks usually get you a bow with more advanced technology, better materials, added features, and higher-end add-ons. Whether the goodie package is worth it is up to you. Most manufacturers offer packages at several price points; as an example, here's a look at the line from TenPoint.

GOOD Starting at $599, the Titan Xtreme is a workhorse crossbow with a 180-pound draw weight that pitches bolts at 333 fps, a decent scope, a 3-arrow quiver, and exactly enough bolts to fill it. (TenPoint makes all high-end stuff. Other companies offer serviceable packages for well under $500.)

BETTER For around a grand, the compact Shadow Ultra-Lite weighs a mere 6.4-pounds, measures just 34.4-inches long, and fires arrows 350 fps. The package includes a scope, 3-arrow quiver, and 3 arrows.

BEST For a little bit under two grand, you're buying a flamethrower. The Venom is a 185-pound high-end bow with a bull-pup stock and carbon fiber barrel that shoots 372 fps. It's equipped with a top-end scope, AccuDraw cocking system, a quiver, and 6 bolts.

128 RIG IT RIGHT

If you buy a kit, it will include a few of these items. If not, you'll eventually need almost everything on this list.

GET COCKY The basic rope cocker will greatly reduce the effort needed to cock a crossbow, as well as ensure that the string is properly aligned, and most bows come with one. To make it so easy a child could cock your crossbow, there are also winch-style cranking devices.

SCOPE IT OUT Red-dot sights are perfect for close-range hunting and fast target acquisition. But for greater precision and long-range accuracy, go with a scope. There are numerous crossbow-specific scopes with graduated reticles on the market today.

FILL A QUIVER Three-arrow quivers that mount on the stock with screws or bolts are standard-issue, but there are quick-detach models that mount with a clip or magnet system.

SLING IT Crossbows are a pain to carry, so get a sling. On extended hunts in rough country, a pack built for toting a crossbow is even better.

GET WAXED Neglect to frequently wax your string and cables, and you'll reduce their life by at least 20 percent. For the price of a new string and cables, you can buy enough wax to last you for years.

LUBE UP High-quality lubricants along the rail reduce string wear and can increase accuracy.

GET ON TARGET You need a target capable of handling the hard-hitting, deep-penetrating bolts of a crossbow. As with a vertical bow (see item 105), a bag target is great for field points. You'll need a layered foam target for broadheads. And 3-D targets are just plain fun.

DISCHARGE IT You can use certain targets for discharging a bolt at the end of a hunt. If you don't have a target handy, use a heavyweight, blunt-tipped bolt to unload your bow.

CARRY SAFELY Soft-sided cases are perfect for protecting the bow and accessories on hunts near home, but for airline travel, get a hard-sided, locking case.

STICK IT OUT As with a rifle, you'll shoot better from a rest. Shooting sticks can greatly increase accuracy and shooting comfort.

Your crossbow probably came with a few arrows, but you'll soon need new ones. Most important, don't get arrows any shorter or lighter than what's recommended in the owner's manual. If you do, you're asking for a broken bow—maybe a broken face. Beyond that, you've got a few decisions to make.

MATERIAL Aluminum bolts are a great value for the money. They have superior weight consistency, and being shorter and thicker than vertical-bow shafts, aluminum crossbow bolts are not so apt to bend. Carbon bolts are most popular. They come in a wider range of weights and are exceptionally durable. Easton's Full Metal Jacket bolt combines the two to marry the best qualities of each.

FLETCHING Crossbow arrows typically come pre-fletched with 2-, 3-, or 4-inch plastic vanes—3 inches being most common. As a rule, they are low-profile and fletched straight (no offset or helical) to ride in the bolt track.

DIAMETER This is pretty standard at $^{11}/_{32}$nds (often expressed as $^{22}/_{64}$ths). While micro-diameter arrows are all the rage for vertical bows, most will fall through the rail an x-bow. The exception is the Victory VAP Voodoo, which rides the rail on two bumps on the otherwise ultraskinny shaft.

LENGTH Crossbow arrows range from 16 to 24 inches, with 20 and 22 being most common. Don't go any shorter than the ones your bow came with. You can go longer, though, if you want more weight.

SPINE This is a non-issue with crossbow bolts.

FRONT OF CENTER Because you can't stabilize a crossbow arrow in the rear with offset or helical fletching, steering it with extra weight up front, via brass inserts or a heavy head, or both, is a good idea.

NOCKS Crossbow arrows typically come with either straight or half-moon nocks. Just get what the manual calls for.

WEIGHT Most bolts weigh between 8 and 14 grains per inch. Your owner's manual will recommend a minimum weight, but this can be inordinately light so as to achieve impressive speed claims. Usually, it's best to go at least a little, if not a lot, heavier. A heavier arrow transfers a crossbow's energy more efficiently. It also retains more momentum downrange, helps quiet the bow, and mitigates wear and tear.

As crossbow sales have skyrocketed, more and more broadhead companies have introduced crossbow-specific models. The question is: Do you need them?

In a word, no. You can, if you want, screw the heads out of your vertical-bow arrows and into your crossbow bolts and go hunting.

The crossbow-specific ones just fit a little better, as they're made to sit flush against a bolt's thicker shaft. Most of them weigh 125 grains (or more), since more weight up front helps steer a bolt.

GO FIXED Fixed-blade models are typically fairly compact, with slightly smaller cutting diameters and in some cases canted blades that help spin the arrow. Why? This is because big blades tend to plane in flight—especially at crossbow speeds—and you don't really have the option to improve stabilization at the rear of the bolt. A more compact fixed-blade has less surface area to create drag and cause issues.

GO MECHANICAL Mechanical broadheads often follow the exact opposite formula. Since they're folded during flight, they basically eliminate arrow plane issues. Many of them (though not all) have extra-large cutting diameters to take advantage of a crossbow's extra speed and kinetic energy. Most have beefier blade-retention systems than standard mechanical heads to keep blades from deploying during flight.

So which should you choose? As with the broadhead selection for vertical bows, the choice is really up to you because either style works just fine on game. Mechanical broadheads, as a rule, cut larger holes, which spill more blood. Does the energy required to open them mean they have less penetration potential than a fixed-blade? Perhaps. But modern crossbows shoot so hard that, so long as you aren't using an ultra-light bolt, lack of penetration is rarely going to be an issue.

Fixed blades provide the utmost reliability. They don't have any O-rings or retainers to keep blades from deploying during flight and ruining the shot. If maximum penetration is your goal, they're probably the best choice.

No matter what model you choose, don't assume—as many people with crossbows do for some reason—that your broadhead will hit in the same place as your field points. They often don't, which means you'll need to adjust your sight slightly.

"BOLT" OR "ARROW"

Dave Hurteau on

Both are correct. Lately, the needle has been edging toward "arrow." But that's a political thing, wherein crossbow proponents seem to believe that calling the implement a bow and "arrow" will make it easier for other archers to embrace. Nonsense. "Bolt" is a perfectly fine word that in many cases avoids confusion. If anyone tells you it's wrong, you can tell them where they can stick their "arrow."

131 BABY THAT CROSSBOW

Vertical bow fanatics tweak their setups between practice, and some gun nuts clean and oil their rifles more often than most folks brush their teeth. But outside of an occasional practice round, the average crossbow spends most of its life hanging on a hook, ready to hunt. Fact is, crossbows are so user-friendly that they're easy to ignore.

But a crossbow begs for some occasional TLC. Violent forces are at work with every shot, and all that downtime between shooting sessions can create problems Follow the tips below for proper care of your crossbow.

WAX THE STRING Crossbow strings and cables wear fast, from exposure to the elements. Replace them as soon as you notice signs of wear because when they break, it's unpleasant. Until then, apply string wax frequently and liberally to the entire length of the string and cables, remembering to leave a gap right above the shooting rail. Wax here could gum up the trigger mechanism.

KEEP IT LUBED Most crossbows are shipped with rail lubricant included. If not, get some (lip balm will work in a pinch). Apply a good smudge of lube to the middle of the rail and spread it along the entire length every 15 to 20 shots to reduce friction on the string.

BLOW IT OUT Woods and range time will result in accumulated dust, dirt, and debris in the rail and in other crevices. Use a can of compressed air to evict these invaders.

KEEP IT OILED Damp weather during a hunt (and in the storage shed or garage) will start corroding exposed bolt heads and the trigger box. Periodic oiling with light gun oil at these points will prevent rust.

CHECK THE LENS Treat your crossbow scope the same way you would your rifle scope. Keep fingerprints away, and avoid cleaning the lenses with your shirt. Instead, use a soft lens cloth in the field, and when in storage, use scope covers.

CASE IT Even when I'm taking a 20-minute trip to a deer stand, I protect my bow or crossbow with at least a soft case. Sure, it's a little extra hassle, but you're dealing with precision gear that deserves protection from the dings, nicks, and bumps that can occur in truck beds and trunks.

TIGHTEN UP Check for loose bolts on the stock, barrel, quiver attachment, scope mounts, and trigger assembly every 50 shots or so, and tighten when needed with the appropriate screwdriver or hex wrench.

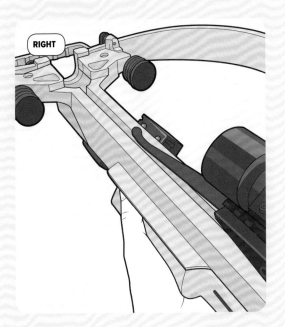

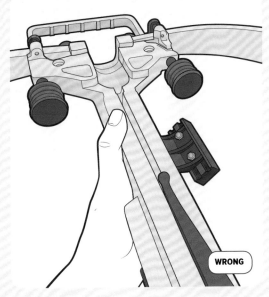

132 DON'T SHOOT YOUR THUMB OFF

Many first-time users are a little nervous around crossbows (even if they have a lifetime of vertical bow and firearms experience) for good reason. A cocked crossbow is under tremendous tension, and careless handling can put you in the hospital, the same as a gun. You needn't fear your crossbow. Simply respect it and remember these safety rules.

KEEP YOUR FINGERS Perhaps the most common injury involves people getting their fingers between the rail and the cocked string. If this happens and you fire the bolt, your fingers, or at least bits of them, will go with it. Most of today's crossbows have flared forends or guards that make it difficult to put your hand in the wrong spot—but it still happens on occasion, especially when shooting from a rest. Watch where you put your off hand.

CHECK YOUR BOLTS A cracked carbon arrow fired from a crossbow can leave shards of graphite stuck into your face. Check to ensure that your bolts are in good shape, and that they're heavy enough (see item 129) for your crossbow.

WATCH YOUR BACKDROP Crossbows shoot hard. I've killed quite a few critters with them, but have only found my passed-through bolts a few times. Be sure you have a good backstop when shooting a crossbow, same as you would if shooting a rifle.

DON'T DRY-FIRE All decent crossbows these days are equipped with an anti-dry-fire device that will not allow you to fire the bow unless a bolt is in place. This is a critical piece of safety equipment. If the bow you're thinking of buying doesn't have it, find a different one.

WHEN IN DOUBT, SHOOT IT OUT You can de-cock some crossbows, particularly recurves, with the aid of a rope-cocking device. This isn't particularly hard to do (instructional videos abound on YouTube), but the penalty for doing it wrong even one time could be a dry-fired bow hovering directly over your foot. The far safer way to de-cock a crossbow is to keep a target or discharge bolt in the truck and shoot it at the end of the day.

DON'T BE AN IDIOT I once saw a fairly well-known outdoor TV host carrying a cocked crossbow by the rail—his entire hand through the string—on his show. That's a perfect example of being an idiot.

133 PULL IT TOGETHER

If you buy from a big box store or online, your crossbow will likely come unassembled. Putting it together typically involves little more than attaching the bow to the stock via a large bolt or two, attaching the foot stirrup and quiver mount via a couple screws, and, in some cases, mounting a sight. Just follow the owner's manual directions carefully.

Buying from a local bow-shop pro has two upsides: First, the crossbow will be correctly assembled for you, and second, if there's a problem you can easily take it back for a quick fix. Buying from a bow shop might cost you a few bucks more, but may well be worth it.

134 GET ON TARGET

Almost without exception, today's crossbows come with either a red-dot sight or an optical scope. These in turn feature either a basic reticle with a single dot or crosshair or a multi-reticle with several graduated aiming points under the top dot or crosshair. This will become important in a bit. For now, begin with these three basic steps.

GET CLOSE Start by shooting your crossbow from a steady rest at just 10 yards, using the top dot or crosshair if you have a multi-reticle. If the arrow hits the bull's-eye, great. If not, shoot it once more to make sure it wasn't just a bad shot. If you're way off at 10 yards—like a foot or more—double-check that the bow is correctly aligned with the rail, and that the scope is correctly installed.

MOVE IT Assuming you hit in the same place, move the windage and elevation adjustment dials as needed. With some high-end crossbow scopes, one click moves the point of impact $1/2$ inch at 20 yards—or $1/4$ inch at 10. Otherwise, one click equals $1/4$ inch at 100 yards, which is $1/40$ of an inch at 10. In this case, if your arrow is 2 inches to the right of the bull, you need to turn the windage dial left 80 clicks.

FINE TUNE Next, you need to decide if you want your main dot or crosshair to be sighted in for 20 or 30 yards. Most guys choose the former, but I like the latter if I'm shooting a fast bow. Either way, step back to that distance, shoot a group of three arrows, and then fine-tune the windage and elevation until you're dead on.

135 SHOOT AND SEE

With most crossbows, the arrow starts dropping pretty quickly after 30 yards or so. How you sight in for longer distances depends on what kind of reticle you have. So let's take the types one at a time.

SINGLE DOT OR CROSSHAIR Step back 5 yards and shoot a group to find out exactly how much the arrow drops at the new distance. Let's say it's 1 inch. That's how high you have to aim to be dead on. But don't assume anything. Shoot a second group at that distance, aiming 1 inch high, to verify. Then step back 5 more yards and do it again—and again, all the way out to the maximum distance you plan to practice. Write everything down and make sure to use the same range finder you'll use when hunting. Individual range finders may read a yard or two differently—and that makes a big difference when you're shooting an arrow from longer range.

MULTI-RETICLE Once you've sighted in the top dot or crosshair, the graduated ones below show you the proper hold for longer ranges, in roughly 10-yard increments. "Roughly" is the key word here. Arrow trajectory can vary greatly depending on speed and shaft weight, so the only way to find out exactly what ranges correspond with those dots or hashes is to shoot until you figure it out—precisely. Then memorize those distances, and write them down in case you forget.

136 SIGHT IN FAST

To get your scope close quickly, set up a bench rest 10 yards from the target. You need something solid, like a Lead Sled loaded with lead, so that the crossbow absolutely will not move. Shoot your first arrow. Then, keeping the bow perfectly still in the rest, use the windage and elevation knobs to reposition the crosshair or dot so it lines up perfectly with the first arrow. Now back up to 20 or 30 yards and shoot; you should be close enough that you need to make only minor adjustments to get dead on.

137 SIGHT IN FASTER

The best crossbow scopes not only feature rugged construction and superior glass, but actually make sighting in faster and easier. Windage and elevation dials that move the point of impact ½ inch per click at 20 yards put you on target in no time. Also, many of these scopes allow you to dial in your arrow's speed, which automatically sets the graduated dots or hashes for specific distances, out to 60 yards or more. Just make sure you verify arrow speed through a chronograph, and hit the range before you hunt to check that those dots or hashes really are dead on for their corresponding ranges.

138 TAKE A DEEP BREATH

Two keys to good marksmanship are to shoot on "empty lungs," as they say, and to shoot quickly. So here's a great routine to practice. When you acquire your sight picture, take a deep breath, slowly let most of it out, take the shot, and then try to keep the crosshairs on target afterward. Once you let your breath out, you will have about 7 seconds to shoot before your vision starts to deteriorate. So discipline yourself to aim, breathe, and get the shot off fast.

139 ASSUME THE POSITION

Just like any rifleman, you need to master the four key shooting positions. Here's a quick breakdown.

PRONE If you can get on your belly and still have a good view to the target, this is the way to go. Rest the forend on a pack if there's time. In the short grass of spring, for example, prone is the perfect position for plunking field gobblers from behind a tail fan.

OFFHAND Only shoot offhand if there's no time to take a rest and the shot is fairly close. It's important to practice this position because things often happen fast in the field. But be sure to practice it correctly. Don't try to hold the sight perfectly steady on the target; that's impossible. Instead, try to draw smaller and smaller circles around the target with the reticle until it's in the black—or the kill zone—and then pull the trigger.

KNEELING This is often the steadiest position you can take while still seeing above taller grass or brush in the field. Use sticks and put a butt cheek on a heel—the lower you can get, the steadier you'll be.

SITTING This is the next steadiest position after prone—it's a whole lot steadier if you can put your back against a tree and/or use shooting sticks. If you're hunting from a treestand with a crossbow, bring sticks and use them.

140 SHOOT IT LIKE A RIFLE

You often hear that one of the big advantages of a crossbow is that, as with a rifle, all you have to do is look through the scope and pull the trigger. Compared to a vertical bow, it's a fact that a crossbow is indeed easy to shoot with decent accuracy right out of the gate. But if you really want to be hell on wheels with a crossbow, you need to apply two of the same simple but key principles that expert rifleman do.

GET A REST Without a good rest, a crossbow is no more accurate than a vertical bow. With one, it kicks the vertical's butt. When you're about to shoot a crossbow in the field, your first thought should be the same as any rifleman's: Where and how can I get a better rest?

SHOOT A LOT A crossbow actually has an advantage over a rifle here in that, once you have arrows, it costs nothing to practice. In addition, firing your .30-06 in the backyard is likely to annoy your neighbors—but they'll probably never notice you shooting your crossbow any time of day or night. So there's no reason not to shoot all summer to make sure you'll be on your A-game come fall.

141 TRIGGER EASY (OR NOT)

There are two schools of thought when it comes to tripping a crossbow trigger, just as there are for rifles. The first school recommends slowly squeezing the trigger so that the shot surprises you. The second argues that, because you can never hold perfectly steady on your target in a hunting scenario, you should pull the trigger sharply the second the sight picture looks perfect.

Having tested both extensively, we think the best policy is to use the former when you have a solid rest—such as prone, sitting with sticks, and especially when sighting in from a bench—and the latter when you don't. The real key is to practice both ways, and find out what works best for you.

142 TROUBLESHOOT YOUR BOW

The surefire way to keep your crossbow clean, well fed, and on target is to read the damn owner's manual—that little book that anticipates most of the ways one can mess up a finely tuned machine. Unlike a vertical bow, a crossbow simply doesn't have much the average user can tune to make it perform better.

But hey, when something goes awry, we want to roll up our sleeves and fix it ourselves. In fact, you've probably already lost your manual, which is why you're referring to this item. So here's a shot at guiding you through a fix you might be able to pull off yourself—or to encourage you to seek professional help.

THE PROBLEM

HOW TO FIX IT

	FIX NO. 1	**FIX NO. 2**
ERRATIC ARROW FLIGHT OR POOR GROUPING	Check the front-end assembly (near the cocking stirrup) and tighten any loose bolts (crossbows vibrate a lot, loosening bolts). Make sure the bow is aligned properly with the barrel. Do the same for places where the barrel or rail attaches to the riser. Do the same check to your scope rings and bases.	Make sure your arrow isn't rotated slightly and preventing the cock feather from dropping perfectly into the flight groove. Then mark the proper nock position with a Sharpie. Or you cocked the bow by hand and pulled the string up unevenly. Use a rope-cocker or learn to pull evenly.
SERVING IS WEARING OR UNRAVELING	When servings go bad, it's time for a pro-shop visit. To extend serving life, use the rail lube recommended by the bow company. In a pinch, you can replace worn servings with dental floss in the field—but be aware this is only a temporary fix.	If you're a he-man who ignores a rope-cocking device to cock your bow, you might be pulling up on one side of the string harder than the other (if say, one arm is stronger, or longer, than the other), in which case the cocking device won't contact the serving at true center. Use a rope-cocker or learn to pull evenly.
THE STRING IS WEARING AND FRAYING	If the string isn't too far gone, applying wax to it and the cables (not the serving—that can gunk up the trigger) and lube to the rail will reduce friction and increase string life. If any strands are broken, it's time to buy a new string, which—unless you own and know how to use a press—means a pro shop visit.	Inspect the rail for nicks or burrs that could be chewing on your string with every shot. Some can be repaired by a light file or coarse emery cloth, but others will require a shop visit.
THE CROSSBOW WON'T COCK	On some models, you need to have the safety off, or in the "fire" position, for the bow to cock properly (most, but not all, crossbows automatically engage the safety when you cock them). Check your owner's manual to see if this applies to your bow.	The trigger mechanism might be dry, rusted, or otherwise malfunctioning. A few drops of lightweight gun oil near the safety might loosen things up. But if you used a heavy lubricant on the serving, it may have gummed up the trigger, in which case a technician will have to take the trigger housing apart and clean it.
THE CROSSBOW WON'T FIRE	Is the safety on? Otherwise, the retention spring is bent or broken and isn't seated firmly on the arrow. This spring pushes the arrow against the anti–dry-fire mechanism, disengaging it. You may be able to bend a metal spring back in place. If it's plastic and broken, you need a replacement.	If you tried to fire the bow without an arrow (or accidentally pulled the trigger), the anti-dry-fire device engaged and remained there. You need to reset the trigger. Use the rope-cocker again to pull the string up until you hear a "click." Reload and try again.
THE SAFETY MECHANISM IS STIFF OR HARD TO MANIPULATE	Dirt and debris can accumulate in the trigger housing, gumming up the safety and other moving parts. Use a can of compressed air to blow out this gunk by shooting air at various access points around the housing. If that's unsuccessful, take your bow to the shop.	If you tried to fire the bow without an arrow on the rail (or accidentally pulled the trigger), the anti–dry-fire device engaged and remained there. You need to reset the trigger. Do so by placing your foot in the stirrup. Put a rope-cocker on the string, and pull up just slightly until you hear a "click." Reload an arrow and the crossbow should fire.
SCOPE DOESN'T ADJUST FOR WINDAGE OR ELEVATION	Some higher-end scopes adjust for the slow velocities (compared to a rifle) and short ranges associated with crossbows. A click might move the point of impact $1/2$ inch at 20 yards. If your scope is one of these, check to ensure that the mounts are tight and that everything on the bow is in order.	Other scopes use the standard rifle-scope adjustment of $1/4$ inch at 100 yards per click, and it can take a lot of clicks—20 or more—to move a group 1 inch at 20 yards. If it seems you're about to make a complete revolution on that adjustment ring, you probably are. That's O.K. Keep clicking until your arrows hit where you want them.

HUNTING

LIKE MANY BOWHUNTERS, I STARTED HUNTING WITH A GUN

When I picked up the bow I learned one great truth in a hurry: at the point where many hunts with a firearm end, a bowhunt is just beginning. To get within bow range of a game animal, you must first beat its senses, which are hardwired for survival and used for eluding predators every day of its life. Bowhunting is not a game for the lazy, the sloppy, or the seekers of instant gratification. The learning curve can be long, and frustration comes by the bucketful.

I certainly had my share of frustration, maybe more than my share. At least, it felt that way to me at the time. Two weeks into my inaugural bow season, I learned that I moved too much and apparently stunk pretty bad. The stands I used for gun hunting were fine for seeing deer, but hopelessly misplaced for getting a bow shot. And when I finally did sit still, master the wind, and set the right stand, I learned what a heavy dose of buck fever can do to my archery form. I whiffed a 9-yard shot.

But oh, that first success. Kill a game animal with an arrow and it will change your life, or at least how you view hunting. Bowhunting, whether you use a vertical bow or crossbow, is the most intimate and personal form of hunting out there. Once you're hooked, you may find that the rush of adrenaline felt when you're hunting with a gun is just no longer the same. To get your fix, you need your bow because you're no longer just a hunter. You're a bowhunter. Here's how to become a better one.

143 BOWHUNT WHITETAILS

Fred Bear had it right. Though Bear claimed bow-killed trophies from across the globe, he knew that his Michigan-based Bear Archery company must market bows, arrows, and gear to people who hunted deer, specifically those going after whitetails.

Whitetails are perfectly suited for bowhunts. They're abundant and widespread, and their behavior and favored habitats are ideal for arranging a close-range encounter. They're capable of meeting the demands of any skill level, technique, or desire. Whether you're a beginner hunting venison for the freezer or an expert wanting to tag the most demanding trophy, whitetails can provide.

Sure, there are bigger, sexier, and more dangerous game animals. But for all-around bowhunting appeal, nothing matches up to the whitetail, an animal tailor-made for bowhunters. God bless 'em, and I hope they never go away.

144 GO EARLY

I love the rut as much as anyone, but my records don't lie: I've arrowed my four largest bucks during the first two weeks of the season, which occurs mid-September where I live. Those animals have convinced me that a mature whitetail buck is far more vulnerable at this time—when the rut is weeks away and the weather is more like summer than autumn—than at any other phase of the season.

Early season can be magic because whitetails, including mature bucks, are often on a semi-predictable bed-to-feed pattern, usually at a visible food source like an alfalfa or soybean field. They haven't been hunted in months, so they're more relaxed and vulnerable. And finally, the lush vegetation this time of year allows for a quiet, hidden approach to your stand, and extra concealment once you're set. A bowhunter can't ask for much more. These strategies capitalize on all those advantages, so read up.

145 PATTERN AN OPENING DAY GIANT

Bob Borowiak has tagged 30-some Pope and Young bucks, several on the very first day of the season. Here's his blueprint for taking a quick buck.

STAKE THEM OUT Many of the fields Borowiak hunts are easily visible from a road, so he starts by glassing from the cab of his truck. "Bucks are relaxed and coming out long before dark to feed," he says. "I'm looking for some good bucks that show a consistent pattern."

GET A CLOSER LOOK Out in the thick, wooded terrain he hunts, it's often impossible to see the exact route a buck takes to a feeding area. So he moves closer. "I look for a tree where I can hang an observation stand that lets me view the action a little better," he says. "But you need to be able to sneak

in and out without the buck, or other deer, seeing or smelling you."

SET THE TRAP Within a week before the opener, Borowiak hangs a hunting stand. "I've usually picked the tree during one of my glassing sessions," he says. "Many of my spots have a brushy hillside or an old apple orchard where bucks stage before hitting the feed field. The best ambush is apt to be here, rather than right on the field edge."

He hangs the set at midday and returns as soon as the season is open and the wind is right. "Early-season bucks may not hit the field night after night like they did in summer. So don't panic if he doesn't show on the first hunt." If you stick with it, you'll almost always get your chance.

146 BET ON BEANFIELD BACHELORS

Sometimes you can't spend all summer glassing bucks—but don't despair. Bucks travel in bachelor groups in the early season, and a little knowledge of their behavior can help get you into bow range fast. When time is limited, follow this plan.

SEEK SOY If you haven't a beanfield to hunt in September, try to find one. They're the surest early-season food source out there. "Shedding the summer coat and growing the winter one requires even more protein and energy than developing antlers," says noted deer biologist Dr. James Kroll. "When you see deer's coats going from red to gray, they're seeking out protein. Soybeans are about 34 percent digestible protein; that's why deer swarm to them early in the season."

STRIKE FAST Bachelor groups often hit the same field two, occasionally three, evenings in a row—but seldom four. When you see that 10-pointer step into a beanfield with his homeboys on the opening afternoon of bow season, don't dally. Move in to kill him the next afternoon. If the wind won't allow a treestand setup, hunt from the ground.

RECOGNIZE TOADIES Young bucks in bachelor groups are "toadies" that mature bucks love to use as sentries. That's why the young bucks are usually the first to appear in a field. Study your trail-camera photos carefully and learn exactly what the toadies running with your shooter look like. When you see them, clip your release to the string.

147 CHECK IT

Most hunters think of corn as a food source, but when it's standing tall and green, mature bucks often bed in the corn and travel through woodlots and hedgerows to hit alfalfa and beans. Scout carefully before setting up.

148 LURE IN VELVET BUCKS

Any state that opens up to bowhunters on or before September 15th offers a great shot at a velvet whitetail. But the odds really rise when you can use attractants. Carl Doron, of Snipe Creek Lodge, guides 20 clients per day during the first week of Kentucky's early-September bow season. He won't sit anyone in a stand without knowing at least one velvet P&Y buck will be coming along. Here's how he does it.

GET YOUR LICKS Doron rarely sets hunters in a beanfield corner where bucks are moving, because the animals would quickly catch on. Instead, he lures them to an area 100 yards or more off the main trail with attractants—particularly salt licks. These licks will be in areas hunters can access undetected.

WATCH THE SALT Set licks in early spring, and freshen them a couple of times before season. Set a stand within bow range, with the lick behind a large tree to keep you hidden from the many deer that will visit. Monitor it with a trail cam, but don't be too aggressive. If a buck gets squirrely around your camera, pull it out. You already know he's there.

SWEETEN THE DEAL As the season nears, Doron scatters shelled corn at the lick every few days. This isn't legal everywhere, but effective where it is. From there, killing a big buck is a matter of persistence. You might watch a bachelor group at 100 yards three evenings in a row and then on the fourth, they decide they want some salt and corn. As long as the wind is right, you'd better be in that stand.

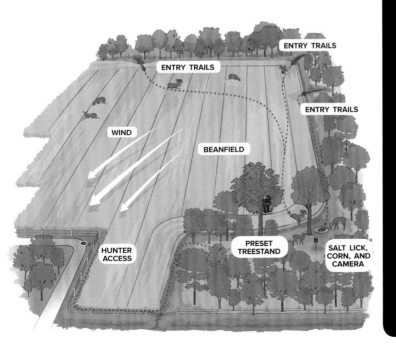

149 GET THE EDGE

Many key early-season food sources are found in the fields, but figuring out exactly where to set up on those fields for a bow shot can be maddening, especially since bachelor bucks are notorious for using a different path each evening. Here are two solutions to the problem.

CHECK THE PERIMETER An oak that's dropping good acorns on the edge of a beanfield is like the fried chicken tub at a Southern buffet: It pulls all sorts of creatures into the area. Such oaks will concentrate deer. One way to find the best trees is to walk the edge to look for acorns and feeding sign. Another is to watch the deer in your field. It's not at all uncommon to watch deer run full-bore across 200 yards of beans to hit an oak on the far side. If you see that, you know where to go the next evening.

GET EARLY PICKINGS Deer swarm to fresh-picked corn to clean up the waste grain. Typically, farmers with large fields will plant 16 to 32 end rows paralleling the field edge, and these are often the first ones picked. Suddenly, you have open shooting to a hot food source, located between the standing corn and the treeline, which is rarely more than 40 yards across. If deer are coming from the woods, focus on the best trails and set up in the treeline. But a bachelor group is just as likely to step out of the standing corn, so if the wind is more favorable for a ground setup from the stalks, pack in a folding chair and settle in two or three rows deep. The opportunity is short-lived, though—sometimes just an evening or two before the farmer combines the rest of the corn. But one good evening might be all you need.

150 FOOL 'EM WITH A FEMALE

A doe decoy can work wonders during early bow season. Her nonthreatening, unalarmed posture seems to calm real-life does and fawns, even on pressured properties. They might stop and stare for a few minutes, but they almost always accept the interloper and approach to feed nearby. If you want to deke a doe—and draw the buck that may be watching her into bow range—use a decoy doe.

Remember to never place any decoy in a spot where it could surprise approaching deer. Agricultural fields, clear-cuts, pastures, power lines, and other open areas are best. Stake the decoy upwind of your treestand by 15 or 20 yards for an easy bow shot, and turn the fake so that its full profile will be clearly visible to deer that are approaching from the most likely direction.

Once a deer commits to your decoy, it will feed downwind of it before getting licking-distance close. Any human scent on or near the faux doe will cause the real thing to bug out. Handle the decoy with gloves, and liberally spray it—as well as your clothing and boots—with scent-elimination spray.

That feeding-doe deke is a cool way to fill an antlerless tag, but it can also pull in bucks. The antler size and posture of most buck decoys intimidates $2\frac{1}{2}$-year-old or younger deer—which very well could be shooters for you. To lure in any and all deer, a feeding doe decoy is the way to go.

151 CLIMB FAST

A climbing stand can be a mobile bowhunter's best friend. Here's the skinny on the shimmy.

PACK IT IN Get a pack with a buckle loop on the top, or attach a rubber-coated carabiner. Then clip the pack to the stand's platform and throw the whole thing on your back for the walk in.

GET TREED You need a straight tree trunk free of large, low limbs (you can saw off small limbs). Avoid slick-barked trees such as sycamores and beeches, which keep your stand from getting a good bite into the trunk. Beyond that, find a tree that forks at about 20 feet to provide a little more cover at your back. If possible, seat the platform over a small knot in the tree, to give you rock-solid footing from which to shoot.

TAKE COVER Scale a trunk next to a leafy sapling and position your stand just above it so you can see and shoot over the foliage while it blocks the deer's view of you. If a pine or cedar is right behind your stand tree, even better: Deer won't see you from behind, and the other tree breaks up your silhouette from the front.

GET AN ANGLE Most trees are wider at the base than at 20 feet up. You absolutely do not want your stand's platform angling downward and you can't adjust the angle on most stand platforms once you're climbing, so you need to start with it angling upward at the bottom. At height, secure the seat portion with a strap or tighten it a notch so it has a good bite and won't come loose.

HANG UP Use two bow hangers: a small one to hang your pack on the right side (reverse for southpaws) at hip level where you can access your gear quickly; and a larger, folding model for hanging your bow on the other side, slightly above you, within easy reach. You'll be ready to shoot at a moment's notice, even if a buck slips in silently.

152 HANG AND HUNT

For hit-and-run deer hunts, I used to be strictly a climbing-stand guy—largely because it took me a half hour, on a good day, to hang a lock-on. But that changed once I learned to hang a stand quickly. The upside is obvious: You're not limited to straight, branchless trees, as you are with a climber, and you can hunt from whatever perch puts you in the absolute best spot to tag your buck. Here's how to hang one in less than eight minutes.

Pick a lightweight lock-on stand with a cinch strap (not a ratchet). A light model is easier to pull up and position, and the cinch strap is quicker and quieter to secure. Before you start, make sure everything you may need—extra steps, clippers, a saw, a safety line—is at hand in a fanny pack.

To climb, use three or four portable climbing sticks. They're much faster and safer than screw-in steps. Save yourself extra trips by tying one end of a pull-up rope to your stand, the other to your safety harness. Do the same with your bow, making sure the arrows are secure. Attach one climbing stick to the base of the tree with your feet on the ground. Grab the second stick in one hand. Clip the third to your safety harness so that it will be easy to grab with one hand when you need it.

Climb halfway up the first stick. Attach the second stick and go halfway up that. Unclip the third from your harness and attach it. This will get you maybe 15 feet up. If you want to go higher, add a fourth stick.

Finally, pull up the stand and hang it. Get in. Sit down. Now just pull up your bow, nock an arrow, and wait for a good buck to show.

153 DON'T BE LULLED

In the "October Lull," whitetails seem to enter an inactive phase. This frustrates the heck out of bowhunters, and inspires all sorts of theories. Some make sense; others—like "bucks are resting up for the rut"—are just nutty.

Meanwhile, telemetry studies largely pooh-pooh the notion of a lull; biologists tell us that once a buck sheds velvet, his movement does nothing but increase until the rut is over. I'm not entirely sold on the lull, but I do believe whitetails go through a period of big change as autumn settles in. If you're aware of those changes, you can use them to your advantage.

154 FIND THE ICE CREAM TREE

One potential common cause of October lull is an abundant acorn drop. Whitetails simply don't have to move far to find food, and hunters struggle to stay on the most active deer. Scouting for the "ice cream tree"—that one oak (or group of oaks) with the best-tasting acorns—is a key to beating the lull.

Acorns without caps are an obvious sign of a sweet oak. Though they look perfectly healthy, capped acorns are invariably rotten or wormy inside, and whitetails avoid them.

Sometimes the hottest oaks have no acorns at all beneath them because the deer eat them as fast as they hit the ground. In that case, read between

the lines and look for other evidence: churned-up leaves and droppings that indicate feeding activity, or other buck sign.

My bowhunting buddy Tom VanDoorn used this trick a couple years back as we hunted northern Wisconsin's big woods. Though we found multiple oaks dropping acorns, VanDoorn set up near a tree almost absent of nuts, but with gobs of buck sign. He shot a 150-class 12-point that night, one of four bucks that came in, waiting for the next acorn to fall.

155 FIND ONE HOT BUCK

Three vicious rubs marked a trio of cedars; the pair of scrapes I found nearby smelled of earth and musk, their overhanging limbs twisted and raked by antlers. The sign belied the calendar—October 8—and so I was tempted to dismiss it. Then, that evening at dusk, I saw the buck.

The next day I hung a stand there for my father, and he still talks about that hunt. Twenty minutes before dark, a chocolate-antlered 8-point emerged from a thicket, worked a scrape with gusto, and jumped the fence into the field. By the time Dad gathered his wits, the buck was 100 yards off and walking away. Dad blew a grunt tube and the buck whirled to face him, then pawed the ground like a bull ready to charge. The giant eventually walked within feet of Dad's tree. Unfortunately, it was too dark to shoot.

Stuff like that is not supposed to happen during the lull. Mature bucks spend most of their time bedded, and when they do move, it's in vampire mode. Hunters who stick to their stands focus on shooting does; most grab a grouse gun or fishing rod and "wait for things to get good again."

I've hunted long enough to know that plenty happens to throw a buck off in October; hunting pressure increases, food sources change, warm weather can settle in, and falling leaves transform the landscape.

But I also know this: the October lull can be a self-fulfilling prophecy. Of course bucks aren't as visible and predictable as they were during the early season. And yes, the frenzy of the rut is weeks away. But as Dad found out with the giant 8-point, there are always a few does on an early estrous clock. If you find hot buck sign now, hunt it immediately. Your odds may never be better.

156 GET PUMPED FOR THE PRE-RUT

It's pure magic. The pre-rut is that 10- to 14-day stretch just before the breeding begins, typically in late October or very early November. Rubs pop up like mushrooms after a spring rain. Bucks scrape almost on reflex, pausing during a feed to scratch the dirt. Trail cameras light up with daylight buck activity. The woods positively pulse with energy.

Right now, a buck will respond readily to a grunt call, some rattling antlers, or the challenge of a snort-wheeze. He might walk in to check out a doe decoy, or barge in to challenge a buck decoy. But the truly exciting thing is that most bucks are still working their home ranges, and not yet bouncing all over the landscape like some hormone-propelled ping-pong ball. If you know anything at all about a particular buck, he's vulnerable to the most exciting tactics in a bowhunter's playbook.

157 SET A TRAP

Rich Baugh, an Iowa land agent for Whitetail Properties, spends all year preparing a big-buck trap. And it works. Here's the scoop.

GO THERE "I drive through my farm all year long," Baugh says. "Deer won't spook from a vehicle if they're used to it, but they won't bed in an area you're driving through every day, either. I don't want deer bedding right next to my favorite stands."

SET THE TRAP Baugh scouts year-round to pick the best funnels for his stands. In spring and summer, he makes those funnels better. "I block all the trails within 50 or 100 yards of a funnel with a wall of cut brush," he says. "I'm not afraid to choke a buck's route to within 15 yards of my tree."

CAM IT "I set my cameras in open, easy-to-access areas where I can check them from the window of my truck or seat of my tractor, which they're used to seeing," says Baugh. Food plots get most of his focus in the pre-rut, but he also sets cameras over active scrapes if possible.

STRIKE Baugh stays home until he's confident he can kill a particular buck. "Once they start cruising a little bit, there is a short window of predictability," he says. "Some bucks are on their feet two hours before dark, and your odds of killing them are outstanding. This activity usually starts around the 25th or 26th of October, but it can be sooner with a strong, early cold front."

By then, the trap is already set. "Bucks are usually in their beds before daylight, so I'm hunting evenings only," Baugh says. "I hang back, watch the wind, and when I get a favorable afternoon, I slip in knowing that I'll probably get a shot."

158 STALK A BUCK WITH A BUD

Rick Hanson's buddies used to laugh at him for belly crawling across the South Dakota prairie, bow in hand and whitetail buck in mind. Now they ask to tag along—and he lets them. "This is simply the best way to kill a big buck in open country," says Hanson, who has stalked and arrowed a 200-incher, not to mention numerous 150-class bucks. "Hunting with a good buddy can really help, too." Here's how it's done.

PICK A SPOT "Whether you have big crop fields mixed with woodlots or rolling prairie, you need open country with lots of small breaks or contours so you can spot bucks and get close." Though it can work anytime, Hanson loves to use this tactic during the pre-rut, when bucks are responsive to calling.

BUDDY UP Once you've chosen an area, it's time to grab a friend and glass from afar. "When you find a good buck, sneak in together to within 200 yards of him," says Hanson. "If I'm the shooter, my buddy gains a vantage point where he can see the buck and direct me into range." Hanson then starts crawling and never looks up to check on the deer; instead, he depends on his partner's directions. "He's the coach."

CALL HIM CLOSE With a bedded buck, Hanson will crawl all the way into bow range. But more often, he stops 60 to 70 yards from the deer, gets to his knees where he can't be seen, and makes a few aggressive grunts. "When you're calling from within a buck's safety zone like that, he'll usually come right to you for an easy shot. Meanwhile, your buddy can watch exactly where he's hit and where he goes down."

159 HUNT THE RUT

I was 17 when I shot my first archery buck. The 8-point was walking past at 100 yards when he smelled a rag that I'd soaked in doe-estrus scent, dragged through the timber, and hung from a limb 5 feet off the ground. The buck trotted into range, stopped broadside at 9 steps, and only flinched a bit when I sailed an arrow over his back. He stared blankly at me as I popped another arrow from my quiver, nocked it, and drew. I settled down enough to make the second, 11-yard, shot.

I adore that hunt not only because it was my first archery buck, but because it was also a classic archery rut hunt. When the first round of does comes into

estrus, whitetail bucks lose some of their notoriously cautious habits. I've watched bucks charge in to rattling antlers and smash decoys. I've seen them chase does down paved roads in broad daylight. I've seen bucks fight other bucks so viciously it scared me.

Of course rut hunting is no slam-dunk. Even hormone-addled deer remember the danger of human scent. And the chaotic behavior that's so fun to watch can make getting a bow shot difficult, and patterning individual bucks impossible. But for sheer excitement, coupled with the occasional golden opportunity, nothing beats the magic month of November.

160 PHASE YOUR RUT STANDS

For consistent success, you need to understand the general progression of the breeding season—a method to all that madness—that dictates how deer behave. Understand that, and you can develop a solid strategy for hunting each of the rut's basic phases. Here's your rut-stand game plan.

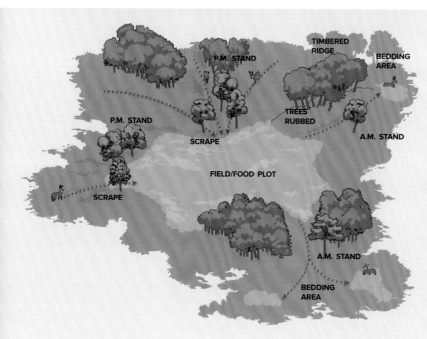

LATE PRE-RUT

THE SIGNS: Fresh rubs and scrapes appear almost daily, with bucks working them consistently.

THE DEER: Bucks of all ages appear at major food sources, checking for the very first estrous does. Young bucks badger does by running at them, while older studs linger to study body language and scent clues.

YOUR MOVE: Place stands near the most popular local food sources. You'll determine specific sites based on fresh scrapes or rub lines near these food sources. Afternoon stands can go right on field edges, while morning sets should be back in the timber, between the food and a known bedding area.

PEAK BREEDING

THE SIGNS: Once-fresh scrapes go dead and rubs are getting glossy with age.

THE DEER: Buck-doe pairs are the rule here, as well as multiple bucks clustered around a single hot doe. With 30 to 40 percent of area females in heat, bucks are far more concerned about finding a doe that's ready to breed than they are about laying down fresh sign.

YOUR MOVE: Bucks are either going to be with a doe or looking for one. Either way, you want to be in thick cover, such as a known doe bedding area, and sit as long as you possibly can.

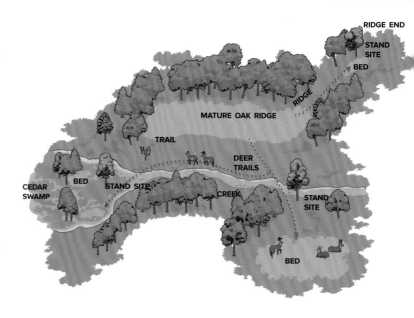

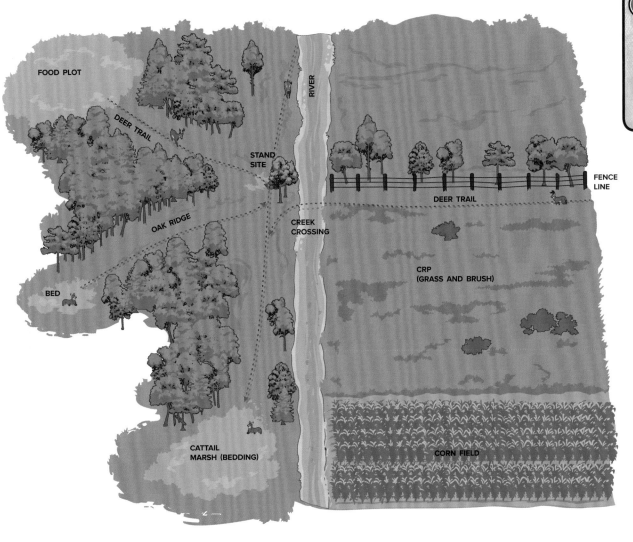

FOOD PLOT

DEER TRAIL

STAND SITE

OAK RIDGE

CREEK CROSSING

RIVER

DEER TRAIL

FENCE LINE

CRP (GRASS AND BRUSH)

BED

CATTAIL MARSH (BEDDING)

CORN FIELD

IMMEDIATE POST RUT

THE SIGN: Some scrapes, usually large ones situated in or near deep cover, start showing use again. Rub lines (often in terrain funnels) may open up or show reworking.

THE DEER: Don't expect to see much action anywhere on open food sources such as crop fields and large food plots. Does and fawns are just plain tired of the harassment they get from bucks every time they poke their nose from cover. Young bucks are tired from chasing. It's

not unusual to see an older buck out during the middle of the day, searching.

YOUR MOVE: Many hunters get discouraged now, as the frenzy of peak breeding has passed. But your chance for a truly big old whitetail may never be better than now. Set up in terrain funnels that connect several doe bedding areas. Mature bucks—animals that have the drive and stamina—will be covering ground, looking for the last available does.

161 DEAL SOME DECOYS

If you want to experience the most dramatic whitetail bowhunt of your life, stake out a decoy during the rut. I've seen bucks trot across 300 yards of prairie to duel with a fake intruder, and sometimes even leave a doe after a snort-wheeze drew their attention to my deke.

But the most intense clash I've ever seen occurred the first year Dave Hurteau hunted with me. We staked a deke near his evening stand close to a food source, and just before dusk a dandy 8-point spotted the imposter, sidled over—making every aggressive body posture in his genetic code—and smashed the decoy so hard the head, ears, and tail came off. Hurteau zipped an arrow through the buck seconds later. Sound exciting? Here's how you set up just such an encounter.

❶ THE DECOY

Use a buck decoy with small- to medium-size antlers. You want to punch a bigger buck's aggressive buttons. Plus, does will usually avoid a buck but harass a doe decoy, which they'll eventually sniff out as fake. Their snorting and stomping could alert other deer and wreck your hunt.

❷ THE PLACEMENT

Keep the decoy in an open area so that your buck has had time to size up his opponent.

Position the deer so it will be staring down oncoming bucks; they interpret this as an aggressive behavior and will usually respond, especially to a smaller deer.

Have the decoy 15 yards, give or take, upwind of your stand or blind. If the buck decides to circle downwind of the deke before smashing it, you've got a perfect broadside shot.

❸ THE STAND

Set your stand in a tree with good cover. Since you may incorporate rattling into your plan, a distant buck could spot movement when you do this, and may spook.

Keep some kind of obstacle—a fence, steep creek bank, some very dense brush—behind and downwind of your stand, to prevent a buck from making a wide circle around your setup and smelling you.

THE ACCESSORIES

The decoy is only part of your setup; use the following gear to seal the deal on a rutting whitetail.

Rattling antlers Sometimes getting a buck to see the decoy is the biggest challenge. Grab his attention by rattling.

Grunt tube and/or can call You can also try grunting or bleating with a call.

Bottle of deer urine Many hunters like to place scent wicks soaked with deer pee near the feet of the decoy. As the buck circles downwind, the scent acts as a "closer" to convince the buck his opponent is real and randy.

Rubber gloves and/or no-scent spray bottle Try to keep your decoy as free of human scent as possible. Wear rubber gloves during transport, and mark it with no-scent spray after you stake it out.

READING BUCKS

■ Scott Bestul on

One of two things usually causes a failed calling attempt: Either the deer didn't hear the call, or he's not in the mood. Here's how to handle those hurdles.

Deer will always give some indication they've heard your call. They'll turn and look, twitch an ear, bristle up, or change their body posture in response. If you don't spot any of those signs, the deer hasn't heard you. Wait until the buck stops, or simply call louder.

If the buck stares or takes a step toward you, he's likely ready to come to the call. But some bucks need coaxing; if he turns his head away or gets into some brush, work him some more. If he tucks his tail or raises it slightly, back off immediately. Try him another day, when he's feeling a little more frisky.

162 BASH THOSE ANTLERS

When bucks bang heads, other deer often come running, like kids who can't resist rushing in to watch a playground fight. Imitating these brawls with a pair of real antlers or a rattle bag can be an excellent way to bring a buck into bow range. Start with a sharp, aggressive whack of the antlers, and then slide off into a series of lighter bangs and bonks to mimic two bucks beating on each other. Keep your bow handy; more than once I've had bucks run in so quickly that I had to scramble to prep for a shot, and once I was simply caught flat-footed mid-sequence. I had to watch as the buck stared at me, realized he'd been fooled, and spun to leave.

A mature buck, especially, is apt to circle downwind of the sound. So try to set up upwind of an obstacle that will prevent or discourage him from swinging around and getting your wind (see item 157). One great solution is to put a buddy downwind of the horns to stop a circling buck cold.

163 MAKE THE CALL(S)

Deer are highly social critters that "talk" to each other all the time. Bucks will have their ears peeled for any deer vocalization during the rut, so luring in a buck can be as simple as mastering these three basic sounds here.

BLOW A BLEAT The go-to sound deer make to greet or stay in contact with each other. As the name implies, the bleat is a soft, sheep-like "baaah." It's most easily mimicked using a tip-over call like The Can, but reed-style calls offer better control of sound, inflection, and volume.

GIVE A GRUNT While does grunt too, the sharp "uurp" (yup, it sounds like a belch, and sometimes a loud one) of a rutting buck is unmistakable. There are scads of effective, user-friendly grunt calls out there on the market.

SOUND A SNORT-WHEEZE Bucks who are either seriously pissed off or sexually frustrated make this sound. While this is a last-ditch challenge call, a snort-wheeze will often bring in a buck when nothing else will. Happily, you don't have to buy anything to make this sound. Just inhale, rest your top teeth on your lower lip, and breathe out a sharp, three-note, phh-phhh-phhhhttt.

164 SET SOME SCENT

There are three basic methods for attracting a buck using scents during the rut. While there are many types of deer pee marketed under many names and types (doe, buck, estrous, and so on), straight deer urine will usually work fine. Experiment with different types until you find a favorite.

DRAG A RAG Apply some deer urine to a clean patch of material (cotton cloth, felt strip, and so on) attached to a sturdy line. As you walk to your stand or blind, drag the rag behind you, letting it touch the ground so it leaves a scent trail. Stop every 50 to 75 yards and freshen the rag with more pee to "heat up the trail." A lot of bowhunters like to walk the rag in a figure 8, with the intersection right in front of their stands, so that no matter where the buck picks up the trail, he'll wind up in bow range.

SET SCENT WICKS Hang scent wicks soaked with pee 5 or 6 feet high on branches within shooting range (and upwind) of your stand. Any deer walking downwind will catch the scent of these

"bombs" and approach. (If you've used a drag rag, you can simply hang up the rag when you reach your stand for the same effect.) These dangling lures are a good way to get a buck into position for a good shot.

MAKE MOCK SCRAPES Bucks are visually attracted to scrapes during the rut. Some very successful hunters like to create one or more mock scrapes of their own within shooting distance of the stand, and then treat them with deer urine for a double-bang effect.

165 STAY ALL DAY

When testosterone tells a buck it's time to chase love, the last thing he looks at is the clock. He's as likely to move at 10 or 2—when most of us are taking a break at camp—as he is at daylight or dusk.

Enter the all-day sit, a unique form of torture seemingly designed to either kill a midday buck or break the hunter's spirit. Manning a stand or blind from dawn to dusk is a highly effective tactic during the rut, but there's no sugarcoating the difficulty. You'll endure boredom, claustrophobia, and doubt as you wait for the midday giant. But waiting is the only way to get him.

166 HUNT THE RIGHT SPOT

As a rule, avoid open-cover food sources such as food plots or farm fields; bucks don't like exposing themselves in such areas during daylight, and most does won't be eating there unless the sun is low in the sky. A secluded food source such as an oak stand or clear-cut edge can produce all-day action. The best ones usually have fresh buck sign and evidence of recent feeding.

Some of my best all-day stands are in doe bedding areas or terrain funnels that connect bedding areas. Rutting bucks like to cruise between bedding areas searching for does all day. I like to use a no-bust stand, as bucks may enter a bedding area from multiple directions. I also like to rattle and call during an all-day sit, and doing so from a no-bust stand (see item 174) makes good sense.

167 PACK THE RIGHT GEAR

People have teased me for carrying enough gear to stock a small mail-order catalog, but on an all-day sit, I tote a pack that could fill an entire store. Clothing is the main item; since I usually have a long walk to the stand, I dress very lightly on the trip in, and then layer up when I arrive. I also bring extra layers for any weather fronts (predicted or not; in the upper Midwest in November, things can turn crappy in a real hurry). To carry this load, I like a big, roomy daypack with external straps for tying on bulky coats and cold-weather bibs.

Food and drinks are another big consideration. Not only is eating important for maintaining body heat, but snacking can also relieve boredom. I carry a small, insulated lunch sack that holds a can of soda, a couple of sandwiches, some dried fruit or an apple, and a bag of chips. And that's just the midday meal; I also tote a bag of trail mix, some dessert (cookies, candy bars, and so on), and a large bottle of water or sports drink. I've tried toughing out an all-day hunt with less food, but I have learned that I need a fairly constant intake of calories to fend off the cold. Plus, I use food as a reward: When I make it to midmorning I eat some trail mix; two hours after lunch, it's time for a cookie; and so on.

THE BREAKING POINT

Dave Hurteau on

Let me offer another perspective on sitting all day: Don't. Or at least, don't if you're wired like I am. Some of us just can't sit much more than four or five hours without beginning to really loose it. I'm not talking just boredom; I mean serious existential angst. If, however, I take a short break, maybe change locations quickly or have lunch at the truck, I'm good to go for another long stretch. If that means I'm not as hardcore as some, I can't say I give a rip. And you shouldn't either if you can't sit for 10 hours. Remember, bowhunting is supposed to be fun.

168 FIGHT BOREDOM

I fight the war against boredom on several fronts. Books are my main line of defense. When it comes to all-day sits, I'd be lost without a good novel. Some folks pooh-pooh reading in a tree, afraid that paying attention to the page would make them miss seeing a deer. I can't say this has never happened to me, but the losses have been worth it; reading has kept me in the stand for hours where I've seen many deer. And instead of costing me deer, books have actually put me on to them.

The other defense, in recent years, has been my phone. I don't live with it in my hands, but I do text friends—usually hunting buds who are also biding time in a stand—and play a game or two. Finally, I'll crawl down the tree once or twice in a 10-hour day, simply to get my land legs back and relieve some stand-induced claustrophobia. I don't care if I'm settled in to the largest hang-on stand going; after five hours it feels like a postage stamp. After I climb down, walk around the tree a few times, or even stretch out on the ground for a quick nap, I can ride out the rest of the day, alert and relatively refreshed.

169 LOVE THE LATE SEASON

After the rut, the following weeks are the final phase of deer hunting, and so they're called the late season. Like the early season, this phase is all about finding food. Whitetails pack on calories to replenish fat reserves lost during the rut, or they might not survive the winter. To a bowhunter, this means they become more predictable than they've been since September.

This hunt is no slam-dunk. After months of hunting pressure, deer are wired. I've spooked them from 100 yards away by simply brushing a glove against a tree limb, a sound they'd have ignored in September. They typically congregate near the best food, too; you're not only dealing with uber-sensitive deer, but lots of them working together to avoid danger. Winter hunting can also mean brutal cold and deep snow, factors that make travel to stands—and staying warm when in them—a huge hurdle.

Those challenges aside, I look forward to late season. It's a tough but simple challenge of finding an appealing food source, and then setting up to avoid the sharp senses of multiple whitetails. Cold keeps most people out of the woods, so there's rarely competition. It's just me, the deer, and the puzzle of getting close enough for a shot.

170 SET AN EYE-LEVEL AMBUSH

"Killing a mature whitetail at eye level is the ultimate challenge with a bow," according to bowhunting legend Barry Wensel. "I'd rather kill one deer this way than 10 from a stand." Eye-level hunting also happens to be a highly effective method in the late season. When pressured bucks aren't reaching their target food source until dark, Wensel slips a little closer to the bedding area and sets up quietly in a natural blind.

If there is no snow, he wears a ghillie suit; otherwise, it's snow camo, and he carries pruners to cut branches for cover or to clip a hole in a fallen treetop or thicket.

"I spend a lot of time figuring out my setup, picking a spot where everything is right for me and almost right for the deer. I want a fairly flat area, so I get a true wind. And I want the terrain or cover to funnel deer past a specific spot, but the funnel can't be too tight or a mature buck won't feel comfortable walking through it. I may drag a couple of big limbs to block the edges of a bench, for example, so a buck has to walk down the middle and within range of my hide."

171 STOMP A TRAIL

Crunchy, ice-covered snow is common during Midwestern winters. Wensel deals with this by going out ahead of time and stomping a trail to the spot where he plans to sit. "I just place my boots right next to each other and kind of shuffle in there, with no pretense of being quiet. And then I do the same thing on the walk out. When I return to hunt the next day, I've got an almost silent walking trail."

172 GET AGGRESSIVE

Some smart late-season bucks will not come out to a field or plot during daylight. Here's how Illinois guide Joe Gizdic hunts them.

A perfect example, he says, was a 240-inch nontypical he hunted a few seasons ago. Gizdic had planted 3 acres of beans with the sole purpose of putting a client on this buck in the late season, but the deer would not come out no matter how cold it got. "Odds are a buck like this is hitting a secondary food source in the woods—acorns, soft mast, or browse—until dark," Gizdic explains. "So I walked into the timber and found a brushy draw littered with honey-locust pods."

Gizdic warns that your approach has to be spot-on when you move in on a late-season buck. Give yourself plenty of time to hang a stand silently and pick a spot with cover that shields you in the direction of the buck's likely bedding area. Most important, set up where you can kill the buck, not just see him; you may not get another chance.

"Don't second-guess yourself. I learned that lesson the hard way," he adds. "I had two good stand trees to choose from and I picked the more conservative one." A half hour before dark, the monster rose from his bed and walked right under the other tree.

He eventually worked his way to the beans on a different trail, right at dark, and Gizdic never got another chance at him. "I've killed other good bucks this way, but you should learn from my mistake: If you decide to get aggressive, go all the way."

173   BLOCK A BUCK

When you can't use a natural terrain break to keep your scent above downwind deer, do the next best thing: Set up with a creek, fence, ledge, ravine, or open field on the immediate downwind side of your stand to discourage or physically block a buck from getting to where he can wind you.

174 DON'T GET BUSTED

A tree stand where deer can't wind you, no matter what direction they come from, may sound too good to be true. But it's actually quite feasible on many hunting properties. All you need is a sharp drop in terrain, a steady prevailing wind, and a good tree where you can hang your perch.

I have several on my own lease. My hunting buddies and I call them our "no bust" stands.

The idea is simple: Just place your stand at the edge of a terrain break so that there's a steep downhill slope on the downwind side. Your scent will remain above downwind deer. Some hunters try to achieve the same effect by hanging their stands very high, but this creates a poor shot angle. Besides, your scent will soon fall to the ground in flat terrain, and a smart buck can still bust you by circling far enough downwind. But deer can't do that with a no-bust stand, thanks to the elevation drop.

This illustration details one of our favorite no-bust stands, called Bobcat. Use it as a template to create scentproof setups on your own hunting area this fall.

SET A NO-BUST BOWSTAND Bobcat **(3)** is located on the end of a ridge, just before the terrain drops sharply downhill. In the morning, deer travel from agricultural fields **(1)** toward a thick bedding flat **(2)** west-southwest of the stand. You'd hunt this stand only with a southerly wind. Most deer heading to bed remain on the upwind side of the stand. But big bucks especially love to travel along a bench hidden on the back side of the slope **(5)**.

During the rut, bucks may show up from anywhere. And deer responding to calls or rattling are apt to circle the stand. But in every case, a steady southerly wind will carry your scent **(4)** well above downwind bucks, keeping you in the game.

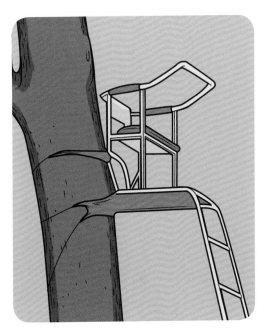

Buck bedding point

Evening feed: green forb

Stand

Nighttime feed: cut corn

175 HUNT SOUTH SLOPES

"Late-season deer need to feed every six hours, and they seek foods that are high in carbs and protein," says Neil Dougherty, one of the nation's top whitetail consultants. A field of corn or beans is perfect. But pressured deer know better than to expose themselves in daylight. So the trick is to find quality forage where deer feel secure.

One of the most overlooked late-season food sources is forbs, which make up 60 percent or more of what deer eat throughout the year, he says. "The key to finding them now is sun-drenched southern slopes, where weeds and wildflowers—maybe 100 edible species—are still green and growing, providing deer with the nutrition they need now."

Any south-facing slope can be good, but those facing straight south or southwest are usually best. "These can be 6 to 8 percent warmer than any others," says Dougherty. Also, target hillsides with a somewhat open canopy, he advises, where the sun reaches ground plants and keeps them alive and growing.

These slopes set up perfectly for a late-season afternoon hunt. "Most of us have a prevailing wind from the west," says Dougherty. "So slip in from the east and below the point of the ridge, where bucks love to bed, just out of the wind. Quietly hang a stand overlooking the greenest forbs, or find some good nearby cover that will let you hunt from the ground."

SNOW

■ Dave Hurteau on

The best part of the late season is snow. By then I'm often struggling, frustrated at trying to figure out where pressured, post-rut bucks have disappeared to. But give me a few inches of freshly fallen snow, and I feel brand new—because suddenly the mystery of what bucks are up to is plain to see, written over the clean, new layer of white, in deep-set hoof prints. Some quick scouting, and I'm right back in the game.

176 BRAKE WITH A FAKE

When I expect I'll need to make a running buck stop short, I stake a decoy nearby. Even a sprinting deer is going to slam on the brakes when he sees that deke. It works every time. For safety reasons, I always wrap an orange shirt around the decoy's neck.

177 BE THE FEED FIELD

You've heard the cliché: Whitetails know their turf like you know the layout of your living room. But when someone rearranges your furniture unexpectedly, you might find yourself sitting on the coffee table. It's the same with deer, says Primos Pro staffer Keith Beam, who primarily hunts in Nebraska and Kansas and who has arrowed more than 50 P&Y-class bucks from the ground. "When a farmer cuts a cornfield, it changes the whole immediate environment, and it takes a little while for deer to get their bearings. You need to seize the moment."

A lot of farmers leave crops standing well into the late season, so knock on the door or give them a call to find out exactly when they'll be harvesting and be ready to go as soon as the combine changes the scenery. "Grab a ground blind, build a brushpile, or dig a hole out in the field near where you've seen deer entering the standing crop."

A new covering of snow has the same effect. "It's the perfect time to put on some snow camo and set up right where they feed," Beam says. "The bottom line is that the best time to set up in a hot late-season feeding area is when the whole field changes its look. Deer will walk right up to you."

178 HUNT ALL DAY

Whitetail hunters typically associate all-day sits with the rut, when a revved-up buck may run under a funnel stand at any time. But a similar approach can put you on the biggest bucks in the late season, says Washington guide Gary Greenwalt. "By the time I can hunt, our deer are in post-rut, winter-feeding mode, and our food plots can draw in the best bucks from 5 or 6 miles away. When it's cold—and I have a year's worth of trail camera photos to prove it—those tired, hungry, older bucks will bed tight to the feed and walk into the plot at all hours."

To tag one of these bucks, you need to be there when he comes out to grab a bite or follow a late-cycling doe to the feed. "I wait until an hour after first light so that any dawn-feeding deer are off the plot and back in the timber. Then I crawl into a stand overlooking the feed and wait."

Greenwalt sets up so that the wind blows his scent where deer are least apt to approach, such as a steep hill or ravine. "I know there are bucks out there. That and some high-quality winter clothing make it easy to sit all day. I just enjoy the woods and let things unfold."

179 MAKE A FIELD OF DREAMS

Post-rut bucks want a secure thicket on a sunny hillside and a short walk to prime feed. Here's how to give it to them.

Before the season, hinge-cut trees to enhance winter bedding sites roughly 200 yards from a field or plot. Then find a funnel to the feed, such as the head of a wash, or make a route by blocking existing trails and clearing new ones. Finally, in late fall, scatter winter rye over the existing crop, right where you want a big buck to feed. It comes up bright green in the late season, and deer will head right for it.

Set up where the funnel meets the field and within range of the new planting. You've created the ideal conditions for a big buck to move into the area and follow that funnel right under your stand. But even if he does enter the field some other way, the rye will entice him.

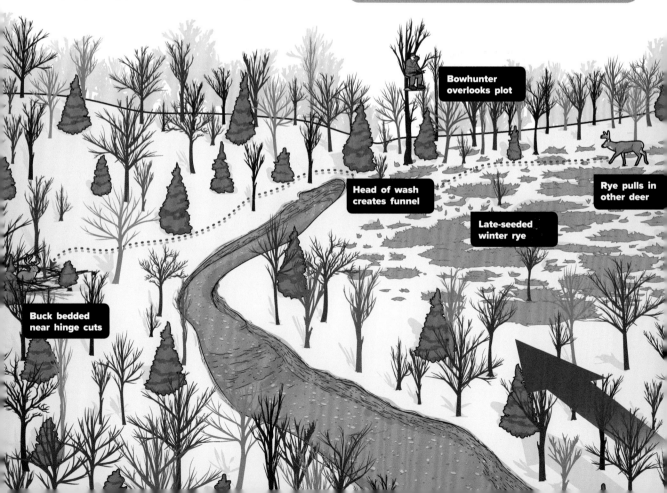

Bowhunter overlooks plot

Rye pulls in other deer

Head of wash creates funnel

Late-seeded winter rye

Buck bedded near hinge cuts

180 SWAP SCENT

One of Alabama hunting guide Steve Maxwell's favorite tricks for hunting in the later post-rut season is to use the scent of a killed buck or doe. When you or someone in your camp kills an estrous doe during the rut, carefully remove the bladder and bottle the urine, he says. If someone kills a rutting buck, cut off and save the tarsal glands. "You can keep them in the fridge for post-rut pickup breeding or the second rut."

The key, he says, is to use them in the same general area where they were taken. "Bucks in the doe's area know her by smell and will still be looking for her. The ones in the buck's area know him, too, and may still have a score to settle."

Maxwell runs the doe urine on a drag rag and then hangs it up 50 to 75 yards out in front of his stand in a crosswind. He hangs buck tarsal glands the same way, but in this scenario he rattles from the ground.

"Start with three or four minutes of rattling, crashing brush and raking branches, and then give it a rest for 15 minutes or so." Do that three times, he advises, and then try a new place.

"I've had bucks come in so hard that they had to skid on their hooves to keep from running me over," says Maxwell.

181 GET DOWN AND SNEAK

"I enjoy the challenge of the late season," says Kentucky guide Pat Willis. "I love figuring out offbeat ways to kill the toughest bucks."

Where he hunts, deer are just about guaranteed to hit a hot food source when it's cold out, but the smartest ones never seem to enter in the same spot twice, making it tough to get your stand in the right place. Willis's answer: "Let him come out, and then go get him."

Of course, that only works if you've got cover to hide your approach. So Willis makes cover by

dragging brush, cedar trees, and hay bales out into the field, creating a sort of man-made hedgerow. He gives the deer a day or two to get used to it, then sits in his best stand. "If the buck I'm after comes within range, great. If not, I climb down and use that cover to sneak in close enough for a bow shot."

Another option, he says, is to set two or three ground blinds along the introduced cover. "Start with your best guess, and if your buck comes out way off, crawl to the blind that gives you the best chance." Willis pulled this hedgerow trick on a 140-class 6-pointer last year. "I crawled to within 40 yards of him but misjudged the distance, and my arrow went just under his belly. Finally, in January, I snuck along the same cover into chip-shot range— only to find that the son of a buck had dropped one of his antlers."

LAST RESORTS

Dave Hurteau on When hard-hunted, late-season deer go completely nocturnal, there's one last-ditch trick that sounds crazy, but can really work. If you know your ground well, I'll bet can pinpoint a few dependable late-season bedding areas. Grab a stand and your bow, go there at midday, and purposely bump the deer. Then set up. If you approach from downwind, so the spooked deer don't smell you, odds are they will come right back to the spot that kept them safe through the heart of the hunting season. And you'll be waiting.

This is Rule #1 if you want to get into bow range of a whitetail. A deer's sense of smell is nothing short of spectacular. Bloodhounds—the legendary sniffers of dogdom—are thought to have 200 million olfactory receptors. Deer have an estimated 297 million. In the right conditions, a downwind deer can detect your scent from more than 300 yards away and can smell where you've been long after you've left.

A multimillion-dollar industry—selling everything from skunk-pee cover scent to b.o.-busting bubble gum—exists with the sole purpose of defeating a deer's ability to smell an upwind hunter. The question is, does any of it work?

To find out, over the past several years I've enlisted the help of several cop buddies and their drug-sniffing K-9 partners. Here's a breakdown of some of the more interesting tests we've done.

TEST #1
DOG: BLITZ

SCENT PRECAUTION: RUBBER BOOTS
Many bowhunters insist on wearing knee-high rubber boots, believing it keeps foot odor from deer noses while walking to and from stand sites. So I laid down two trails. First, donning old, smelly leather boots, I zigzagged along a field edge for 100 yards and then looped wide to avoid a backtrail. Next, wearing knee-high rubber boots that I'd thoroughly scrubbed with a paste of baking soda and then air-dried outdoors, I walked quickly along a snowmobile trail of very short grass. Blitz nailed both of these trails with ease.

THE TAKEAWAY: A deer can smell where you've walked whether you wear rubber boots or not. So be careful not to walk in the area from which you expect deer to approach.

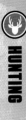

TEST #2

DOG: CHANCE

SCENT PRECAUTIONS: SCENT-CONTROL SOAP, SHAMPOO, DETERGENT, SPRAY, AND CLOTHING

For this test, we ran a training exercise called the "Hot Box," in which six plywood boxes are spaced evenly in two rows across a field. Hunters get in all the boxes for a couple minutes to "heat them up" with human scent. Then, all but one leaves, and the dog has to find him.

First, a hunter who had not taken any scent-control measures stayed in the box. It took Chance 20 seconds to find him. Next, the test hunter took a no-scent shower and dressed in camo clothes washed in an unscented detergent. It took Chance 18 seconds to find him. Finally, in addition to the shower, the hunter wore two layers of activated-carbon clothing. I literally soaked him with a scent-killing spray, and he even chewed a wad of gum designed to eliminate breath odor. It took Chance 13 seconds to find him.

THE TAKEAWAY: All the scent-reducing measures in the world didn't make a bit of difference to our dog—and probably wouldn't to a deer, either.

TEST #3

DOG: IKE

SCENT PRECAUTIONS: COVER SCENTS

Sticking with the Hot Box test, we ran four trials. First, a hunter using no cover scent stayed in the box, and Ike found him in 6 seconds. Next, the hunter sprayed down liberally with earth scent. This time, Ike ran past hunter's box and had to double-check it before finding him; elapsed time: 25 seconds. The third hunter used acorn-scent wafers and sprayed down with acorn scent. Here, Ike had even more trouble, eventually finding him in 45 seconds. Last, the hunter used enough skunk scent to gag an outdoor writer. Again, it took Ike 45 seconds to find him

THE TAKEAWAY: Cover scent clearly buys you time, maybe enough to shoot.

TEST #4

DOG: CHANCE

SCENT PRECAUTION: BAKING SODA AND OZONE-GENERATING PRODUCTS

Baking soda is well-known for controlling odors and used by many hunters. Ozone is claimed to contain an extra molecule that attaches to other stinky molecules—say b.o. molecules—changing their structure to eliminate odor.

Again using the Hot Box test, we first ran a control with a hunter wearing untreated street clothes. Chance found him in 14 seconds. Next, a hunter took a shower in no-scent soap mixed with soda and then dressed in clothes washed in a similar solution, plus powdered in soda. Chance found him in 19 seconds. The last hunter ran an Ozonics unit for a minute inside the box before the test began, and left it on throughout. It took Chance 50 seconds to find him. Even the handler was stunned at how confused his dog was.

THE TAKEAWAY: Baking soda wasn't very effective, but ozone confused that super nose for nearly one minute, which amazed everyone. Nothing completely covers human odor. But if you can muddy the olfactory water for 50 seconds, you'll almost certainly shoot more downwind deer. Still, your best bet is to avoid getting upwind of a whitetail.

183 DON'T BLOW IT

The buck approaching your stand has Pope and Young record book written all over it. All you need is a clear shot—and a way to avoid the blunders bowhunters often make at these critical moments. Here's how to avoid the four most common gaffes.

HOLD THE GRUNTS A grunt call can bring deer closer, so it's tempting to use it the instant a buck shows. But hold off; don't draw attention to yourself if a buck is already coming to you. Even if the buck pauses, don't call unless he starts off in the wrong direction or wags his head and neck back and forth, which often precedes a change in course.

DRAW RIGHT There are two essential parts to solving this problem. First, anticipate obstructions that will shield you from a buck's line of sight, and draw when he's behind one. Second, draw sooner when a buck is moving quickly— and take your time when he's taking his. You can improve both skills dramatically by drawing on every deer that walks under your stand, whether you intend to kill it or not.

GET IN RANGE Don't complicate a great opportunity by trying to guess how far away your buck is. Get it right ahead of time by planting yardage stakes or by scanning key landmarks with a laser rangefinder. Take extra care with the latter method to avoid false readings from stray twigs or grass.

GET A CLEAN SHOT There may be no worse feeling in all of bowhunting than the nauseating regret that comes from making a bad shot on a trophy animal. Carefully monitor a buck's body angle as he approaches, and wait for a double-lung shot. As you take aim, consider where your arrow must exit to pierce both lungs. Presumably, you've done everything else right if you've gotten this far. Don't forget this last crucial step.

184 DRAW AND QUARTER

A bowhunter's best two shot angles for deer are broadside or quartering slightly away; both provide a large target and a direct path to the vitals, unobstructed by heavy bone. The quartering-to shot, we're told, is low-odds. That's just not true—and it's still about 6 inches in size, the same area as a hog's vitals (and much bigger than the largest gobbler's dead zone). Deer are wounded with the quartering-to shot because most hunters aim at the wrong spot. The target isn't behind or through the shoulder; it's in front of it. I've killed lots of deer with this shot, and so can you.

BE PICKY Take this shot only if you can arrow a softball every time at 20 yards. Even so, that's the maximum range. I've taken the quartering-to shot only when I've already drawn on a deer moving quickly toward my tree.

AIM FORWARD If you aim behind the shoulder, you'll shoot down the side of the deer's rib cage and hit one lung at best. You'll rarely recover that buck. Instead, shift your focus to the front edge of the shoulder, in the crease where the base of the neck and shoulder blade meet. The kill zone is a circle extending from the crease to the center of the deer's chest. Aim for the middle.

DO NOT PASS You'll rarely get a pass-through. The arrow will clip the edge of the foreshoulder or center in the opposite shoulder. Either way, it's a short distance to the heart, lungs, trachea, and several major blood vessels at this angle. Though I killed one of my best bucks ever using a mechanical broadhead with this very hit, I like the added penetration assurance of a fixed-blade.

HIT THIS SPOT

185 TRAIL A BUCK

Hit a deer perfectly and all you need to do is walk a red line to your prize. Hit a deer poorly, however, and he will break out a battery of tricks to elude you. He'll line out, veer sharply, backtrack, swim, circle, hide, and more. As long as there's good blood, you still need only follow it, if a bit more carefully. But with a light, spotty trail, you'll have to rely on your own battery of skills to recover that buck. Here's how to follow the trail to its end.

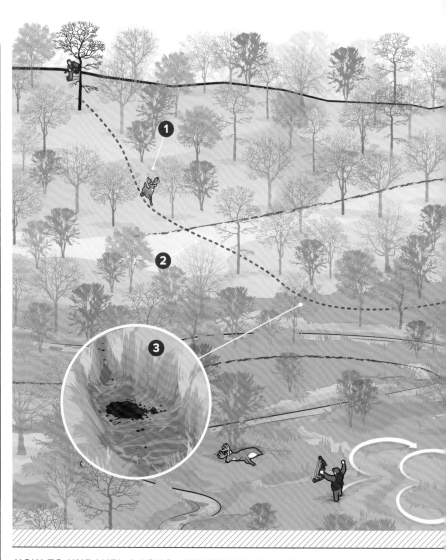

HOW TO UNRAVEL A LONG, INDISTINCT BLOOD TRAIL

❶ THE HIT

Watch the impact as closely as possible, and note the deer's reaction. Pick a mark where you last saw the animal. After 15 minutes, go to the hit site and look for the arrow. If there's no blood on the ground here, walk slowly to your "last-seen" mark, searching for blood, tracks, or scuff marks.

❷ THE DASH

Most deer make a brief, panicked run, usually downhill toward water or thick cover. If there's no blood at the last-seen mark, check trails leading in these directions. Once you find blood, note which side(s) of the deer it's coming from and how high it is on the grass or brush. Mark each spot with toilet paper to help you see the path.

❸ THE EMPTY BED

Finding a bloody bed within the first 300 yards is a mixed blessing. A buck that beds this quickly is hurting, but you likely bumped him. If you can't find a blood trail exiting the bed, the chances of recovery have plummeted. Either way, examine the blood to get a better idea of the hit, and then back off for several hours.

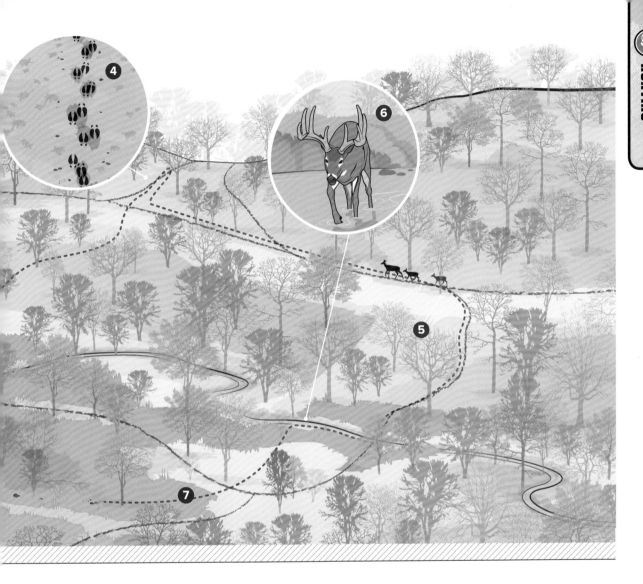

4 THE BACKTRACK

When a blood trail seems to dead-end, odds are the buck backtracked. Catching this is easy if you know which side he's bleeding from; suddenly there's blood on both sides of the trail. Or search for identical fresh tracks in both directions. Otherwise, walk it back, searching for where more blood veers off the trail.

5 THE LINEOUT AND CIRCLE

A wounded buck may take a straight-line path of least resistance. Usually at the end of a lineout there will be a dead buck, an end to the blood, or a change in direction. Slow down, stay on the blood, and remember that an injured buck has a tendency to circle, especially if that leads him back downhill.

6 THE CROSSING

Wading or swimming is a classic move that poses a major challenge. Make sure your buck didn't stop, get a drink, and backtrack. If you spy aquatic vegetation showing blood, wade in and stay on the trail. Otherwise cross, if possible, and comb the banks, examining crossings and trails for where he came out.

7 THE LAST BLOOD

Sometimes, you just can't find another drop of blood. Don't panic. Mark the last drop, and start walking in widening cloverleaf circles; walk a ways, circle back, and walk another circle, looking for any sign. Keep an eye toward water and thick cover. Check blowdowns and thickets; with luck, you'll find your trophy.

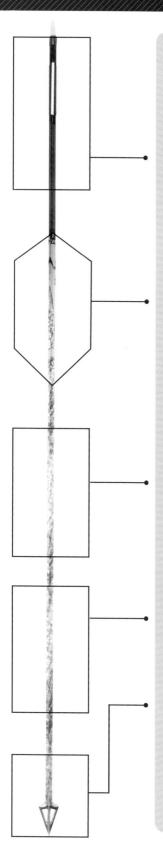

186 EXAMINE AN ARROW

An arrow recovered after a shot tells a tale. Here's how you can read it.

VIEW THE VANES They may hold the most blood. For the last buck I killed, my arrow was wiped nearly clean on the exit. But the 4-inch feathers didn't lie; they were soaked in blood. A single bloody vane can indicate a grazing hit.

SEE THE SHAFT Blood from tip to nock means a pass-through. Otherwise, the end of the blood reveals the penetration depth. Take the sniff test: Pure blood has a musty, rusty-iron smell. Gut hits will smell like regurgitated salad. A shaft coated with whitish fat or sinew usually portends a poor hit.

GET A GOOD BREAK If your arrow breaks here or higher, your broadhead likely penetrated deeply enough to hit vitals. If it looked like a good shot, odds are it hit the off shoulder, and you'll have a quick recovery.

BEWARE A BAD BREAK If the arrow breaks off around here or lower, you've hit a shoulder blade or other major bone—not good.

EXAMINE YOUR HEAD Broadhead blades grab bits of meat, tissue, organs, or hair that help reveal exactly where your arrow hit. Nicked or dinged tips or blades indicate bone contact. A single bloody blade suggests a grazing hit.

187 FIND SOME BLOOD BROTHERS

When blood-trailing, it can really help to have a buddy or two along. Here's how to choose and use them correctly.

THE SEASONED HUNTER You're still amped up from the hunt and apt to charge forward too quickly. Let a hunting buddy you trust take the lead. That is, of course, unless you know a real pro (see below).

THE PRO This is the guy you really want to call. He's a calm, experienced tracker who is even less emotionally invested than your hunting bud. If he answers the phone, put him up front.

THE EAGER ONE This guy (usually a newbie) practically begs to help, but he's impatient and charges forward, passing the blood. Best to leave him home. Otherwise, he belongs at the back, on toilet-paper duty.

188 GET A DOG

Sometimes even the very best blood trailer can't find a very dead deer. But if you live in one of the 27 states that allow the use of tracking dogs to aid in big-game recovery, you can call a member of an association such as the United Blood Trackers and get some canine assistance. Since a tracking dog doesn't need blood to follow an animal's scent, it can find your buck when all else seems lost. UBT (and other associations) provide contact information on certified trackers in participating states, as well as information on training your own dog.

189 KNOW THE HIT

If you watched him crash after a double-lung hit, go ahead with the fist-pump. Otherwise, you can follow this chart to evaluate your hit and plan your next steps.

HIT LOCATION

	A) LEG/SHOULDER	B) GUT	C) LIVER	D) BACK	E) NECK
DEER REACTION	Sprints off, hobbling.	Hunches up, and then slowly walks off, twitching tail.	Speeds off, then slows, twitching tail.	Drops immediately or runs off quickly.	Sprints off or drops in his tracks.
BLOOD/SIGN	Audible crack at shot. Broken arrow with minimal penetration. Blood tapers off quickly.	Arrow shaft or the first blood smells distinctly barflike. Expect blood on both sides of trail.	Dark, thickish blood, usually on both sides of trail roughly 3 feet high on branches and brush.	Dark-tipped hair with gray guard hair visible at hit site. Little blood. A tough recovery.	Dark gray or brown hair at site of hit. Dark red blood within 75 yards.
YOUR MOVE	Get on the track fast and stay on this deer. Your best chance is a follow-up shot.	Wait at least five hours. If temps allow, wait overnight on an evening hunt.	Wait three to four hours, and get help if possible. The hit is fatal, but the blood trail may turn difficult.	If you spined and dropped the buck, take an immediate finishing shot. If not, wait several hours.	Heavy blood means an artery or throat hit and a quick recovery. Light blood means muscle or spine; go for a follow-up shot.

OFF THE MARK
WHAT SHOULD YOU DO IF YOU HIT ANY OF THESE SPOTS? SEE ABOVE.

D

E

A

B

C

A

190 QUIT DREAMING AND GO GET YOUR ELK

For more and more bowhunters, calling a rutting elk into archery range is atop the wish list. Don't tell me you've never closed your eyes and envisioned a pissed-off, slobbering herd bull screaming in your face at 20 yards. But the real beauty of this dream—besides the slobber—is that it's so attainable. If you're short of cash but long on motivation, killing an elk is an affordable, feasible goal.

First off, in most states archery tags are the easiest kind to get. Second, most bow seasons take place during the peak of the elk rut, when bulls are bugling and highly active. Also, archery seasons see only a fraction of the pressure that occurs during gun hunts.

But it's no gimme. With a dream so popular and attainable, the number of bowhunters roaming the high parks and timber has shot up in recent years, and the elk have also wised up fast. You'll need to keep some cutting-edge tricks up your sleeve—but of course we've got you covered there.

The best news of all? Elk numbers are at or near all-time highs in the West, and many of those animals live on public lands—vast stretches of country open to any hunter with the ability and attitude to get there. You ready?

191 BOW BEFORE THE BUGLE

In many states, the archery opener precedes the peak rut by weeks. "You can wait for bulls to start bugling in earnest, but you'll miss a lot of great hunting," says Chad Schearer, Montana elk expert. Here are his tips for arrowing a pre-rut trophy.

FIND THE HERD "Getting into animals in the early season is the toughest part," says Schearer. "I climb to a high point where I can glass 3 to 5 miles. If I don't find elk nearby, I move until I do."

BEAT THEM TO BED Early-season elk are all about feeding, and one of their favorite sources is lowland alfalfa. "They'll travel miles to hit a field and get back to the mountain by daybreak," Schearer notes. "I glass until I find a good bedding area and learn how elk approach. Then I try to cut them off the next morning."

CALL THEM CLOSE The predictability of the feed-to-bed pattern makes it easy to get close to a bull now—but not always close enough. Soft calling can close the deal. "I'll set up as close as I can along a trail near an opening where I've got good shooting. Then I use soft chirps and mews to pull a bull those last few yards for a clear shot."

WAIT OVER WATER Warm weather makes drinking water highly attractive. Look for fresh tracks to reveal which sources are getting hit hardest, and then set up in the afternoon. Also look for wallows (which bulls use well ahead of the rut) on north-facing slopes in or near dark timber. Where legal, put up a trail camera set on video mode to find the hottest wallow. Then pack in a lightweight treestand or build a blind within bow range.

WATER BAR Find where elk drink and wallow to get close to big bulls.

192 GET A BULL IN BED

One way to arrow a trophy pre-rut bull is to cut him off on his way back to bed in the morning. Another—bolder but highly effective—way is to climb right in bed with him. Bulls don't like having other bulls in their personal space. With the timber to cover your approach, sneak in and challenge him to a fight.

GLASS Well before dawn, position yourself on a ridge overlooking open meadows or lush valleys—prime elk feeding zones. When a shooter shows up, keep glassing until you see him enter a patch of timber and not come out the other side.

STALK Once the bull has settled in the timber, move in. Look out for cows and raghorns standing sentry. Try to get well inside 200 yards, and then set up in the timber where you have decent shooting lanes.

CALL Let out a shrill bugle and wait for a response. If the bull doesn't answer instantly, grab a sizeable branch and beat on a tree. Once you know the bull is up, call again only if he hangs up—and then really let him have it.

KILL As the bull closes in, don't make the mistake of hiding behind cover. Trust your camouflage, clip your string, and just try to hold it together.

193 ROOST AN ELK

When elk are leaving the fields and meadows prior to first light, waiting until dawn to locate the herd puts you behind the game, says Arizona guide Jay Scott. Try driving forest service roads through good areas in the middle of the night, stopping every four to five miles to listen for bugling and talk from cows. When you locate a herd, you can bet they won't be far away at first light, giving you a great starting point. Scott tells any hunter new to the area to do their initial scouting this way for best results.

1 Be in position to glass at first light. Elk are likely already moving toward the bedroom.

2 Close the distance, mindful of the wind. Ditch your pack at 200 yards and get low.

3 Call loud. Call scary. Call big. It's no time to be timid. You're throwing down for a fight.

4 The bull will come in fast and hot. Range several references in clear shooting lanes ahead of time.

194 STAND UP TO THE FARM BULL

Hunters romanticize the elk as a majestic mountain species, but in fact these prized trophy animals are increasingly adapting to the encroachment of agriculture. Colorado guide Mike Miller says more farmers are finding elk herds in their corn, turnip, and alfalfa fields. As a result, Miller has adapted the whitetail tactics he learned growing up in Pennsylvania—including hunting fields and food plots—to get bow-close to big bulls. Here are the keys to his success:

REVIEW THE SEASONAL MENU Before the season begins, talk to the farmer who's given you permission to hunt on his property about his crop-rotation plans. An elk's changing tastes dictate where to hunt and when. "As turnips and sugar beets emerge, elk will move in to feast on the tender tops," Miller says. "Then they'll hit those fields hard again after fall's first frost."

KNOW WHICH WAY THE WIND IS BLOWING Count on the fact that fields in the foothills are susceptible to swirling winds. Identify ridges, draws, and other changes in topography that will affect wind direction. One tool Miller relies on to figure out the wind is the Mossy Oak Hunting Weather app. "I'm skeptical of technology," he says, "but it's surprisingly accurate."

SET UP A FARM STAND Miller sets a treestand on the field edge within range of where the elk enter as they come out of the mountains in the afternoon. Falling thermals make hunting a field in the early morning, when the elk are already on the field, next to impossible. Here, the best option is a ground blind or stand set a couple hundred yards back in the timber, where you can ambush elk coming back to bed late in the morning.

195 GET A JUMP ON THE RUT

New Mexico guide Tom McReynolds says it's a rule that bowhunters always want to call in and kill a screaming, crazed bull elk in the peak of the rut. "That's what they see on TV," he laughs. But for a true trophy, he swears by the week- to 10-day period prior to breeding.

"That's when a big bull is highly vulnerable. He's hanging fairly close to cows, but he's not yet obsessed with gathering and keeping them close. If he's truly big, he'll be alone. Glass him from a distance. Study where he lives and how he moves through that area, and you'll find he's highly predictable," he says.

"He's not going to have the eyes, ears, and noses of other elk to help him, so it's just a matter of slipping in to one of those spots he already wants to go, and everything is in your favor. Give me some time to watch a bull like that, and I'll bring a hunter in and kill him in one day."

■ Dave Hurteau on

THE PERFECT ELK SETUP

Any decent whitetail bow will work just fine for elk, but given my druthers, I'll take a speed bow that lets me shoot a heavy arrow—for better penetration—while maintaining a fairly flat trajectory—for longer shots at a bigger target. Give me a 32- or 33-inch axle-to-axle length and a mass weight of 3.8 to 4 pounds (bare bow)—which is light and short enough to hike with but long and heavy enough to provide a stable shooting platform. And I'll take hard-hitting micro-diameter arrows tipped with 125-grain cut-on-contact, fixed-blade heads. Thank you.

196 FIND ELK WITH TRAIL CAMS

Jody Smith, who guides hunters for Roosevelt elk in Oregon, hangs trail cameras in traditional bedding areas to watch some elk while he's glassing for others.

Smith's elk go to bed late, so he can get in there to set his cameras while they're still feeding. He starts hanging cameras just before the season and waits about a week before he checks them. When he hunts with clients, he'll hunt a different herd for the first few hours, waiting for thermals to start rising later in the morning. If he doesn't get his client on a bull early, then he heads for the deeper cover where his cameras have marked animals. "By about 8 a.m. the winds get more consistent, so I can get in there undetected," Smith says. "I don't call—I just sit and wait. It makes for an exciting hunt. It's so dense in there, by the time you get a shot, the elk are unbelievably close."

197 TRY A CLASSIC

Elk hunting's surge in popularity has made for smarter bulls, and savvy hunters have upped their game with all sorts of innovative tricks and new deceptions. But don't forget that the classic bow-season method of locating a rutting bull, setting up close, and calling him into your lap still works.

THE CALLS At minimum you need a bugle tube and a few cow calls. The former is often only a tube used to amplify a diaphragm mouth call, but models with the latex reed built into the mouthpiece are easier to learn to blow. You can also use mouth calls to make cow sounds, but, here again, bite-and-blow models are easier to master, and a push-button call, like the Primos Hoochie Mama, is the easiest of all—and the most commonly heard by educated elk.

THE PLAN Simplicity itself. Climb high in the mornings to glass for elk moving uphill to bedding timber and to listen for bugling bulls. In the afternoon, position yourself to catch them moving down from the high timber to feed. Use your bugle tube—sparingly—as a locator call. In each case, when you pinpoint a bull, figure the wind, cut him off, get as close as you dare without letting him get wind of or see you, and—much as with turkey hunting—set up to call him in. That simple plan has killed thousands of bulls, and will kill thousands more.

198 BUGLE HIM

A decade ago, bugling for rutting bull elk was the hottest tactic in big-game archery. Today, more and more hunters are reaching for cow calls instead. "Not so fast," says veteran guide Al Bousley. "At the right time and place, there's no deadlier call than a bugle."

And there's no rush like a tree-bashing bull charging in to meet your challenge. Remembering his first, Bousley laughs. "That giant sounded like a train wreck. I was so shook I missed him clean at point-blank range." Hunts like that keep Bousley's bugle tube close at hand.

199 KNOW WHEN TO BLOW

When should you bugle? Here are Bousley's top tips.

PLAY THE JEALOUSY CARD "If you want to push a bull's buttons, make him think he's in danger of losing his girls," Bousley says. "And the best way to do that is to get between them." When a herd bull drifts away from his cows to feed, drink, or wallow, the guide runs into the void and lets a power bugle rip. "I'm telling you that bull is going to come in—and he's not going to be shy about it."

CLOSE THE DISTANCE Another great time to bugle is when you need to steer a close bull even closer. When Bousley sees a herd moving toward a saddle, for example, he gets ahead to cut them off. Usually, the approaching bull isn't quite in bow range, but a bugle will pull him in. "If a bunch of cows have already come through, I scream at him," Bousley explains. "If he's near the front of the herd, a whistle or short bugle does the trick."

BRING HIM BACK Finally, bugling is the ultimate last-ditch call, according to Bousley. "Sometimes an approaching bull will suddenly get goosey," he says. This is a perfect time to bugle. "I've had bailing bulls stop in their tracks, turn around, and trot right back in. It's like the bugle makes them forget they're spooked." At the very least, the bugle will usually stop him. "And if he's in bow range, you may still get your shot."

200 TREE AN ELK

One surefire way to amp up the realism of your calling is find a good tree to thrash. Try this routine, designed to sound like an excited subdominant bull trying to move in on one of the big boy's cows.

YOUNG RUB Grab a bat-size branch, and kneel near a small tree. Start with a high-pitched squeal of a satellite bull, followed by some light cow calling. Then rake the tree with the branch, loudly scraping the bark. Mix in some grunts and blowing. You want the herd bull to think you're flexing for one of his girls.

BATTER UP If the bull hangs up, get aggressive. Pound the branch into the ground or swing it against the tree like a Louisville Slugger. The louder you are, the angrier the herd bull will get.

SHAKE IT If you can do it without the bull seeing you, shake the outer limbs of a tree. A visual cue is often the final touch to bring the target bull those last few yards into bow range.

201 DEKE A BULL

Today's educated bull is infamous for hanging up out of bow range, looking for the "cow" that called to him—and leaving when he doesn't see her. That's why so many hard-core elk hunters these days carry a lightweight silhouette cow decoy. The basic method is to simply stake the fake 10 or 15 yards upwind of your calling position, much as you would with a deer deke, but there are several ways to make it even more convincing.

HOLD IT Instead of staking an elk deke, Dick Dodds, the owner of Elkhorn Outfitters in Craig, Colorado, holds the fake in front of him, turning it to impart movement. He puts his hunter about 40 yards upwind and to the side for a broadside shot at any incoming bull.

HEAD GAMES Heads Up Decoys makes a highly portably and realistic silhouette of nothing but a cow elk's head, which you can attach to a tree, work with one hand, or fix to your bow via a special attachment. Just be careful, as a rut-crazy bull can get too close in a hurry.

DOUBLE UP One of Dodds' favorite tricks puts a twist on the typical two-man setup. "More than ever, bulls don't approach from upwind, but try to circle downwind instead," he says. His solution is for both hunters to have decoys, calls, and bows. "You set up as usual, with a primary shooter out front. But now, if a bull circles and comes in angling from behind, the two hunters can switch roles. The primary shooter becomes the caller and decoy man, getting the bull's attention so his buddy can take the shot before the bull gets directly downwind."

202 CROSS THE STREET TO BUGLE

Got a herded-up bull that answers your calls but won't come in? You can't really blame him, says Colorado outfitter Dick Dodds. "Think of it this way," he explains. "If you're walking with your girlfriend down one side of the street and some guy is cat-calling at her from the other side, you'll probably just keep walking. But if that guy crosses the street . . . well, now you need to do something about it."

Dodds charges in. "I try to get right on the edge of the herd, usually within 100 yards of the bull I'm after." Then he starts screaming. The trick, he says, is to sound as big as the herd bull (in order to present a legitimate challenge) but no bigger (so as to avoid running him off). "I listen closely and try to sound exactly like him," says Dodds. If satellite bulls come in first, Dodds either stands up or waves them off. "Then I bugle real hard to make the big bull think the youngsters got their butts kicked." Then he goes silent.

"That bull will assume you—a rival—are busy with one of his cows, and he'll come to the exact spot where he last heard you."

203 LEARN TO SQUEAK, GRUNT, AND GLUNK

Years of hunters blowing on bugle tubes and mewing on cow calls has reduced the effectiveness of those sounds, says guide Tom McReynolds. So he likes to get tight—often within 40 to 60 yards—to a bull and work him with a few low-volume calls. Here are his favorites.

SQUEAK "This is an abbreviated, softer version of the standard cow call, but the proximity and reduced volume add realism."

GRUNT "It doesn't take a bugle to piss a herd bull off. A short uh-uh-uh grunt—like a bull does before a full bugle—on a diaphragm will convince a herd bull that he's got competition."

GLUNK "A bull that's really hot and ready to breed makes a glunk. I mimic it by popping my hand over the end of a bugle tube. When a herd bull hears it, he'll leave his cows to come in."

204 BE A LOST CALF

As the rut progresses, a herd bull assembles a larger and larger harem, making him even tougher to call. Montana outfitter Chad Schearer says the sound of a lost calf can get the bull's attention in this situation. "Cows will come running for the calf, and the herd bull will follow them."

First, Schearer finds an active herd—usually on an afternoon jaunt toward food or water—and follows, staying about 500 yards upwind. "I tag along until I come to any feature that funnels the animals past a specific point—a single trail through downed timber or a difficult-to-access bowl," he says. Then he sets up to call the elk back to him. Using a double-reed diaphragm call, he makes a high-pitched cow call and applies increased tongue pressure to make the short, nasal *nyah* sounds of a lost, left behind, and scared calf. "I've had as many as 20 cows come back to my calls before the bull gets there. So you have to be extra careful."

The incoming cows will focus on the caller, giving the shooter—who's tucked in cover 60 to 70 yards between the caller and the herd—the chance at the bull. It's the best way to get past the eyes, ears, and noses of cows searching for that calf. The bull will be looking for his cows, so the shooter needs to have a diaphragm call in his mouth. "As soon as the bull hits an opening, squeak or chirp to stop him for the shot."

205 TRY THE CHAOS AMBUSH

Arizona guide Jay Scott has figured out a clever and effective technique for pulling a herd bull away from his cows—a simple three-step method that mixes passive and aggressive tactics.

WAIT FOR IT "I hang back and wait for a satellite bull to crash the party. That forces the big old bull to do some housecleaning—getting that smaller bull out of there and rounding up his cows again," he says.

MAKE THE MOVE Scott then gets into position. "When I see this chaos happening, I get the wind and head straight for the elk at a good clip, getting as close as I can. I don't worry much about noise because the elk are already making a racket."

CLOSE THE DEAL "Once I'm tight to the herd," he concludes, "it's just a matter of setting up and making soft cow calls or subtle bull grunts before I've got an excellent chance of a close-range shot at a bull."

206 GO LATE

HIS HIDEAWAY
Post-rut bulls are likely to be hiding out and recovering.

The breeding season may be the most intense time to be in the elk woods, but for really big bulls, Colorado guide Mike Miller loves to hunt the immediate post-rut. After a grueling month or more of gathering a harem, chasing off rivals, and avoiding hunters, a trophy bull is so tired and beat up, Miller says, he often wants nothing to do with the rest of the herd or with human pressure. So he goes into hiding. And Miller knows just where to look for him. "In the week or so after the rut, and before they start gathering in winter herds, I find big bulls laid up by themselves in remote areas," he says. "They definitely don't want to hear a bugle or a cow call."

There are, however, two things they still need:

"I look for food, and I look for water. Find one or the other and a bull is probably close, but if I find those two things right next to each other, that's money. I know a big boy will come to loaf there awhile." Miller has a few go-to places—wet meadows and wallows just off field edges—that he hunts post-rut every year, but he and his hunters stay on the move to find other hidey holes. Miller glasses a lot of country, hoping to catch a bull on his feet. When he finally does, he knows the hunt is all but over. "Those bulls are so worn out, they'll stay right in that area and be very predictable. They're almost easy to hunt." Just as with the pre-rut, pattern the bull's feeding and watering habits, and then set up an ambush along his approach route.

207 CALL QUIETLY

Because by the late season most bulls have felt hunting pressure, a lot of hunters completely avoid calling then. But Jay Scott says it can work like a charm as long as you're not too aggressive. "Bugling isn't very effective after the rut, but elk herds are constantly communicating with each other using quiet nasally sounds."

After a short period immediately following the rut, elk become especially gregarious again. Mimic this herd talk by making soft chirps, fluctuating the pitch and tone to sound like more than one elk. Having multiple callers is especially deadly. Set them up 50 to 75 yards behind the shooter and try to pull the bull toward this new "herd."

208 FIND A MIGRATION

I've bowhunted many North American deer species, but none I consider as picturesque as the caribou. A large bull's sweeping antlers and white mane are striking, and caribou country—be it the tundra of the Northwest Territories, the mountains of Alaska, or the taiga of Quebec—is a fitting backdrop.

Five caribou subspecies live in North America, and while do-it-yourself opportunities exist, a guided hunt is probably best for your first adventure. Most caribou populations are slightly down from the booms hunters enjoyed in the 1990s, and besides, most caribou are migratory. Keeping track of where herds are moving is a constant challenge. A well-established outfitter can almost always get you on animals faster than you can do by yourself.

That said, most outfitters are content to get you on animals and then leave the hunting up to you—a perfect system in my book. When I hunted the Northwest Territories, our guide would motor us out to one of several lakes near camp and help us find caribou. Once we spotted a herd, the final approach and shot was up to us; the guide would swing back

into action after that to dress, skin, cape, and quarter the bull.

At first, the relatively treeless tundra seemed a pretty daunting place to get within bow range of a bull, and the fact that I was the only archer in a camp of 12 hunters didn't fuel my confidence. But bowhunting is all about challenge, so I gritted my teeth and plunged in. After a couple of blown stalks and bungled opportunities, I managed to punch one of two bull tags. I'd have filled the other, too, but I air-balled a gimme shot on the last day. And that archery intimidation deal? It disappeared quickly; the constant presence of so many animals, and the many wrinkles in the terrain that allowed for stalking, made my "handicap" evaporate by the end of the first day.

209 GET MOVING

There are two main tactics I've used to bowhunt caribou on the tundra. Not surprisingly, both of them involve spotting the animals first.

When groups of caribou were traveling, I used a "mobile ambush" approach. Once I located a herd, I spent time glassing them from a distance. I would try to project their path and pick out some sort of terrain funnel that they would be passing through. If I could beat them to that funnel, I could get a bow shot. The "mobile" part of the ambush occurred when the caribou veered, or I simply mistook their path. Then, my original hide would be in the wrong spot ... and so I was on the move again.

By watching cows or smaller bulls—which frequently lead the mature animals as they travel—I could cut down the learning curve on the right setup. I studied the herd leaders through a binocular, looking for a rock outcropping, ridge saddle, or entry into a waterway preferred by the cows, and then I hightailed it to arrive ahead of the bulls, because migrating caribou move a lot faster than they appear to. Even an apparently dawdling bull can walk faster than you can hope to match on rugged tundra.

I was also able to pull off several stalks on animals that were feeding, bedded, or loafing. At first glance, the tundra may seem as featureless as the sea to the uninitiated, but it's actually full of wrinkles: rocks, ditches, ridges, creek beds, and brushy lakeshore that can all make perfect cover for slipping up on stationary animals.

The bull I killed was one we spotted from the boat, and as the big animal fed on some shoreline vegetation, the guide dropped me off 400 yards away on a rocky beach. By using rocks and brush as cover, I was able to slip within 30 yards and make the shot.

CARIBOU CAMP

■ Scott Bestul on

Of the dozen men in our camp, most brought both a bow and a rifle. "I'm going to kill a bull with a rifle first," a Michigan hunter announced the first morning. "Then I'll switch to the bow." All heads nodded in agreement. But of the 23 bulls taken that week, mine was the only bow kill. It was a simple lesson in human nature; if the temptation for an easier path exists, almost everyone will take it. So if you're serious about killing a caribou with a bow, don't even pack a gun.

210 GET 'BOUED UP

Gear for a caribou hunt is straightforward, with a few important details. Bulls are actually not as big and tough as they appear; your whitetail setup will work just fine. Clothing, however, can require some forethought. Most caribou hunts are held in August and September, so warm weather is the norm. That said, storm fronts and cold weather blow in quickly in this country, so layered clothing is a must. (I prefer synthetics, such as polar fleece, that can dry quickly.)

Good boots are critical as well; your outfitter should advise you on the proper footwear for the region. I'm never without a day pack that can hold extra layers, a spotting scope, and plenty of snacks and water. Caribou hunting can be physically demanding, and the days are very long. I simply hunt harder and longer if I stay hydrated and fueled with high-carb snacks.

Finally, a good camera should be part of every caribou hunter's required gear. Getting to the remote places where caribou live requires more effort and money than most of us can invest every year. You'll want reminders of that amazing hunt you took, and those photos will certainly inspire a return trip to hunt the prettiest deer species of all.

211 FIND YOUR MISSING MOOSE

I marveled at the profile of the first moose I ever saw; even that junior-sized bull resembled a boat house on the lakeshore. But when I paddled in to hunt him a month later, it was as if the country had swallowed every moose in existence. Friends from Alaska and Canada report the same bewilderment. It seems impossible for such a leviathan to disappear, but moose can evaporate into the huge, rough, country they call home. Unless you are insufferably lucky, it will take days of scouting, hiking, paddling and glassing to get one bull into bow range. Which is exactly as it should be.

212 RULE THE MOOSE

This fall, you're finally going to fulfill a lifelong dream. You're going to call a bull moose into bow range and take it down with a well-placed arrow. You may never get this chance again. To help make sure you don't blow it, expert moose hunter Peter Brown, CEO of Extreme Dimensions Wildlife Calls, offers the following rules of thumb.

MAKE SOME NOISE Moose make a big racket as they move about. Raking brush, cracking branches, and splashing water can make your other calls sound more realistic.

BE THE COW An estrous-cow call—a long, nasally bellow—should be your go-to vocalization. If you're near a pond or lakeshore, try using a water bottle or other container to make the sound of a cow urinating in the water.

GO ELECTRONIC Where legal, during the rut, try an electronic rendition of two bulls battling for breeding rights. You can lure in a bull that's already with cows using a digital recording by a digital recording of two moose mating.

BE PATIENT A bull may take 45 minutes to an hour to respond to your calling.

BREAK THAT RULE A bull with an estrous cow won't come far in response to calls. So go after him. Rake brush with a stick and grunt. Moose have poor eyesight; as long as you stay downwind, he might let you get close enough for a shot.

DON'T RUSH YOUR SHOT When the time comes, take a minute to calm down. You usually have plenty of time, so take a deep breath, collect yourself, and then make the shot count.

MOOSE MOXIE

Scott Bestul on Moose hunters need special gear to make a short blood trail. Ramp up your draw weight. Opt for a heavy arrow, and consider a heavier broadhead while you're at it. Use a cut-on-contact fixed-blade style, and be sure those blades are sharp. When a bull comes barreling in to a call, be patient. Those vitals are big, but they're protected by thick hide and big bones. Broadside is the only shot.

213 FIND A BLACK BEAR

Getting on big boars doesn't require a guide or a high-dollar outfitter. Start by researching state game and fish websites for potential hotspots. Then hit social networks, archery forums, and hunting chat rooms to talk with other archers; don't be afraid to check Facebook for intel. Ask about units and past hunts. If you're able, get on the ground and scout the old-fashioned way, too. When the season finally rolls around, follow this three-pronged plan:

HUNT OVER BAIT If it's legal in your area, set up a bait pile. Stop at a grocery store or donut shop on your way in. Most stores will gladly donate a pile of stale leftover pastries. Dig a small hole deep in the timber. Make a teepee out of logs to cover up those crusty Boston creams. Note the prevailing wind direction and set up your stand accordingly. Give the pile a day or so to molder.

SPOT AND STALK While you're waiting for the bait to settle, head for the high country. Gain a good vantage point and put your glass to work. Focus on meadows, logged slopes, and rotted-out timber fields where bears can root for grubs. If you spot a bear, don't rush in. Wait for him to bed down, and then get the wind right and ease in after him.

FIND WATER If water's scarce, a water-hole ambush can work well. Use a topographical map to locate water sources and take time to investigate each one. If you find fresh tracks and scat, set up a blind and nestle in. Brushing in the blind is always good practice, but if it isn't an option, don't fret. Bears typically don't spook at a new pop-up in their area. Sit the water mornings and midday; hit the bait in the evenings.

214 COMPARE BEARS

If your goal is to arrow a Pope and Young black bear, you'd better learn to distinguish a mature boar from a mature sow in the wild. Of the nearly 8,000 current entries in the club's records program, only 85 are females. That's barely 1 percent. Because the gender of black bears is notoriously difficult to judge in the field, you can't rely on any one feature. So here are 10 to consider closely before shooting.

1. HEAD The large, pumpkin-shaped head of a big boar sometimes has a crease running down between the ears, from the forehead to the back of the head, as well as plenty of scars on the face and ears. Sows' heads are smaller and rarely have a head crease.

2. EARS If these seem to be situated on the side of the bear's head and appear small, shoot! Trophy bears typically show a 7-plus-inch span between the ears. Sows and smaller boars have large ears that sit on top of the animal's head.

3. NOSE A mature boar has a short, massive snout; a sow's or young boar's is long and narrow.

4. HEIGHT A bear that stands 3 feet high when on all fours is a contender for the record book. If you are hunting over bait, a standing 55-gallon drum makes a handy guide: If the bear's back is near the top of the barrel, go ahead and shoot. If it's only halfway up, pass him up.

5. BODY SHAPE Adult males have long, blocky bodies and appear to have no neck. Think NFL lineman. Adult females are only a little longer than they are tall when on all fours. Their body contours appear softer and rounder.

6. HINDQUARTERS A boar's rump is wide and blocky; a sow's is comparatively narrow and more rounded.

7. BELLY A mature boar's stomach is massive and often appears to be dragging on the ground. Not so with females.

8. FOREQUARTERS A boar's front legs and shoulders are well muscled and squared off and look very powerful. A sow's appear more narrow and rounded. A dominant boar often walks pigeon-toed, with an air of authority.

9. FEET The front pad of a book boar (measured horizontally just beneath the toes) will go at least 5 inches—considerably larger than that of a sow. If the front feet look small, don't shoot.

10. SEX ORGANS Boars have a penile sheath, just like a dog's. Their testicles are clearly visible in spring but shrivel up somewhat in fall. Females have a pointed patch of fur extending from the vulva below the tail. It often shines after urination. If you think you can identify the sex organs of a big boar, and you can confirm your guess with any one or two of the features above, go ahead and take your P&Y bruin.

215 GET TERRITORIAL WITH A DECOY

Trophy boars are smarter than your average bear. But even the savviest old bruin has a few weaknesses that you can exploit with decoys. For example, you can take advantage of his territoriality. Big boars are solitary animals and will claim a food source as their own, commonly defecating along entrance trails to warn other bears away. Stake a small bear decoy near the food source, with its head down and its backside facing the direction from which you expect a boar to approach. Attach a few strips of black cloth to the decoy's ears and tail for added realism. Use a plastic bag to collect some bear scat from another area—preferably from a boar—and transplant it to the entrance trails.

Any wise old boar that might otherwise camp just off the food until nightfall is almost sure to investigate when he sees your "intruder." A boar may visit a food site daily or stop by every second or third day while patrolling his home turf. Be patient, and don't let your guard down.

216 OFFER AN EASY MEAL

Black bears are fond of fresh meat and will drop their guard to capture an animal in distress. A small, furry decoy, like those used for foxes and coyotes, wiggling about in plain sight is sure to draw attention. With a little luck, the bruin will move in quickly to finish off what he thinks is hapless prey. If he hangs up, add a few squeals from a dying-rabbit call to entice him.

If whitetails are prevalent in your area, a fawn decoy can be too much for a hungry black bear to ignore. Try a few fawn contact bleats; if that fails, use a fawn-in-distress call. Nock an arrow and get ready. The bear will come in fast, so prepare to shoot pronto.

217 FIND A FEMALE

Black bears rut in late spring and early summer and will visit bait sites, looking for a sow in heat. If baiting is legal in your area, set a small decoy with its head in the bait barrel, and hang a few scent canisters soaked with sow-in-heat urine a few feet off the ground. Odor control is critical: During setup, wear rubber gloves and spray the decoy liberally with a good scent remover. The boar will approach warily. Don't rush the shot. As he investigates, you'll have plenty of time to draw.

218 AMBUSH A BEAR IN THE CORN

Looking to arrow a bruin snacking in a grain field? Follow these instructions and you'll tag your corn-fed bear in no time.

FIND THE BEAR ZONE Talk with your local biologist or warden to learn where bears are most plentiful. Then locate the remotest parts of those areas, with few roads, lots of unbroken timber, and some cornfields.

SCOUT FIELD EDGES Farmers will probably be happy to tip you off to the bear-damaged spots in their corn. If not, search the perimeters of cornfields that edge up to remote, hilly woodlands.

FIND THE SIGN When bears feed on corn, they can tear up, knock down, and roll over swaths of 150 square feet or more. It's easy to recognize, but they may walk in a few rows before they create such chaos. When you find a few trampled stalks on the edge, move in closer.

ANALYZE THE PRINTS You don't want to set up on a sow and her cub. Make sure the paw prints are of one size only. The toe span should be at least 4½ inches; this tells you it's a big bear, likely a boar.

CHECK FOR SCAT A pile the size of a Big Mac is from a baby. A heap nearly the size of a loaf of bread is from the bear you want.

FIND THE ENTRY TRAIL Undisturbed bears tend to follow the same route day after day. They may walk through open timber along part of the trail, but they like having cover as they approach the corn. Look for a matted-down entry trail through shrubs, briars, and brush on the field's edge.

MEASURE CLAW MARKS Bears often claw trees before they enter a field. Look for raked bark 6 to 7½ feet high to confirm you're onto a shooter.

BACKTRACK AND SET UP Follow the bear's trail back until you locate a good downwind stand tree or blowdown to camouflage a blind. Your bruin may not show on your first sit, but a three- to four-day effort should result in a plush rug and some bear steaks.

219 BAIT A BEAR

Bears love donuts, but you don't need to raid a Dunkin' dumpster for bait. We asked three of North America's top bear outfitters to reveal their single favorite bait ingredient, to give bears a bow-range food coma.

MAKE LICORICE George McQuiston of Wild Idaho Outfitters buys liquid anise extract online by the gallon and dilutes it by 70 percent with clean vegetable oil. "I put it in a spray bottle and spritz it while walking through the woods and all around the bait site," he says. "The whole spot will be crawling with bears exclusively from that black licorice smell."

POP SOME CORN Looking for an inexpensive bulk filler, Trevor Kunz of Wyoming's 5K Outfitters discovered popcorn. "It's cheaper than dog food or grain," says Kunz, who runs 35 bait sites over a 40-mile area in the rugged Bridger-Teton National Forest. Popcorn won't fill a bear's stomach for long, so he'll return to the bait site more often.

SUGARCOAT IT Kevin Barber of Hunt N It Outfitters in New Brunswick tops things off with straight sugar. "I can turn any bait into bear cocaine by adding copious amounts of white sugar," says Barber. At less than 50 cents per pound, pure cane sugar can be bought by the pallet at most warehouse stores. "Bears have a real sweet tooth," Barber says. "So many people lean on donuts and cake, but you can save money and make a more concentrated bait by using the main raw ingredient."

220 GET A BEAR WITH YOUR BUCK

Deer hunters have always taken their share of black bears just a matter of happenstance. But with bruin populations growing within or expanding further into whitetail habitat almost everywhere these days, your chances of arrowing a black bear from your deer stand are better than ever. Both species favor some of the same foods and travel through many of the same natural funnels, so when you hear a snap and turn your head, you may see either trophy walking into bow range. Follow these steps to set up a stand for both bucks and bears.

FIND FOODS Scout for food sources that both species favor, including standing cornfields, beech ridges, abandoned apple orchards, grown-over clear-cuts, oak hollows, grape vineyards, and oatfields. Deer sign should be easy to find, but look closer to locate bear spoor, including claw marks on trees, beds, tracks, coils of dung, and fur caught on the trunks of rough-barked trees and on barbwire fencing. Set up trail cameras to verify that both deer and bears are hitting the same groceries and to learn where their travel routes overlap, or are at least within bow range of each other. In lieu of trail cams, you can scrape or rake away forest duff where sign suggests that deer and bears routinely pass, and then look later for tracks in the fresh earth.

PICK A LANE These two species may use different routes from bed to feed, but if there is a funnel or pinch point just off the food, both will use the same narrow travel lane. That's where you want to set up your treestand. Ravines leading downhill from high bedding sites toward known feeding areas are good ambush sites for both species. So are fingers of brush that extend into cornfields, creek crossings, wooded ridgelines that rise out of swamps, hedgerows that separate grainfields, and strips of uncut timber crisscrossing clear-cuts. Set up, wait for a good wind, and be prepared for buck or bruin; you may even tag both before the season is out.

221 BLINDSIDE A PRONGHORN

Sitting over a waterhole while the sun turns your popup blind into an oven is no fun, but it's undoubtedly the most effective way to arrow a pronghorn buck. Ron Gehrke, Flambeau pro-staffer and a veteran of many DIY hunts for Wyoming antelope on public land, outlines his favorite setup.

SCOUT THE WATER In a dry year, even a puddle will attract thirsty goats. But when an area has several ponds, antelope invariably have a couple favorites. Gehrke spends the first day of the hunt glassing for watering goats and noting at what times they visit certain ponds. "I've seen herds hit a waterhole like clockwork at a certain time every day, but they're not always predictable," he says. "You have to be ready to sit as long as it takes."

HUNT COVER Gehrke tries to avoid ponds on featureless prairie. "It can take pronghorns a few days to get used to a blind sitting in the open," he says. "So if you've the time to stick one out and wait to hunt it, fine. But most of my trips are short; I need to set up and kill one quickly. I look for a waterhole with some type of cover; a willow tree, a rock ledge or ditch, even a big patch of sagebrush, that I can tuck the blind against for cover and eliminate the silhouette. I also like to tie vegetation up against the blind. One of the best setups I have is a willow tree that grows 30 yards from the waterhole. I stick the blind right up against the trunk, and the drooping limbs just hang down and conceal the blind."

STAKE A DEKE Gehrke likes to place a decoy within easy bow range of the blind to complete the setup. "It's usually the rut when I'm out there, and the bucks are very aggressive when they see competition, especially if they're traveling with does," he says. "I use a buck decoy with smallish antlers so a mature buck will want to run him off. But even if the rut's not rocking, the decoy seems to relax the animals, and they're not as hesitant to approach the water."

WAIT FOR IT Even a parched, thirsty pronghorn is a bundle of nerves at a waterhole, so be patient and wait for a perfect shot. "They'll usually do a couple head-bob fake-drinks when they first approach the water. I hold off until I see the buck stick his nose in the water and his neck muscles working to drink. Then I figure I have 20 to 30 seconds to draw, aim, and take the shot."

PASS THE DAY You can't sugar-coat it; hunting from a blind can mean a hot, boring wait. "You have to bring water and snacks," Gehrke says. "Some guys bring a book. Wear light, breathable clothing, but I pack some layers, too, in case a front blows through and cools things down. Wear a facemask or camo paint, and gloves. Antelope have amazing vision; you don't want to blow hours of waiting because a buck saw your face at the last second."

222 PRACTICE FOR PRONGHORN

Picture this; rocks and thorns are probing your knees, you're surrounded by sage, sweating like a boxer, and drawing on an animal that can see fleas mate at 40 yards. You've got to train for that moment. Practice from your knees while you're crammed into brush, with the sun beating on you. Draw, aim and shoot within a couple of seconds . . . or hold your draw for as long as you can stand it. And learn to judge distance in open terrain. Rangefinders are great, but when your buck is nervous or simply surprises you, trying to range him will waste time and add movement you simply can't afford.

223 GO GET YOUR GOAT

Hunting hell, if you ask me, is sitting in a ground blind for 12 summer hours, staring at a stagnant stock pond on a barren prairie, waiting for a pronghorn buck. Fortunately, it's not your only option. Colorado guide Miles Fedinec leaves the ground blind at home and takes the hunt to the goats. It's not quite as effective, but it's a ton more fun.

PATTERN PROPERLY You can pattern and kill a pronghorn just as you would a whitetail. "Even in open country, an antelope's home range isn't huge," Fedinec says. "They're normally in small herds this time of year—a buck and several does—and may cruise no more than a square mile. Sit on a hillside and watch them for three days. If you see them feeding on the same grassy flat at 10 every morning, you know that's a good place to get close."

WORK WITH THE RUT When the rut is on, a bowhunter can lure his goat into range. "If bucks are really dogging does, they're distracted," he says. "A decoy can work wonders. Get within 150 yards and challenge the boss with a young buck decoy. They may run right into it!"

DON'T BLOW IT The antelope will bust you most of the time. Far too many hunters either give up altogether or continue dogging the same animal until he moves into the next county, Fedinec says. "A pronghorn is like a cottontail rabbit in some ways. When spooked, he'll run—sometimes a long way. But eventually, after he settles down, he'll begin circling back. When I blow a stalk, rather than chase them, I'll often find a good hiding spot and stay put. I can't tell you how many times I've had the same buck return a couple of hours later."

224 SHOOT LONG

Chances are the ninja-in-camo image you have of yourself is a little overblown. In reality, sneaking within 30 yards of a pronghorn and drawing your bow unseen is nearly impossible. Stretch your effective range by getting a big, round target, so you won't lose arrows. Set it up 10 yards beyond your effective range. In a few weeks, your groups should tighten to where you can hit pronghorns or whitetail. Next, move your large target another 10 yards back and repeat. I routinely practice at 80 yards; 50 is my maximum distance on any animal.

225 HIDE AND DEKE

A rutting buck antelope is ready to go to blows the moment that he sees another buck so much as look at one of the females in his harem. Luckily, that can work in a bowhunter's favor. Play into his jealousy by popping up a pronghorn decoy nearby, and the buck you're after might close the distance from 300 yards to 30 faster than you can imagine. So when he starts charging, you had better have an arrow nocked.

FIND A SPOT First, locate a secure position. Look for terrain with some contours—the down-sloping side of a hill or a coulee—that allow you to get close without being seen. An antelope buck responds to decoys best if you can get within 200 to 250 yards. Any farther and he'll likely gather up his does and run. Get into the zone by crawling as close as possible. From this point on, things happen very quickly, so be ready to react.

FLASH THE FAKE While you're still hidden, have an arrow nocked and range a few close clumps of brush or yucca plants so you have some reference points. Take one last deep breath and pop the decoy into position. Keep the lower third hidden from the buck's view over the crest of the hill or in knee-high grass. You want to anger the buck, not intimidate him.

DRAW AND SHOOT You'll know instantly if he'll choose fight or flight. If it's the former, pick up your bow and clip in your release. As the buck gets close, come to your knees and draw in one smooth motion. When he stops—and he probably will—you have only a second or two to estimate the distance, settle the appropriate pin behind his shoulder, and then squeeze the trigger.

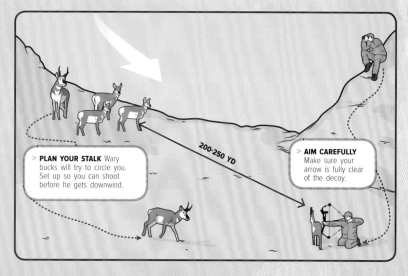

> **PLAN YOUR STALK** Wary bucks will try to circle you. Set up so you can shoot before he gets downwind.

200-250 YD

> **AIM CAREFULLY** Make sure your arrow is fully clear of the decoy.

226 HUNT OUTSIDE THE BOX

When three buddies and I went on a recent Wyoming hunt, we left the pop-up blinds at home and returned to Minnesota five days later with coolers full of meat and three caped-out heads. Here's how we pulled off a memorable DIY spot-and-stalk antelope hunt while on public land.

MAKE A MILK RUN We began by studying a map from the Bureau of Land Management that matched our hunting unit, circling all the tracts that were adjacent or close to roads. Each morning, the four of us would split into two vehicles, and then drive past all those BLM areas, glassing for antelope. There was enough federal land to keep us busy for most of a day.

PICK A TARGET Finding goats was rarely a problem. Picking a buck that was vulnerable to a stalk was tougher. Trying to sneak up on herds of 20 or more animals grazing on pool-table mesas is a fool's game, so we ignored those and drove on. The ideal candidate was a lone buck feeding or bedded near cover or rolling terrain that allowed for a high-odds approach.

PLAN THE ROUTE After carefully glassing the terrain and cover, and giving close consideration to wind direction and other antelope that might spook, we planned a route to the buck. Then one of us began stalking while the other hung back in the vehicle, standing ready to offer hand or flag signals to help keep the stalker on course.

GET CLOSE Sneaking that last 50 to 100 yards into bow range was usually the make-or-break move. Wearing kneepads and leather gloves helped us to crawl close without making too much noise, or

becoming a pincushion thanks to all the sharp foliage. On some stalks, we just ran out of cover. Then it was time to pop up a silhouette decoy and hope the goat would close the gap. I tagged a Pope and Young pronghorn that was feeding up a narrow canyon; I belly-crawled to the edge, rose to my knees, and shot him at 25 steps.

HAVE A BACKUP PLAN If the sneak approach won't work, try an ambush. We shot two bucks at the end of our trip by watching the feeding herd, noting the direction in which they moved, then burying into some boulders downrange. My friend Ron got to kill a great antelope by kneeling down between the rocks and waiting it out.

227 GET A BIRD WITH A BOW

Not long ago, sticking a gobbler was a near-impossible feat. But pop-up ground blinds and ultrarealistic decoys have made getting your bow bird far more attainable. It isn't easy, but what in turkey hunting is? You can do this. Here's how.

WAIT HIM OUT I'll admit that I'm not wild about "deer hunting" for turkeys, but manning a pop-up blind in a green field is simply the best way to kill one with a bow. Toms will walk right up to the thing; you don't have to brush it in or give the birds time to get used to it. Ideally, you'll have patterned turkeys in a particular field ahead of time. If not, any high-traffic field is a good bet. Just get set up before they arrive.

USE A GOOD DECOY You need all the realism you can get to capture a turkey's attention long enough for a bow shot. If you're setting up on a dominant bird, stake a full-strut gobbler decoy with a real turkey fan facing you at 15 yards. A real tom will usually confront a strutter face-to-face, giving you a close shot on a bird that's looking away. If you're not sure where your target bird sits in the pecking order, swap the gobbler decoy for a jake and add a fake hen.

TAKE THE RIGHT SHOT Your deer-hunting bow will work fine, but consider a wide-cutting mechanical broadhead if you usually shoot fixed blades. A turkey's vitals are small, and the bigger the cut, the better the odds. Placing the arrow at the top of the bird's thigh will break bones, hit vital organs, and drop him within sight.

228 CAPE A TURKEY

A gobbler mount isn't cheap. Here's an inexpensive way to create a sharp-looking trophy that'll look good for years.

STEP 1 Make a cut across the back of the neck, where the feathers meet the head. Peel the skin back several inches along the neck and back, working it free with the knife.

STEP 2 On each side of the bird, you'll notice a seam in the feathers just above the wing joints. Cut along those seams.

STEP 3 Skin to the base of the tail, and then cut around it as you would to remove the fan. Avoid cutting through the back skin. Scrape excess flesh off the cape and tail, and rub with salt.

229 GET YOUR BONUS BIRD

You can arrow a fall turkey from your deer stand—but it's no gimme shot. Here's how to do it.

GO CAMO A deer may let you get away with a shiny face or hands, but a turkey seldom will. Wear camo gloves and take a few minutes to paint your face, or grab a mask when you head to your stand.

SIT TIGHT You might stand up when you spot a deer out of range, but that's a game-ender with a flock of turkeys. Don't move a muscle when you see white heads bobbing through the timber, and plan to take your shot sitting.

DRAW STRAIGHT BACK As the birds approach, keep your bow between your knees, shifting them slowly to point the bow toward the incoming flock, and get the release on the string. Draw straight back from your knees, so you don't skyline the bow, and then shoot with the bow in front of you, rather than to one side. It's awkward; practice in the off-season.

TAKE THE MIDDLE If you draw on the first turkey in the flock and spook it, it'll run away and take the others with it. If you spook the last bird, all your other shot opportunities have gone past. Your best bet is to draw on one of the middle birds. Wait until it passes behind a tree or lowers its head to feed. Some of the turkeys will probably see you and start putting, but not all of them will spook at once. Keep your composure and get the bow back. You have nothing to lose at this point. If the bird you're drawing on runs, shift to one that's standing still. Be prepared to shoot fast.

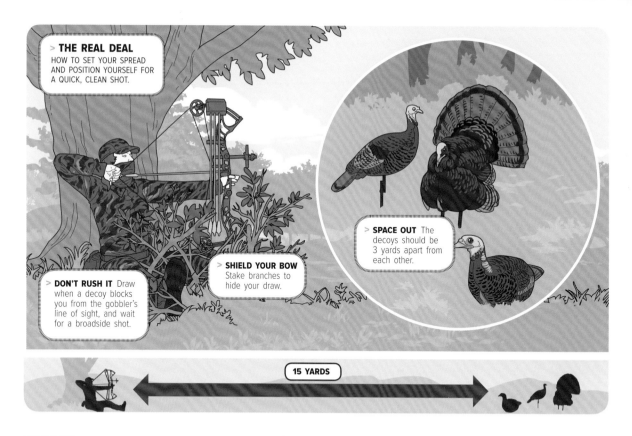

> THE REAL DEAL HOW TO SET YOUR SPREAD AND POSITION YOURSELF FOR A QUICK, CLEAN SHOT.

> SPACE OUT The decoys should be 3 yards apart from each other.

> SHIELD YOUR BOW Stake branches to hide your draw.

> DON'T RUSH IT Draw when a decoy blocks you from the gobbler's line of sight, and wait for a broadside shot.

15 YARDS

230 MAKE A TRIPLE PLAY

Waiting in a pop-up blind is a fine way to kill a gobbler with a bow. It's also really boring. To get the most out of the hunt, you need a strategy. Ask Cally Morris, a world-champion turkey taxidermist, who has killed more than 50 gobblers with a bow—and no blind. His secret? A three-bird spread of realistic decoys. Here's his plan.

SPREAD THE DECOYS With no blind you can go where the turkeys want to be. That might be the edge of the hayfield where you saw a gobbler strutting, or 100 yards from a bird hammering in the timber. While this tactic gives you the freedom to run and gun, you will be packing some decoys. Morris uses three: a full-strut tom, a breeder hen, and an upright hen. He sets the strutter and breeder quartering slightly away from you at 15 to 17 yards. The upright hen is off to the side of them, no farther than 20 yards. The key is to leave enough space—about 3 yards—between each decoy for the gobbler to strut. "They'll rarely commit to the spread otherwise."

GET SET UP Find a large tree and clear yourself a good spot free of leaves and branches. Right-handed shooters should sit with their left shoulder and hip resting against the trunk, feet shoulder width apart, and their left boot pointed right at the strutter decoy. Stake a few leafed-out limbs in front of you, on your left side, in order to mask your draw. Lay a camo bandanna on the ground between your knees so you can rest your bow's bottom cam on it and keep an arrow pointed at the spread. This is all in the service of minimizing motion. Using a 32-inch or shorter bow helps. You'll need to either have a buddy call for you or be skilled enough with a mouth call to bring a gobbler close.

TAKE THE SHOT Once the tom is in range, shut up and let the decoys work. You might watch him for several minutes before getting your chance to draw. "Seventy-five percent of your shots will happen when the gobbler circles the strutter to size it up and either turns his fan to you or gets his head behind the decoy's fan," Morris says. "Some toms will go straight for the hens and try to breed them. That's fine, too. If he's getting it on with the decoy, he's not watching you draw."

231 READ THE HEN MENU

A hen's primary instinct in spring is to gorge on protein-rich foods, which help her produce eggs. That mostly means bugs. "Hens eat insects almost exclusively when they're available in early spring," says Scott Vance, an avid hunter and assistant vice president for conservation with the National Wild Turkey Federation. "Bugs provide not only the protein hens require but high mineral content as well." Hens will scratch through leaf litter, dig under dead logs, and prowl sunny spring fields to catch them. "If you see cow pies flipped over in a pasture, you can be sure turkeys are using it," Vance adds. "They're searching for pill bugs."

Grasshoppers and crickets, commonly plucked from sunny fields, are universal favorites. Figure out which fields by glassing for feeding birds or simply walking through the vegetation to displace insects. Soft grubs and snails, typically pecked from overturned leaf litter, are also choice items. "Look for turkey scratchings

in open hardwoods, especially along creek bottoms," says Vance. "Those damp areas warm up a little earlier and are often the first place turkeys can find bugs." And pay attention to localized insect hatches. "I once killed a gobbler in Missouri that had 37 walking sticks in his crop," says Vance.

In the north, hunters may wake up to snow or freezing temperatures on opening morning. If it's too cold for your birds to find bugs, Vance recommends searching for anything green. "Hens are also looking for foods that are high in moisture content in spring," he says. "Most winter foods—hard mast, waste grain, and so on—are dry. If you find some overwintered clover, alfalfa, or chufa, you can bet that hens will show up there—and bring gobblers with them."

232 GO INTO A FALL FRENZY

For unbridled turkey hunting fun, fall is the dream season. Scatter a flock by running at them, then set up at the scatter site. Within minutes birds will be yelping, kee-keeing, and cutting as they regroup. This is no sly seduction; mimic the turkey sounds you hear, add volume and desperation, and birds will come running. It's a target-rich environment, with plenty of room for spookings, misses, and screwups. Come with a full quiver.

233 ORDER A SPRING SPECIAL

A hen's diet in the spring is important for a couple reasons. For her, finding the right food is crucial for nesting success. For you, finding the right food means knowing where she'll be. That's where you'll find all the gobblers, too.

	GRASSHOPPERS	CLOVER	GRUBS	CHUFA	ALFALFA	PILL BUGS
WHY	Grasshoppers offer a nice crunch with a medley of minerals. They're a big meal.	These protein-rich greens frequently come with a side of bugs.	Grubs offer lots of protein and a creamy texture.	The tubers' nutty flavor makes them worth digging up.	Alfalfa is subject to availability, as it's slow to green up in cool temps.	These tiny, tasty morsels are filled with protein.
WHERE	They tend to be found in and around vegetation.	Clover grows in almost any soil and light conditions.	Grubs can be found on a bed of damp leaf litter.	"Tiger nuts" grow close to the surface in mild climates.	Alfalfa grows worldwide in a variety of conditions.	Turn over a rock, log, or cow pie to find them.

234 GO BIG, GO MULEY

Americans like big things: big houses, big vehicles, big personalities—and big deer. So if you're mostly a whitetail hunter, the draw of the American West's iconic deer is simple: It's bigger, in every way. The average mule deer buck outweighs the average whitetail by about 50 pounds. The heaviest muley ever taken (522 pounds estimated live weight) tops the stoutest whitetail (511). And B&C's highest-scoring mule deer ($355^2/8$) easily outscores the top whitetail ($333^7/8$).

Then there's the muley's home turf—our tallest mountains, our broadest deserts, and the sweeping prairies under our biggest skies. Plus, when you spot this buck in his mostly open habitat, it's not the flick of an ear or the flash of an antler you happen to see. More often, it's the whole shebang. Right there, pretty as you please, larger than life.

If big deer in big country aren't enough to entice any bowhunter, there's also this: You don't even need a treestand.

235 LOOK DOWN THE LEE SIDE

When the wind whips cold over the open prairie, mule deer bucks love to hunker down below the heads of lee-side draws and canyons. Facing downhill, into the bottom of the cut, they can spot danger below, while the slope above and behind blocks the frigid wind. It's a good way to stay warm—but not a great way to stay alive.

All you have to do is break one of the iron rules of hunting and approach from upwind. Wherever a bunch of draws, cuts, or canyons—especially side canyons—cut into a hillside, grab your bow and walk along the top rim, peaking down at the heads to spot a muley buck bedded right below you. While the stiff breeze covers the sound of your footsteps, it also carries your scent right over the top of the deer. In other words, he can't bust you, even though he's technically downwind.

Now just relax and wait for your shot. He has no idea you're there.

236 TAG-TEAM A MULEY

Sneaking into bow range of a bedded mule deer buck is on just about every bowhunter's bucket list. It's far easier to pull off, however, if you've got a buddy along, says Montana guide Al Bousley. Here's his two-man plan.

SLEEP IN "I rarely go out before 9 a.m.," Bousley says. "I want the deer bedded. If you're out at dawn, you're just alerting deer that are on their feet."

GET GLASSING Drive back roads and two-tracks, or hike to good vantage points, and glass for bedded bucks. "Focus on structure and shade," Bousley says. "I find most bucks bedded in a shadow cast by a large rock, bush, or ledge."

CHOOSE YOUR QUARRY "You'll pass some deer before you find one bedded in a vulnerable spot," Bousley says. "You need to approach the buck from downwind and behind its field of vision. The stalker also has to be able to see the spotter, who'll guide him to the deer—the stalker usually won't see the deer until he's very close."

MAKE THE STALK After circling wide to get behind the buck, the stalker should glass back toward the spotter for directions. "I use a flag or rag tied to a pole for signaling because it's highly visible," Bousley says. "The signals are simple: A straight-up flag means the stalker walks directly toward the spotter. A sideways flag means he should correct left or right. A flag that's straight down means the buck is dead ahead and very, very close."

SNAP THE TRAP The final steps are critical. "Most of my hunters either remove their boots or slide on felt booties for the final yards," Bousley says. Hunters who prefer not to shoot a bedded deer should wait it out if possible. If not, Bousley suggests tossing a stone 20 to 30 yards past the buck, which will stand to investigate the sound. "As soon as you throw the rock, draw your bow and get ready to shoot," he says. "In my book, there isn't a more heart-stopping hunt out there."

237 AMBUSH A BUCK

Early last fall, I did some mule deer hunting in Colorado with my buddy Miles Fedinec, owner of FMF Outdoors. He'd been watching muleys by the dozens filter out of nearby cover—cedar draws, sage flats, and a thick river bottom—and into a massive, irrigated alfalfa field. It sounded like a familiar bed-to-feed pattern for hunting whitetails back east.

"Sure, it's not the romantic stalk you envision when you dream of killing your big muley," he told me. "But the fact is, if you can set up and catch that buck on the way to his food, that's your very best chance of killing him."

That evening, Miles pulled his truck to a stop next to a tall stack of hay bales to do some glassing. "There he is," he said after about 2 minutes. Sure enough, with about an hour left of daylight, the buck came out of the river bottom, crossed a dirt road, and strolled into the field.

We went back the next evening and set up a ground blind in the sage about 50 yards from that dirt road. My buck walked into the field with two hours of shooting light left and followed a grown doe and a velvet spike right to me. I had to bleat to stop him at 23 yards. It came together like a classic early-season whitetail hunt.

238 STALK SOLO

Shawn Monsen is a Utah mule deer freak who routinely sneaks within bow range of giant bucks. His muley stalks involve glassing from a distance, and then whittling 1,000 yards down to 50. Here's how to do it.

MAP THE ROUTE "I don't rush into a stalk once I locate a good deer. I map it out, making sure I have the terrain, cover, and route that will put me in range without being seen. Otherwise, I wait for another opportunity."

TAKE A PICTURE Monsen carries a digital camera to keep his bearings. "The landscape will look different as you move, so take several pictures before you begin your stalk, and then stop to reference the landmarks in the photos as you go."

STUDY THE BUCK "You may only be able to see parts of the deer— antler tines, an ear, maybe his back. But make sure you know which way he's facing. Always plan your final approach from behind."

LOSE THE SHOES "Once I'm within 125 yards, I take off my pack and my boots. I put on an extra pair of socks for padding and start to slide into range. You have to get to a comfortable shooting distance, but not so close that you risk making the buck nervous. Being a good shot at long range is a big help."

BIDE YOUR TIME "Once in range, be patient. Keep your bow ready and watch the buck through your binoculars. Draw when he gets restless and starts to stand up. This might take a while. The longest I've ever waited on a buck was nine hours—but I killed him."

239 BE BOLD

After hunting mule deer for the first time, many Eastern whitetail hunters arrived at this conclusion: Man, these big-eared deer are dumb.

That's not entirely accurate, of course. Allow a muley buck to get a whiff of you on a swirling thermal, for example, and he'll be gone just as fast as any Alabama whitetail. But a mule deer is, on average, far more tolerant of seeing you than is a whitetail. That is something a traveling bowhunter definitely needs to know.

When the buck you're stalking suddenly sees or hears you and stands up, it's no time to panic—and certainly no time to stay tucked in behind cover. "You can absolutely be more aggressive with mule deer than you can with whitetails," says Colorado guide Miles Fedinec. "That's a mistake many Eastern hunters make. When a buck stands up before they're ready, they try to hide when they should be drawing their bow. A mule deer will stand there for 5 to 10 seconds regardless of what you're doing, and if you have a good shot, there's no reason to wait."

240 PACK A PHONY

Decoying mule deer has become an increasingly popular tactic with bowhunters because it works—and it does so in a variety of ways. Here are three.

LEAVE IT Maybe you've patterned a buck along a funnel or pinch point, but in muley country these can be 100 yards wide. Staking a doe decoy 10 or 15 yards from your ambush can steer him close where he might otherwise pass out of range.

STALK AND STAKE If you spot a muley buck seeking or chasing does, grab a lightweight, silhouette doe decoy, use the terrain to get out in front of the buck, and stake the fake where he'll see it. Crouch behind and be ready to shoot when he swings over to check out the new "girl" on the block.

HIDE AND SNEAK A collapsible doe decoy can save a stalk on a bedded buck, by hiding you as you move through a spot with no cover, or by calming the buck that becomes vaguely alerted to your approach. The decoy can even hide you as you sneak straight into bow range. Heads Up Decoy, for example, makes a highly realistic mule deer doe head-and-neck deke that attaches to your bow, concealing you as you slip close and leaving your hands free to take the shot.

Mule deer bucks may not respond quite as aggressively to rattling as their white-tailed cousins—but they do respond. Cracking the horns, along with a timely doe bleat, can pull a rutting muley right to you.

First, get to a vantage point and glass for a good buck. Rutting muleys are rarely hard to spot, as they cover a lot of ground. Use the wind and cover to get within 200 yards, and then set up in cover with good shooting lanes.

In open country, where rutting bucks are generally found, use a sizeable set of rattling antlers and clash them violently until your target buck looks in your direction. If he starts heading your way, stop. If he only stares, keep up the ruckus. It often takes several sequences to get a wise brute to start closing, but once he does, drop the horns.

When the buck breaks the 100-yard barrier, his steady walk will often turn to a step-pause-step approach. Don't get nervous and take a distant shot. As long as he's still putting one foot in front of the other, you're good. If he starts looking back or milling side to side, hit him with a whitetail doe-bleat call. The sound of a hot female is often all it takes to bring him those last few yards.

242 GET YOUR MULEY IN A COULEE

The one place that holds big muley bucks more consistently than any other is the head of a coulee. The top of a drainage—be it large or small, and whether you call it a draw, cut, canyon, or coulee—makes a natural bed for a buck. What's more, this spot facilitates several tactics for getting within bow range of a deep-forked buck.

SUNRISE SURPRISE Glass from a distance at midday to find a shooter buck bedded near the top of a coulee, usually near a rock outcropping or a scraggly cedar tree. Before daylight the next morning, slip in from the top or the side and set up near available cover. Rising thermals will blow your scent safely uphill as the buck climbs toward you after daylight.

AFTERNOON AMBUSH Again, spend midday glassing to find a resting trophy. Then take a stand farther down the draw where he won't see or hear you setting up— preferably in an area where the ravine pinches down. Eventually, he'll move down the draw heading toward feed, as afternoon thermals push your scent safely downhill.

SNEAK AND PEEK You'll want to pick a coulee with good cover and slip slowly uphill toward its head, carefully checking side gullies and washouts as you go. Or, cut across a slope with several cuts or canyons, hopscotching from one coulee head to the next.

SPOT AND STALK This classic Western tactic works great for head-of-the-coulee bucks. Glass to spot a buck, and then approach from the side or above, as the buck will generally be looking for danger from below.

243 PLAY THE BAITING GAME

Pigs may be the bowhunter's perfect game. Their wariness and sense of smell put a premium on reading the wind. Their poor eyesight makes it easy to sneak in close and draw your bow. And they're delicious. With their diverse habitat and diet, you can hunt them virtually anywhere, anytime. Here's how to arrow a hog—day or night—from a stand or on the ground.

SET THE TABLE Pigs love corn and adapt quickly to timed feeders. Create your bait site in an area with fresh sign, such as rooting or wallows, in a spot that allows for a good ambush. Pigs like thickets; set your feeder along a thick edge, where they can step out to eat but quickly disappear into cover. Tripod feeders work, but pigs knock them over if they aren't anchored. Hanging feeders are better. If there's no tree limb, drive two 10-foot 6x6s into the ground and secure a third 6x6 across the top with lag bolts. Suspend your feeder with heavy eyebolts and wire.

STAY HIGH Pigs can't see well, so you can get close. I've shot them from a 15-foot ladder stand just 10 wide-open yards from the feeder. The challenge is beating their nose. Set your stand so that you're downwind of the feeder, ideally with a field at your back. Pigs are reluctant to circle into the open in daylight; if you have a field behind you, they'll often swing into range while checking the wind. Set a blind on the opposite side of the bait that you can slip into should the wind change during your sit. Avoid pig trails leading to the feeder: If pigs cross your path within an hour of your visit, the jig is up.

BE A NIGHT STALKER Pressured hogs will quickly go nocturnal—but that's O.K. Hunting at night is legal in primo pig states such as Florida and Texas. You can hunt over one bait site all night, but if you have several, it's more fun (and more effective) to still-hunt from feeder to feeder. Roaming groups, called *sounders*, will clean up the corn from one feeder and move on to the next. Sounders grunt, squeal, and fight as they travel, so they're pretty easy to locate. Choose a night with a bright moon, when you can spot silhouettes and slip along with the wind in your face, listening as much as looking.

244 RIG FOR PIGS

If you bowhunt pigs at night, you need specialized gear. Here are some things to consider.

DRAW HEAVY Shots at pigs are often close and fast. A bow that's handy and smooth is right at home. My hog bow has a 60-pound draw weight, and I wouldn't feel comfortable with anything under 50 pounds.

GET A REST For fast use at close range, in the dark, a capture rest such as a Whisker Biscuit is foolproof.

SIGHT IN Swap your pins for an electronic dot scope dialed in at 15 to 20 yards, best for fast shooting in low light.

LIGHT 'EM UP A stabilizer-mounted light with a pressure switch allows you to aim in the dark. I've also gotten by with taping a powerful, compact flashlight to my stabilizer.

BREAK BONE A pig's vitals are located between his shoulder blades. You want to use a fixed-blade broadhead that'll break bone if needed.

245 QUARTER THAT HOG

A pig isn't hard to kill with a well-placed arrow, but recovering one after a marginal hit is no fun—and it's all too common, since most bowhunters are used to shooting at deer. Aiming just behind a broadside boar's shoulder, as you would to double-lung a whitetail, typically results in a paunch hit. A small portion of a pig's lungs extend slightly behind the shoulder crease, but most of the vital area rests between the shoulders. For a good hit on a hog, keep your shots close and follow these steps.

GET AN ANGLE Wait for the pig to quarter away. The favored shot angle of many whitetail bowhunters is a near necessity on hogs. The angle needn't be sharp—just a step or two beyond broadside is fine.

TARGET THE FAR SIDE Aim at the opposite shoulder. You want a broadhead to exit either through the far shoulder or just in front of it (but no more than an inch or two). If you're behind it, you're likely in the guts. Hitting the far shoulder, even if the arrow doesn't pass through, typically results in a double-lung shot.

HOLD LOW A pig's heart is located low in the animal's chest, in line with the bend of the elbow. If you miss the heart low, you're apt to get a clean miss. If you miss a little high, you'll get lung—and you'll likely get your pig.

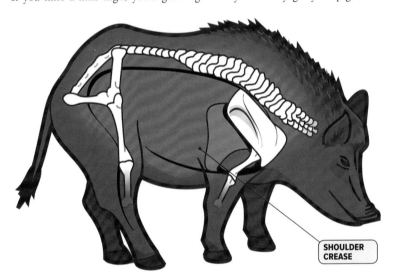

SHOULDER CREASE

246 GET SOME CHOICE PORK

If you're looking for good eating, 50- to 70-pound shoats are tasty, but for the choicest chops, look for an adult sow that's not nursing piglets. She's turning her calories into rump roast instead of milk. Given the pig's year-round breeding schedule, a big, dry sow is a fairly rare find—and the truest trophy in all of hog hunting.

247 DOG A HOG

There are medieval paintings depicting hunters and hounds pursuing wild boars, and the characters almost all wear panicked expressions. Pig hunting with dogs is an intense experience—one that, for centuries, was considered a test of bravery. A cornered hog is as aggressive as any game animal on earth, and today's pissed-off boar is just as capable of hooking your femoral artery and slinging you into the bushes as the beasts in those historical paintings.

Killing a bayed pig with a knife or spear may seem crazy, but the truth is—if you're using a catch dog as most hunters do—it's far and away the safest method for delivering the coup de grace. To really up the ante, trade that knife for a bow, and brush up on your tree-climbing skills. South Florida pig guide Tom Walker says bowhunting hogs with dogs is the most exciting pig hunt there is. Here's how to do it.

HIT SWAMPS AND THICKETS One of the best things about hunting hogs with dogs is that you're probably going to get a hog. Pressured pigs can be tough to bowhunt without dogs during the day, but it's easy for a pack of hounds to sniff them out of thickets and swamps where they hole up. When they do, you'll know; it sounds like a cottontail-and-beagle chase from the bowels of Hell.

HOLD THE DOGS "Most hog-doggers use a big catch dog—like a pit bull—that actually latches onto the hog after it's bayed," Walker says. "That's safest because you can slip in and kill the hog with a knife. You can't do that with a bow because the chances of hitting the catch dog are way too high. Instead,

take the catch dog out of the mix, and take the shot when the hounds bay him and he turns to fight."

You'll need great dogs and nerves of steel. "The dog handler has to be able to call his dogs off to keep them from getting in the way of your shot. Meanwhile, the bowhunter has to be ready—and on his toes. The hog will almost always stand there for a bit, ready to kill everything, including you. That's your shot opportunity."

GET THE ANGLE "There are two shots a bowhunter should take on a big hog: hard quartering away or broadside. You either want the arrow to bury into the opposite shoulder without passing through, or to zip through the pig. You don't want a wounded, charging hog with a broadhead hanging out of his side," Walker says. "I actually prefer a traditional bow for this hunt. A long shot will be 10 yards, and it will happen fast. I like to carry my 50-pound recurve tipped with a big Zwickey broadhead. You get plenty of penetration to kill the pig, but rarely enough to push the broadhead out the other side."

BRING BACKUP "You never know how a dog hunt's going to go," Walker says. "I can tell you a big hog is twice as tough as a black bear, and damn sure meaner when he's surrounded by a pack of dogs. This is the most exhilarating pig hunt there is, but think safety first, both for you and the dogs. You also strive for a quick, humane kill. We bring along guns and spears on every dog hunt. If it's just not right for a bow shot, you have to do what's needed."

248 HAVE A JAVELINA

Some game species just seem tailor-made for bowhunting, and the javelina is just such an animal. They're relatively abundant within their range—in the U.S., that's Arizona, Texas, and New Mexico; there are even more in South America. They don't require specialized archery tackle, and they're reasonably easy to hunt. You can chase them using a variety of bowhunting-friendly methods. They're good eating if prepared properly and—a biggie for me—they don't compete with other animals for your time and attention, since you typically hunt them in January and February.

EAT YOUR JAVELINA

■ Scott Bestul on

Javelina remind me of pronghorn in this respect; far too many people dismiss them as table fare. Hunters in the know follow a simple procedure: take your photos, dress the animal, skin him immediately, and get the meat on ice ASAP. My buddy Jim followed that procedure on his last javelina. Later, he slow-cooked the meat and served it to non-hunting dinner guests, who raved and asked for seconds.

249 HUNT JAVELINA RIGHT

I suspect most bowhunters who've never chased a javelina are just like me: I don't live in javelina country, so they just weren't on my radar. But when an Arizona buddy invited me to his javelina camp in February, I jumped at the chance, and I can't wait to return. The collared peccary (the proper name for javelina, which are not—as they are often called—pigs) is now firmly on my radar screen and will remain there. Here's why I fell in love with them.

GLASS FIRST We'd start each day much as we would a mountain hunt for muleys or elk: glassing from a high vantage point to locate animals. This proved to be tougher than I expected. Though javelina appear almost black in most photos, they actually have a salt-and-pepper coloring that can make them tough to spot. The saving grace is that peccaries typically travel in small herds of 8 to 10 animals, so one of them is usually moving.

MAKE A STALK Once you've spotted the animals, it's decision time. Javelina have keen hearing and a sharp sense of smell, so be mindful of noise and wind direction. Their eyesight is relatively poor, but I've talked to plenty of hunters who've been busted when they relied on this weakness. Javelina can spot movement easily, so creep in and use available cover for camouflage.

CALL 'EM UP Specialized calls are available, but some hunters claim any reed-style predator call will suffice, and javelina are highly susceptible to calling. If a predator attacks one, the rest of the pack rushes to its defense, often presenting a close shot opportunity, 10 yards and under. Some hunters call javelina in from great distances, but you're more likely to succeed if you first close the gap to 75 yards or less. So strong is the herd's protective instinct that every hunter I begged for advice told me, "If you miss one on a call-in, nock another arrow and go for your call again. They almost always come right back, even after you've scared the crap out of them."

250 PREPARE FOR DESERT COUNTRY

I always adore seeing new country, and the Arizona desert we hunted was breathtakingly beautiful; full of ridges, rock outcroppings, and—of course—more kinds of cactus than I had ever imagined.

My first lesson in cactus taxonomy was studying up on the prickly pear, which happens to be one of the favored delicacies of javelina. The rest of the species I learned because they were just as beautiful and a little bit dangerous.

The desert is very frequently a deceiving place to hunt, I soon discovered. Mornings can be chilly, but the terrain warms up fast once the sun rises. You need layered clothing. I heeded the advice to wear light but tough boots, as cactus and other thorns can jab right through a wimpy pair, and I always kept on a long-sleeved shirt to protect wrists and arms from the thorns, spines, and spikes so common in the desert.

You also need quality optics out there. Though a good 10x40 binocular was perfect for the country we hunted, a spotting scope would have come in handy for spying animals in flatter terrain.

251 GET IN SHEEP SHAPE

Extreme altitude. Rugged terrain. Sharp-eyed, ever-wary animals capable of instant escape. Of the 29 species of North American big game, various sheep and mountain goats are perhaps the most challenging for a bowhunter.

Roy Roth, a Wasilla, Alaska, hunter and guide, says "I still feel disbelief whenever I walk up to one I've shot. Where they live, how sharp they are, the difficulty of just getting to them, and the time that can be required to hunt them—I start every hunt wondering how I'm going to pull it off." And yet, he does. Here are his tips for success.

BOOK SMART With a few exceptions, most sheep and goat hunts require an outfitter—and only a handful of these truly understand the requirements of bowhunting. As with any guided hunt, do your homework by checking references. Even with the right guide, sheep and goat hunts still require more effort, preparation, and gear from the hunter.

DROP THE GUN "Leave your rifle behind," Roth laughs. "Most goat and sheep tags are any-weapon. Some guys bring a bow *and* a gun 'just in case.' But when they can't

get within 300 yards of a ram, guess what they reach for? You want to kill one with a bow—bring a bow."

KEEP YOUR BOW Bring the bow you use for whitetails or elk. "I shoot a Hoyt set at 70 pounds, a Spot Hogg sight, drop-away rest, and Rage broadheads," Roth says. "My shots are never farther than 40 yards and sometimes under 10. But I always have an angle-compensating range finder and binocular; the shot angles can be extreme."

GET IN SHAPE Even well-conditioned hunters struggle in the mountains. "Cardio, cardio, cardio," Roth stresses. "And work on walking sidehills. This is days and days of straight up and down in high country. There's no such thing as too much conditioning."

TRAIN YOUR BRAIN A proper mindset is as critical as strong legs and lungs, Roth says. "One guy showed up looking like Mr. Universe. He quit after a day. I think the stress of all the climbing got to his head more than his body. It's day after day of hard

walking and blown stalks and hard living. There are times when sheep hunting is just not that fun."

DRESS RIGHT "I wear polar fleece on the exterior," says Roth, "and synthetics close to my body. Layering is everything. I crawl up the mountain in next to nothing and layer up when I stop to glass or plan a stalk. When my clothing gets wet, I stop and let it dry in the wind or sun. And high-quality mountaineering boots are crucial."

PACK RIGHT Roth carries everything on his back to sleep and live wherever the day's hunt ends. "Hiking back down to a base or spike camp takes too much energy and costs you hunting time," he says. "My pack is 8,000 cubic inches, and I strap my bow to the outside. Inside I carry a sleeping bag, bivvy sack, and tarp. Even on a guided hunt, you need to know you can survive if something happens to your guide. A spotting scope, a hiking staff with an ice axe head, and mountaineering crampons with inch-long spikes are always handy, too. Oh, and a satellite phone."

FUEL UP "You can't take in enough calories," Roth adds. "I like bagels, peanut butter, honey, candy bars with loads of nuts—simple, high-energy, high-calorie food. And lots of water."

STRIKE FROM ABOVE "Sheep and goats have great eyesight and are paranoid of any potential danger they spot from a distance," he says. "But they never expect danger from above, because they live higher than everything else. Plan your stalk to drop in on top of them—meaning far more, and harder, hiking—but it's pretty simple to get within bow range once you pull it off. Once, after a long, looping hike that took hours, I popped over a mountaintop on a ram I'd spotted earlier in the day. When I poked my head over, he was still 60 yards off, bedded, and there was nothing between us. So I just stayed low and kept sneaking. He looked at me several times before I shot him at 30 yards. You get in a certain zone around them and it's like they can't believe you're a threat. It's even easier to get close during the rut. I wear a white polar fleece top, a hat with fake horns on it, and I slip in tight to a billy; when he sees me, he'll run to challenge the 'intruder.' I've shot them at under 10 yards."

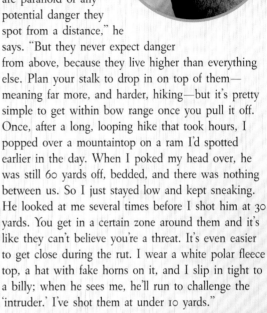

252 BOWHUNT AFRICA

Africa has long held a magnetic pull for the world's big game hunters, but except for a few celebrities, bowhunters weren't part of that romantic picture. That's changed greatly in the last decade; outfitters who understand the challenges and requirements of bowhunting have set up shop across Africa.

Few understand this better than Tim Herald, cohost of *The Zone* TV show, hunting consultant, and veteran of 16 hunting trips to Africa. "Right now, there's no better value for a totally outfitted bowhunt in the world than African plains game," he says. "Many of my clients don't hesitate to spend $4,000 for a five-day guided whitetail hunt every fall. I tell them, "Skip that deer hunt one season and you can take an amazing African bowhunt where you can kill five animals, hunt for seven days, and be treated like a king in the process." Here are his tips for success.

DO YOUR RESEARCH

African outfitters are just like any others: There are some great ones, a few total crooks, and plenty in between. "You're spending lots of money, and you want the trip of a lifetime," says Herald. "Do your research. You want an outfitter who specializes in—or at least regularly takes—bowhunters. Or use a consultant who can find a reputable outfitter who offers the species and style of hunting you want. For example, there are a growing number of high-fence operations; If you don't want one, ask first."

PLAN FOR SUNDRIES Along with the hunt package, be sure to budget for your airfare, an extra night or two in a hotel, shipping of trophies back home, and tips for guides and cooks. "I usually suggest 5 to 10 percent of the cost of the hunt for tips," Herald says, "and at least $1,000 for processing and shipping trophies. Don't forget gifts for loved ones."

BOW UP "Any whitetail bow setup is perfect for plains game, as 95 percent of African bowhunting is over water holes, shooting from a blind 15 to 30 yards away," Herald says. "I prefer a fixed-blade broadhead, especially for some larger species such as kudu or eland. Clothing is simple; all that you wear for deer is fine. Since you're in a blind, lots of hunters don't even wear camo."

PICK YOUR SHOTS "The number one mistake bowhunters tend to make on African game is shot placement," Herald says. "If you shoot plains game as if they were whitetail, you'll gut-shoot them almost every time. The vitals are farther forward on most of the animals; as a rule, on a broadside animal, I just put the pin on the animal's leg, move it straight up, and keep the arrow in the lower third of the body.

The Perfect Shot is a 50-page booklet that I recommend to all my clients. You can take it into the blind with you, and it gives detailed anatomy on every game animal there. It's the best nine bucks you'll spend on an African trip."

ENJOY CAMP Herald says African outfitters offer unmatched hospitality. "I'd love to take some North America outfitters over there once, just to show them how it's done. The food is great. The lodges are neat and clean. They do your laundry every day. You sit around a fire at night and tell stories with other hunters in camp. It's a great experience."

253 HUNT SMALL GAME

Big bucks and bulls get all the glory, but if you shake almost any successful big game hunter hard enough, chances are a small game hunter will tumble out. In areas where upland game is abundant, the fundamental big-game hunting skills of stalking, waiting, watching, and shooting all blossom. But small-game hunting, particularly with a bow, is fun in its own right, too. If you're not already a small game nut, here's how to get started.

255 CHASE A RABBIT

For many years, my cousins and friends owned beagles that we used to chase rabbits, and those hunts—usually conducted in the winter after deer season had closed—remain some of my fondest hunting memories. You don't need dogs to bowhunt cottontails, but they sure help. If you've never hunted bunnies behind a hound, the basic drill is pretty simple: The dogs course through cover until they jump a cottontail (or snowshoe, in the North), and then the chase is on. The dogs howl as they (try to) stay on the track, and the bunny generally makes a loop that heads toward a den or other cover.

The beauty for bowhunters is that, by just listening to the dogs, you can anticipate the direction of the chase and get set up for a shot. Sometimes a rabbit will be running full-bore. But often as not, he'll be plodding along slowly and stopping frequently—presenting a pretty good opportunity for a bowshot. Even if you end up missing, the rabbit will frequently do you the favor of repeating the circle.

254 TAKE TO THE TREES

As a teenager, I spent hours peering into treetops in search of fox and gray squirrels; they were a challenge for me then—when I held a .22 rifle or shotgun—and that challenge only grew in stature when I tried to hunt them with my bow.

Bowhunters can squirrel-hunt using all the familiar techniques. Taking a seat in great squirrel habitat (think woodlots filled with oak, hickory, walnut, and other hard-mast species) and waiting on feeding squirrels to appear is the best bet. Earlier in the season, many shots will be up in the trees, which is obviously not easy. The angles are steep, the target is small, and you'll break or lose arrows in the process.

Truthfully, bowhunters are better off waiting until a bit later in autumn, when squirrels come down from the treetops to forage for nuts on the ground. The best technique is settling in to a good feeding area, waiting for a squirrel to slip to the forest floor and start foraging, and then sneaking in for a shot. Squirrels are paranoid feeders that constantly poke their heads up to scan for predators. Slipping to within bow range and waiting for a clean shot requires woodsmanship and patience.

256 SHOOT ON THE WING

Gamebirds and bows might seem a bad mismatch, since many of us feel lucky to just hit them with a shotgun. But there are diehard archery wingshooters who practice on aerial targets and take birds in flight with arrows.

Wingshooting is best done with specialized archery gear, including flu-flu arrows. These are fletched with 4 to 6 long, bulky feathers with an aggressive helical to create significant drag, quickly slowing the arrow. Flu-flu arrows are accurate at short range, but drop to the ground quickly, minimizing arrow loss. Many wingshooters also use a bird loop: a small-game head with 3 to 4 wire loops designed to snare a bird's head, feet, or wings in the (likely) scenario that the head itself doesn't center-punch the target.

Game birds can also be taken by stalking them as they feed on the ground. But because of the dense cover preferred by most upland species, shooting these birds is a steep challenge with a bow.

257 BE BLUNT ABOUT IT

You'll shoot a few gamebirds, squirrels, and rabbits incidentally while pursuing big game, but using conventional broadheads for this purpose quickly becomes expensive. That's why many archers like to keep an arrow or two tipped with a small-game head in their quivers at all times. Here are the most popular styles.

BE BLUNT A blunt is a flat head designed to stun or immobilize game though shock rather than tissue damage or blood loss. Most are made from steel, but in rocky areas, a rubber blunt means you'll end up with fewer broken arrows.

LEARN JUDO The judo point adds four spring arms behind a blunt head. The springs retard penetration in a hit on an animal, and also grab grass and brush to prevent arrow loss by kicking the arrow upward on contact.

ADD BLADES Some arrows include small blades behind a blunt head. Like a judo point, these shortened, curved blades aid in arrow recovery, as they grab grass, brush, or twigs and prevent the arrow from slipping under leaf litter and grass.

258 GO BOWFISHING!

Flaccid and unused—that's no state to let your bowshooting muscles get into in the summer, because you could be out bowfishing. In this sport, there is no sitting around waiting on a deer to walk by or a fish to bite. There's just a lot of shooting and, on a good day, lots of reeling in big fish.

We've already showed you how to build an awesome bowfishing rig (see item 114). Beyond that, you don't need much. Barefoot women in bikinis go bowfishing all the time. Hell, even watching it is fun. Here's what you need to know.

259 SHOOT THE BIG 3

Bowfishermen target rough fish—which is slang for "not game fish"—but the list of what's legal and what isn't varies from one state to the next, even on individual waterways. In general, the following species are the most popular and most common.

CARP These brutish fighters are found everywhere from turbid ditches to clear-water streams, coast to coast. The best shooting for them is during the spring, when pods of fish spawn in shallow, flooded vegetation. Sneak up on them either by boat or on foot.

SILVERS AND BIGHEADS Commonly called "Asian carp," these invasive big-river fish are primarily found in the Mississippi drainage.

Bigheads can top 100 pounds and are best targeted by easing along riverbanks in the day wearing polarized sunglasses. Silver carp can jump when spooked, and the airborne fish make fine targets.

GAR These prehistoric predators favor slack rivers, backwaters, and lakes. Though the giant alligator gar is the best-known species, it has a limited distribution, and is protected in many areas. You'll frequently encounter long-nose, short-nose, and spotted gar in the shallows, and all are favored bowfishing targets. Avoid gar eggs because they're highly toxic, but deep-fry the backstraps, which taste like shrimp.

260 SHOOT JUMPERS

There are plenty of reasons to bowfish for silver carp. They're grossly overpopulated and destroying some of our best riverine fisheries—and they're not bad to eat. They also grow to 40 pounds and leap 6 feet out of the water—sometimes by the hundreds—when startled. Here's how to get in on the action.

JUMP-START Silver carp jump at the sound of boat motors, but to really get them going en masse, run your boat in shallow water—10 feet deep or less. On major rivers, that might mean pulling into tributary creeks. Trim your outboard up and give it just enough gas to plow a good wake. If there are fish present, they'll be jumping in seconds.

DESIGNATE SHOOTERS Sit at the transom of the boat. Any bowfishing rig will work, but a reel that allows you to retrieve arrows quickly for follow-up shots is a big asset. Most people shoot compounds and keep them at full draw while the fish are jumping, but you can snap-shoot with a recurve, drawing as the fish jumps and shooting just as it falls.

TRUST YOUR INSTINCTS This is reflexive shooting. On a good run, fish will be everywhere, but wait for one to jump near the boat. When it does, hit your anchor point, track the fish over the end of the arrow, focus on a spot just underneath it, and let fly as it falls back toward the water. Do this right, and your arrow your arrow will zip through it and the fight is on. And if you miss, it's not like you won't get another chance.

261 GET THE GEAR

A few pieces of supplemental gear such as the stuff below make a day of bowfishing all the more enjoyable.

WIELD SWEET LUCY I don't remember where I heard the name "Sweet Lucy" as it pertains to a hefty hardwood stob suitable for whacking a 50-pound carp into submission, but I do know that when a giant fish is flopping in the floor of my boat and wrecking gear, Sweet Lucy puts a stop to it.

WEAR SUNGLASSES Shooting on a calm, sunny day can be just as productive as shooting at night. There are fewer bugs, and you can save after-dark hours for drinking beer and celebrating fish-sticking triumphs. For daylight shooting, quality polarized sunglasses are a must. The difference in lens clarity can determine whether you see the fish—or not.

GET A GUT BUCKET Bowfishing is messy business. It's not uncommon for thrashing carp to turn their entrails into projectiles. And their slime, given a little time in the sun, will bake onto your boat's hull like a clear-coat paint job. A boat-bound bowfisherman needs a gut bucket. Heavy-duty plastic lawn and leaf buckets cost about $10 and will do everything a good gut bucket should.

LIGHT UP THE NIGHT Many species are more active near the surface after dark, particularly on lakes and rivers that receive heavy boat traffic. But multiple halogen bulbs powered by a generator, the standard after-dark bowfishing setup, are expensive and noisy. A 6-volt lawnmower battery will fit into a sturdy backpack, so it's handy enough to use from the shore or while wading the shallows. It'll provide silent power to a Q-Beam for a couple hours.

WEAR THE RIGHT SHIRT It can be camo or your favorite beer logo. I've seen some fine shirts decorated with howling wolves and dream catchers. The only thing required of a good bowfishing shirt is that it be thick enough to absorb a full day's worth of carp slime. Keep one clean spot—you're going to need somewhere to wipe your hands on before grabbing a sandwich from the cooler, after all.

INDEX

ABOUT THE AUTHORS

SCOTT BESTUL is a Field Editor for *Field & Stream* magazine. After graduating from Winona (Minnesota) State University in 1985, Bestul had just started a teaching career when he sold his first story to *Sports Afield* magazine. He began freelancing for various outdoor publications soon after and was rescued from starvation in 1996 by the late John Merwin, who recruited him to write for *F&S*'s regional pages. Since then, Bestul has figured heavily in the magazine's whitetail features, covering some of modern deer hunting's top trends, techniques, equipment and hunters. He has chased deer in 16 states and logs hundreds of hours each year scouting, planting food plots, running a chainsaw, and hanging tree stands. Bestul began bowhunting when he was 12; decades later, archery remains his passion. He lives in southeast Minnesota's bluff country and is the proud father of twin teenagers, Brooke and Bailey. With Dave Hurteau, he is co-author of *The Total Deer Hunter Manual* and the popular Whitetail 365 blog on fieldandstream.com.

DAVE HURTEAU is the Deputy Editor of *Field & Stream* magazine. One of eight children, he grew up hunting the boondocks north of New York's Adirondack Mountains. After graduating from the University of Rochester in 1991, he launched *The Finger Lakes Outdoorsman* magazine from an Ithaca, NY, apartment. He moved to Manhattan in 1994 and began his career with *Field & Stream*, working as Assistant and then Associate Editor. Three years later he was back in the boonies, but still writing for the magazine, eventually parlaying a freelance stint into another full-time editorial position. In one capacity or another, Hurteau has been with *Field & Stream* for 20 years, during which time he has hunted and fished throughout much of the country. From upstate NY, where he now lives with his wife and two children, Hurteau handles much of the magazine's hunting coverage. With Scott Bestul, he is co-author of *The Total Deer Hunter Manual* and he and Bestul also co-write and edit the popular Whitetail 365 blog on fieldandstream.com.

ACKNOWLEDGMENTS

SCOTT BESTUL I'd like to thank Mariah Bear and the entire Weldon Owen staff for the amazing effort they put into this book. To the folks at *F&S*—Anthony Licata, Mike Toth, Slaton White, and the entire crew—I'm so deeply grateful for your friendship, guidance, patience, and expertise. Will Brantley was happily editing this work when he was hired full-time as the *F&S* hunting editor; he managed to not only keep his sanity, but do a fantastic job. I want to be Will when I grow up. Dave Hurteau and I have spent hundreds of hours talking archery and bowhunting over the years; his guidance has made *Field & Stream*'s bowhunting coverage the best out there. He's not only a great boss, but I couldn't think of a guy with whom I'd rather share a by-line or, more importantly, a hunting camp.

I dedicate this book to my father and the entire Bestul clan that taught a kid the magic of chasing deer near Iola, Wisconsin; Howard, Dave, Scott, Stuart, Steve, Dale and Danny . . . I'm proud to be part of your crew.

DAVE HURTEAU Thank you to Mariah Bear, Will Mack, Ian Cannon, Liz Fiorentino, and the whole Weldon Owen crew for their tremendous effort—particularly all the eleventh-hour, hair-on-fire scrambling that this book involved. Most of what I know about bowhunting I learned directly from Scott Bestul. I would have no business co-authoring a book on archery without the expertise he has so generously shared. Thank you to my colleagues and mentors at *F&S*, especially Anthony Licata, Mike Toth, Slaton White, the great David E. Petzal, and the late John Merwin and Maggie Nichols. *F&S* Hunting Editor Will Brantley gets special thanks; this book could not have had a more knowledgeable and hardworking Project Editor if I had handpicked him myself. This one is for Hannah and Jackson.

ABOUT THE MAGAZINE

In every issue of *Field & Stream* you'll find a lot of stuff: beautiful artwork and photography, adventure stories, wild game recipes, humor, reviews, commentary, and more. This mix is what makes the magazine so great and what has helped it remain relevant since 1895. But at the heart of every issue are the skills. The tips that explain how to pick the perfect stand location every time, the tactics that help you bag that trophy buck, the lessons that you'll pass on to your kids about the joy of the outdoors—those are the stories that readers have come to expect from *Field & Stream*.

You'll find a ton of those skills in *The Total Bowhunting Manual,* but there's not a book big enough to hold them all in one volume. Whether you're new to bowhunting and archery or an old pro, there's always more to learn, and you can expect *Field & Stream* to continue teaching these essential skills in every issue. To order a subscription, visit www.fieldandstream.com/subscription.

ABOUT THE WEBSITE

When *Field & Stream* readers aren't hunting or fishing, they kill hours on fieldandstream.com. And once you visit the site, you'll understand why.

If you enjoy the skills and opinions in this book, there's plenty more online from our staff of writers and a network of 50,000-plus experts who can answer all of your questions about the outdoors.

Our blogs, written by the leading experts in the outdoors, cover every facet of hunting and fishing and provide constant content that instructs, enlightens, and always entertains. Our adventure videos contain footage that's almost as thrilling to watch as it is to experience. And our photo galleries include the best wildlife and outdoor photography you'll find anywhere.

Perhaps best of all is the community. At fieldandstream.com, you can argue with other readers about the best treestand or the perfect trout fly. It's where you can share photos of the fish you catch and the game you shoot. And it's where you can enter to win guns, gear, and other prizes.

And it's a place where you can spend a lot of time. Which is okay. Just make sure to reserve some hours for the outdoors, too.

CREDITS

Illustrations courtesey of *Conor Buckley*: Hunting Chapter Icon, 50, 54, 59, 63, 79, 80, 91, 139, 175, 178, 214, 225; *Hayden Foell*: 15, 42; *Ryan Kirby*: 148, 185; *Liberum Donum*: 160, 173, 192, 230; *Christine Meighan*: 112, 132, 151, 228; *Robert L. Prince*: 37, 41, 98, 161; *Mike Sudal*: 35, 36; *Pete Sucheski*: 107, 245; *Lauren Towner*: 22, 82, 117, 154, 156, 167, 174, 233, 257.

Photographs courtesey of *3 Rivers Archery*: 86; *Rick Adair*: 114; *Charles Alsheimer*: 170; *Garret Armstrong*: 89; *George Barnett*: 213; *Bass Pro Shops*: 105 (targets); *Bear Archery*: 2 (recurve), 23, 110 (bow, cam serving); *Bowtech Archery*: 11, 84; *Will Brantley*: 146; *Denver Bryan*: 28, 150, 158, 176, 195, 202, 204–206, 236 (hunter), 241 (hunter), 251 (sheep), 252 (kudu); *Denver Bryan / Images on the Wildside*: 69, 190, 226; *Denver Bryan / John Eriksson / Images on the Wildside*: 144; *Denver Bryan / Tim Irwin*: 162; *Denver Bryan / Tre Taylor / Images on the Wildside*: 60; *Tony Bynum / Images on the Wildside*: 237 (upper); *Cabela's*: 1 (broadhead, crossbow), 25, 104, 111 (soft case), 118 (crossbow), 196, 197; *Carter Enterprises*: 52; *Tim Christie*: 229; *Nigel Cox*: 10, 14, 19, 33, 49; *Craig Cutler*: 185; *Peter Eades / Images on the Wildside*: 221 (pronghorn), 225, 236 (deer), 237 (lower), 242 (deer), 251 (inset); *John Eriksson / Images on the Wildside*: 253; *Tim Flanigan / Images on the Wildside*: 219; *G5 Striker*: 45; *Gander Mountain*: 70 (arrowheads); *Cliff Gardiner & John Keller*: 109 (both kits); *Gorman Studio*: 230; *Grizzly Archery*: 2 (recurve); *John Hafner*: Title Page, Table of Contents (bow hunter, crossbow hunter, elk), Anthony Licata intro, Scott Bestul & Dave Hurteau intro, 1, 2, Vertical Bows intro, 3 (hunter), 32, 34, 61, 65 (hunter), 66, 67 (upper), 72, 85, 90, 93, Vertical Bows closing image, Crossbows intro, 118 (hunter), 122 (right), 129, 130 (closeup), 131, 133–135, 140, 142, Hunting intro, 152, 165, 171, 172, 181, 183, 198, 201, 208 (lower), 210, 222, 231 (turkeys), 232, 238, 239, Index, About the Authors, Acknowledgements; *Eric Heintz*: 189 (blood); *Brad Herndon / Bear Archery*: 29; *HHA*: 27; *Hoyt Archery*: Cover; *Brent Humphreys*: 6, 157; *Donald M. Jones*: 97, 143, 153, 155, 169, 191, 192, 211, 218 (pawprints), 220, 234, 235 (inset), 240, 249, Hunting closing image; *Bill Konway*: 63, 67 (lower), 74, 102; *Lance Krueger*: 53, 71, 177; *Lancaster Archery*: 111 (Easton case); *Lon E. Lauber*: 65, 78, 88, Scott Bestul on: Hunting with a Stick Bow, 92, 101, 106, 159, 161, 212 (moose, hunter), 227, 258, 261; *John Lawton*: 4; *Mark Miller / Images on the Wildeside*: 247 (hogs); *Montana Decoy*: 215; *Muzzy*: 115; *Luke Nilsson*: 7; *Tim Pask / Images on the Wildside*: 251 (landscape); *Plano Moulding*: 111 (Plano case); *Carol Polich / Images on the Wildside*: 252 (warthog); *Saxton Pope*: 1 (book cover), 15; *PSE Archery*: Table of Contents (bow), 2 (longbow), 16; *Joe Pugliese*: 2 (compound bow); *Todd Pussner*: 218 (bear); *Travis Rathbone*: 122 (left); *Mark Raycroft*: 58, 189 (deer); *Rose City Archery*: 3 (Howard Hill); *Vic Schendel*: 223; *Scott Archery*: 51; *SKB Cases*: 111 (SKB case); *Gregg Staggs*: 107; *TenPoint*: 2 (crossbow), 127 (all photos); *Kyle Thompson*: 111, 121, 186; *Trophy Taker*: 30; *Wikimedia Commons*: 1 (arrowheads, Genghis Khan, English archer, Kyudo, Fred Bear/Jim Henderson, Olympic archer); *Windigo Images*: 103; *Peter Yang*: 55. All other photographs courtesy of *Shutterstock*.

Text written by *Gerald Almy*: 218; *Jace Bauserman*: 213, 241–242; *Scott Bestul*: chapter introductions, 3–5, 22–24, 47–50, 55–56, 58–59, 70, 73–75, 87–88, 92, 118, 122–128, 142–145, 153–156, 160–171, 173–174, 185–193, 195, 203–205, 208–211, 221, 226, 235–236, 248–257; *Scott Bestul & Dave Hurteau*: 172, 175–181; *Will Brantley*: 1–2, 51–54, 65–69, 71–72, 81–85, 100–102, 108, 113–117, 119, 131–132, 146–149, 151, 157–159, 172, 182, 184, 222–224, 227–233, 237–239, 243–247, 258–261; *David Draper*: 109, 194, 196, 202, 206, 225; *Mike Gutch*: 106; *Bill Heavey*: 93–94; *Mark Huelsing*: 207; *Dave Hurteau*: 6–21, 25–36, 42–46, 57, 60–64, 76–80, 89–90, 95–99, 104–105, 111, 120–121, 129–130, 133–141, 152, 197–201, 234, 240; *Mark Hicks*: 86; *Brian McClintock*: 103; *Jeff Murray*: 183; *Tony J. Peterson*: 150; *Michael R. Shea*: 37–41, 219; *Gregg Staggs*: 91, 107, 112; *Bill Vaznis*: 110, 212, 214–217, 220

weldon**owen**

PRESIDENT & PUBLISHER Roger Shaw
ASSOCIATE PUBLISHER Mariah Bear
SVP, SALES & MARKETING Amy Kaneko
FINANCE DIRECTOR Philip Paulick
PROJECT EDITOR, F&S Will Brantley
PROJECT EDITOR, WO Ian Cannon
CREATIVE DIRECTOR Kelly Booth
ART DIRECTOR William Mack
DESIGNER Liz Fiorentino
ILLUSTRATION COORDINATOR Conor Buckley
PRODUCTION DIRECTOR Chris Hemesath
PRODUCTION MANAGER Michelle Duggan
DIRECTOR OF ENTERPRISE SYSTEMS Shawn Macey
IMAGING MANAGER Don Hill

Weldon Owen would also like to thank
Gail Nelson-Bonebrake for editorial assistance,
and Kevin Broccoli for the index.

© 2015 Weldon Owen International
1150 Brickyard Cove Road
Richmond, CA 94801
www.weldonowen.com

Library of Congress Control Number
on file with the publisher
ISBN 978-1-61628-729-0
10 9 8 7 6 5 4 3
2020 2021 2022 2023 2024
Printed in China

FIELD&STREAM

EXECUTIVE VICE PRESIDENT Eric Zinczenko
EDITOR-IN-CHIEF Anthony Licata
EXECUTIVE EDITOR Mike Toth
SENIOR DEPUTY EDITOR Colin Kearns
MANAGING EDITOR Jean McKenna
DEPUTY EDITORS Dave Hurteau, Slaton L. White
COPY CHIEF Donna L. Ng
SENIOR EDITOR Joe Cermele
HUNTING EDITOR Will Brantley
DESIGN DIRECTOR Sean Johnston
PHOTOGRAPHY DIRECTOR John Toolan
DEPUTY ART DIRECTOR Pete Sucheski
ASSOCIATE ART DIRECTORS Russ Smith, James A. Walsh
PRODUCTION MANAGER Judith Weber
DIGITAL DIRECTOR Nate Matthews
ONLINE CONTENT EDITOR Alex Robinson

2 Park Avenue
New York, NY 10016
www.fieldandstream.com